101 Super Cute
CAT THINGS TO DRAW

Draw, doodle, and color a plethora of purrfectly pawsome felines and quirky cat mash-ups

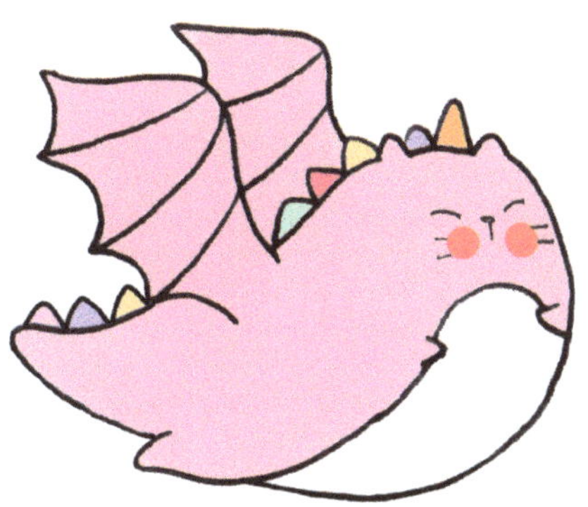

Lulu Mayo

Quarto.com • WalterFoster.com

© 2022 Quarto Publishing Group USA Inc.
Text and Illustrations © 2022 Hsiaochi Yang

First published in 2022 by Walter Foster Publishing, an imprint of The Quarto Group.
100 Cummings Center, Suite 265D, Beverly, MA 01915, USA.
T (978) 282-9590 **F** (978) 283-2742

Walter Foster Publishing titles are also available at discount for retail, wholesale, promotional, and bulk purchase. For details, contact the Special Sales Manager by email at specialsales@quarto.com or by mail at The Quarto Group, Attn: Special Sales Manager, 100 Cummings Center, Suite 265D, Beverly, MA 01915, USA.

ISBN: 978-1-60058-989-8

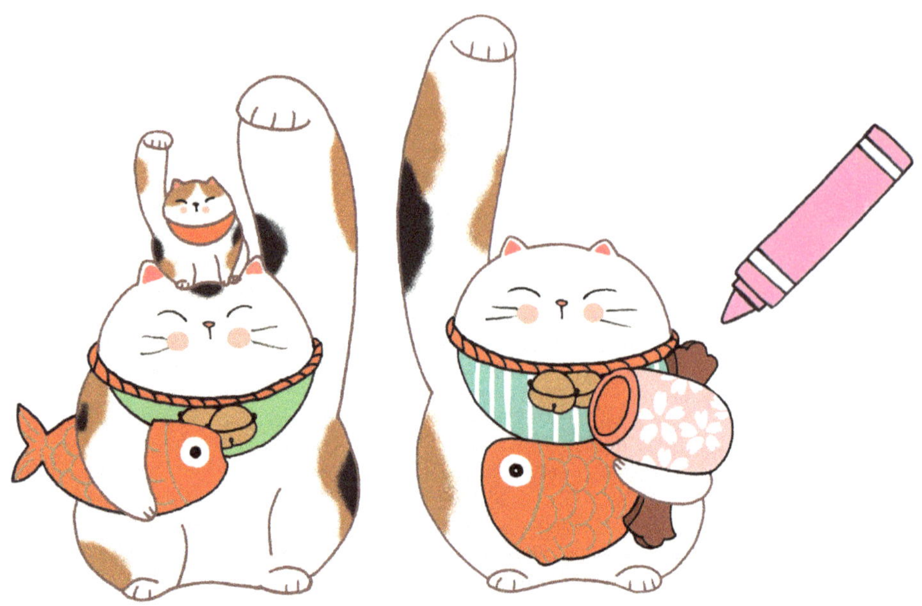

TABLE OF CONTENTS

INTRODUCTION

Welcome to the world of almost unbearable cat cuteness!
Created for cat lovers, doodle enthusiasts, and artists of all ages and
skill levels, 101 Super Cute Cat Things to Draw is where creativity
and fun intersect with fluffy felines in more than a hundred
delightful cat-themed drawing projects, doodle prompts,
and whimsical exercises.

If you are crazy about cats, looking for new ways to get inspired to
draw, or simply want to unwind after a busy day, you are in the right
place. The activities in this adorable book are designed to provide
you an escape from modern life to a relaxing world
of quirkiness and creativity.

I like to bring energy and happiness to my work. My hope is that
when you pick up your pencil and follow along, you will experience
those same feelings.

So let your imagination run wild and lose yourself in doodling!

~Lulu Mayo

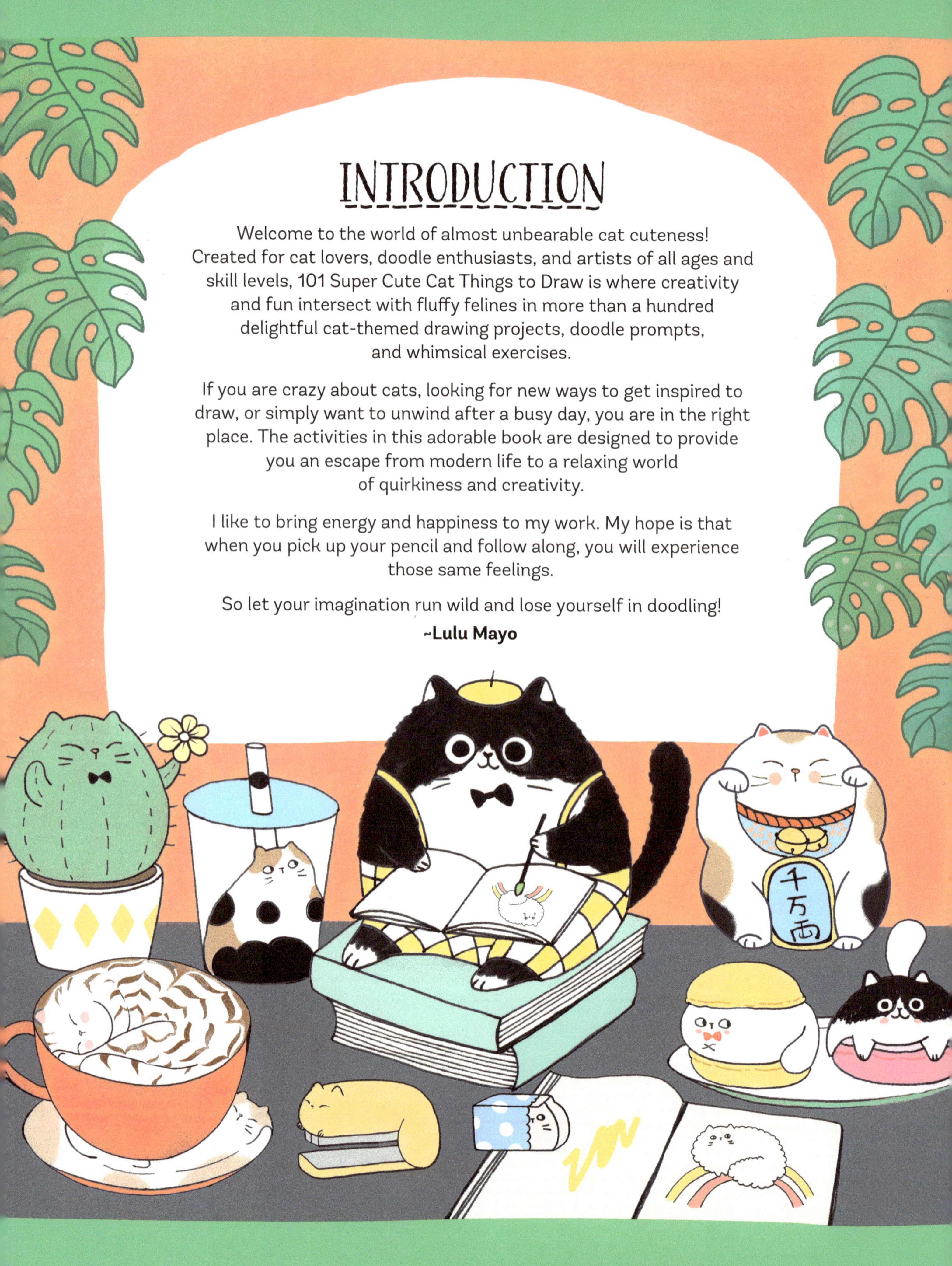

TOOLS & MATERIALS

Here are some basic tools and materials to get you started with the projects in this book.

Colored Pencils – Colored pencils are a convenient and easy tool for applying color. Professional-grade colored pencils have a waxy, soft lead that is excellent for shading and building up layers of color.

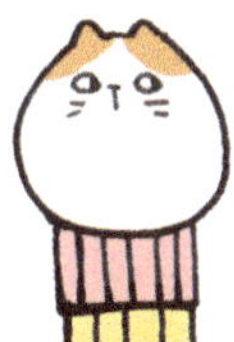

Pencils – Graphite drawing pencils are designated by hardness and softness. H pencils are hard and make lighter marks; B pencils are soft and make darker marks. Pencils range from very soft (9B) to very hard (9H). You can also use a plain old No. 2 pencil if that's what works for you!

Sketchpad – Sketchpads come in many sizes and are great for practicing and doodling.

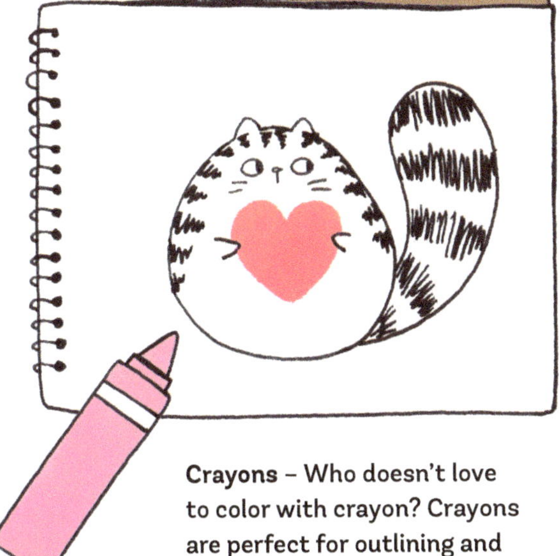

Crayons – Who doesn't love to color with crayon? Crayons are perfect for outlining and coloring in large areas.

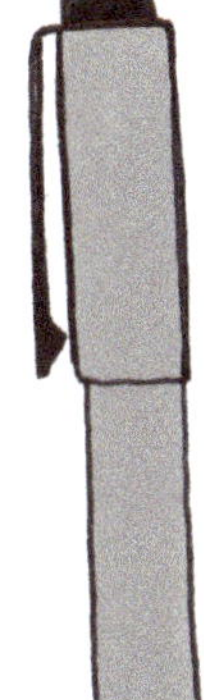

Pigment-Ink Pens – Technical pens are great for adding small details.

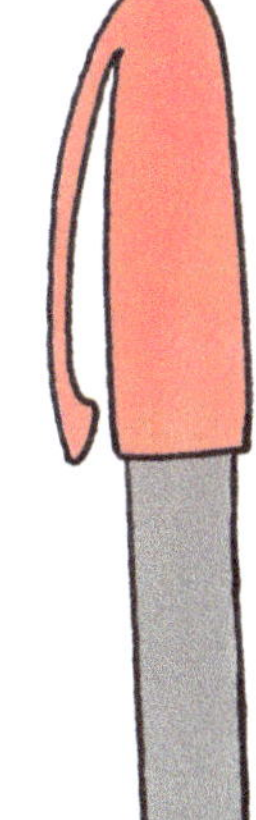

Art Markers – Art markers create bold, vibrant bands of color. They are great for laying down large areas of even color, as well as for shading and creating patterns.

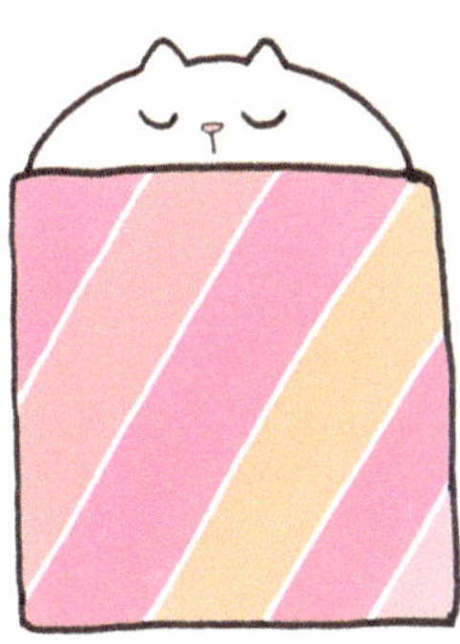

Eraser – Plastic or vinyl erasers are a staple in drawing. They remove graphite without messing up the paper and are best for erasing hard pencil marks and large areas.

GETTING STARTED

All drawings start with a line—and simple lines can be very expressive. You can use them to show emotion, personality, or movement. Here are some examples:

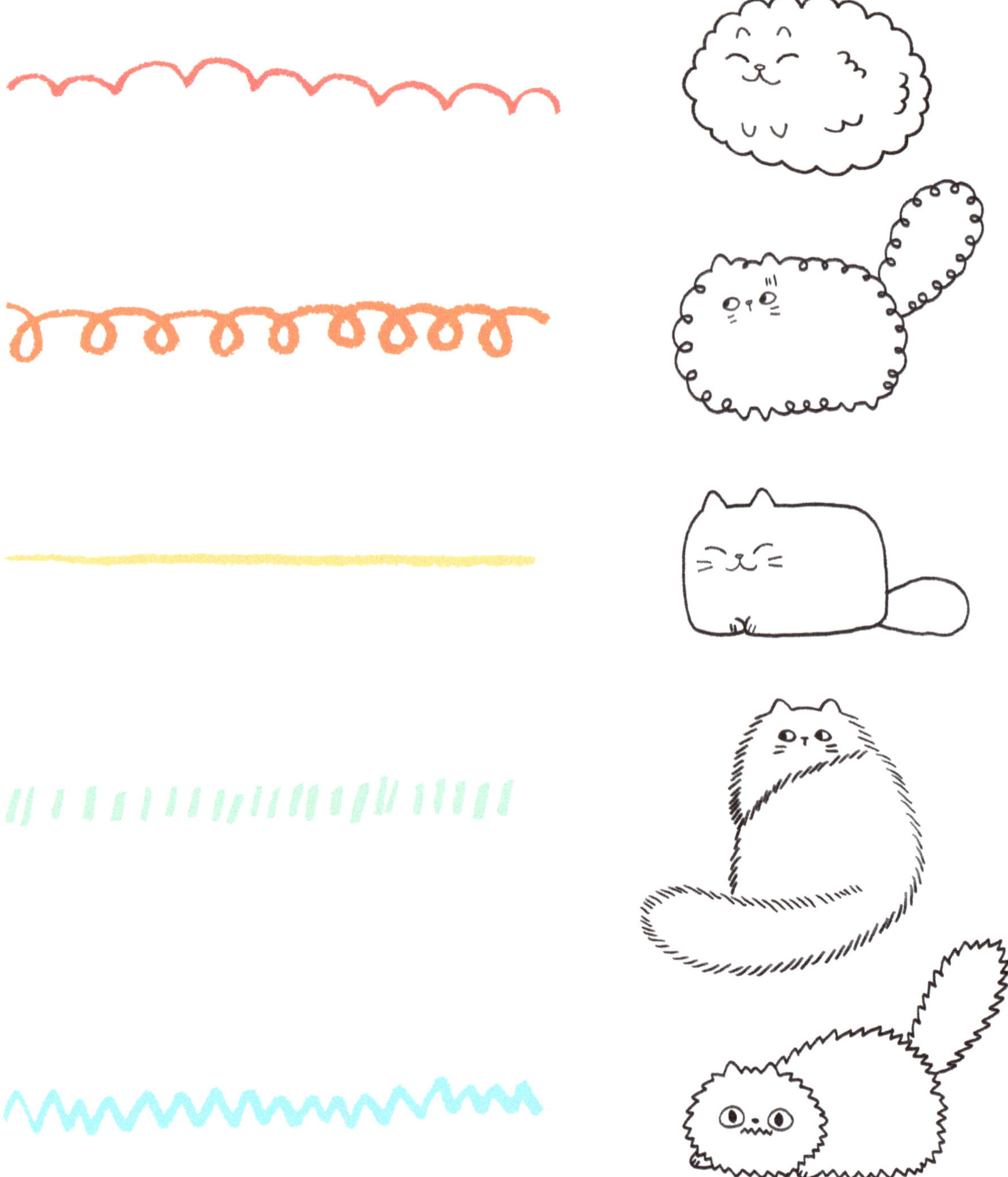

Use this page to practice creating a variety of lines; then turn them into silly, sassy cats!

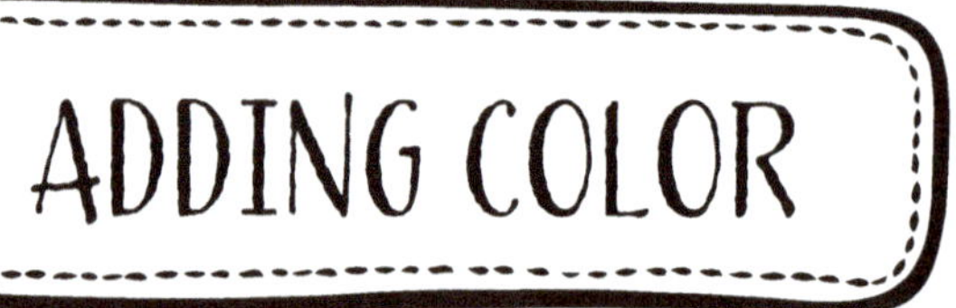

ADDING COLOR

There are many ways to use your coloring tools to create a variety of strokes and unique effects.

TECHNIQUES

Hatching

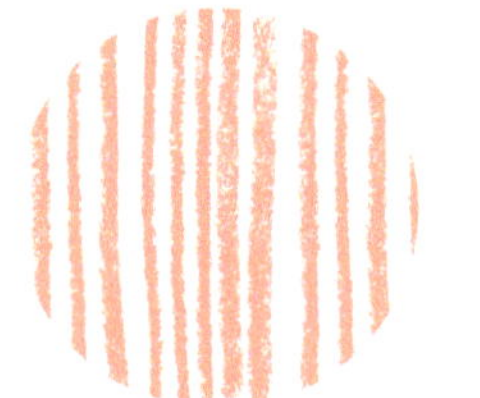  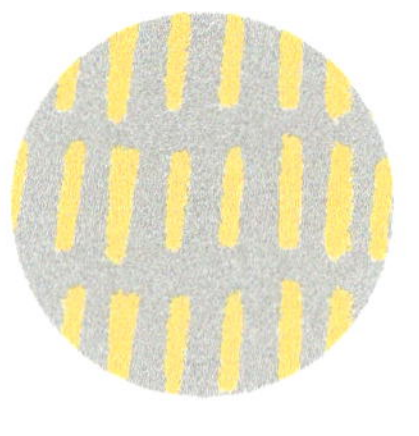 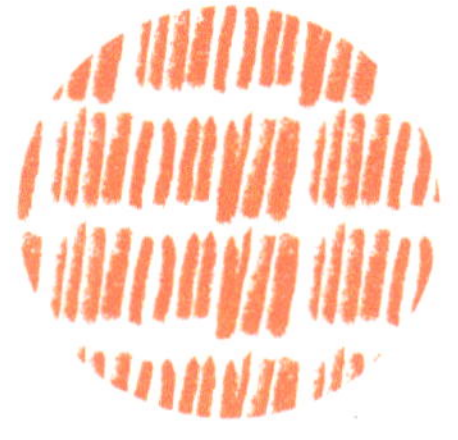 

Hatching is a series of parallel lines going in one direction, either vertically or horizontally.

The closer the hatching lines are to each other, the denser and darker the color.

Crosshatching

Crosshatching involves layering one set of hatched lines over another, but in a different direction.

Scumbling

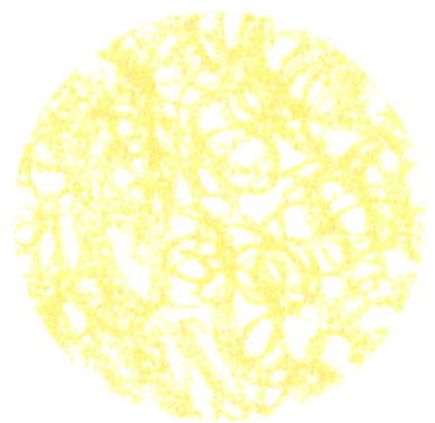

Create this effect by scribbling your pencil randomly to create a mass of color.

Stippling

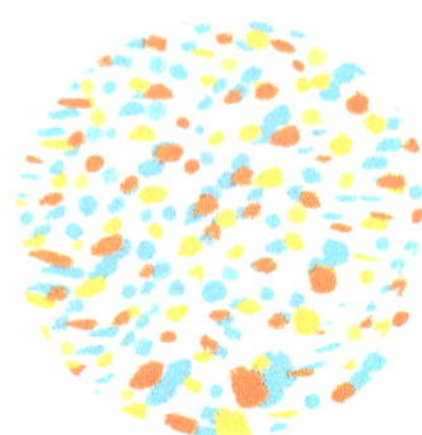

Apply small dots of color close together to create dense color and pattern.

Blending

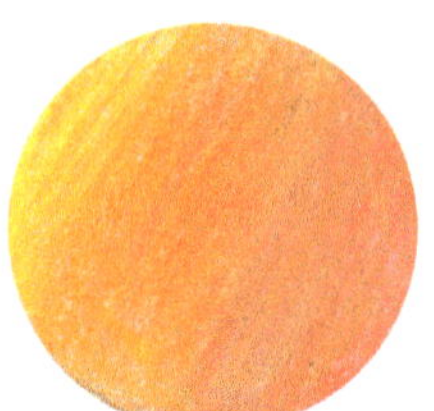

To blend one color into another, lighten the pressure of your pencil and overlap the strokes where the colors meet.

Layering

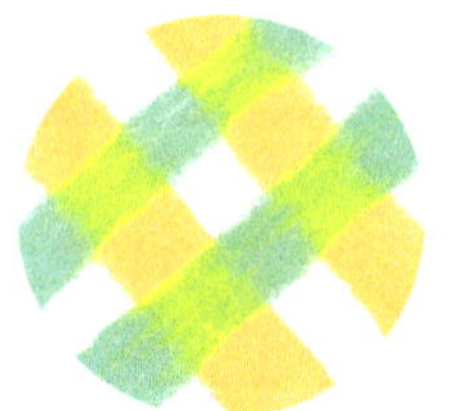

Mix colors of your choice by layering them lightly. In this example, look how layering yellow over dark green results in a lighter green.

Gradating

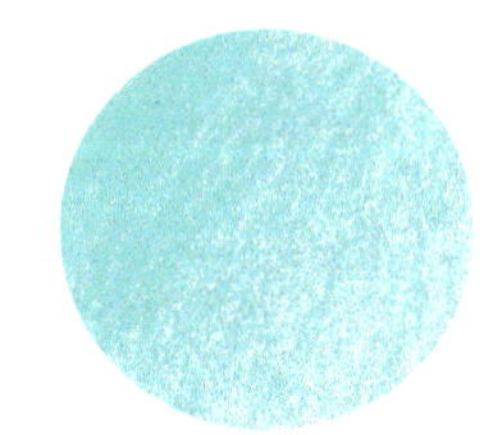

Gradation is a lightening or darkening of a color or the blending of colors. To create a gradation, stroke side to side with heavy pressure and lighten the pressure as you move to show a clear color transition.

COLORING EXERCISE

Warm up your hand by drawing random lines, scribbles, and squiggles. Use the colorful cats below as inspiration, and then practice the techniques you just learned.

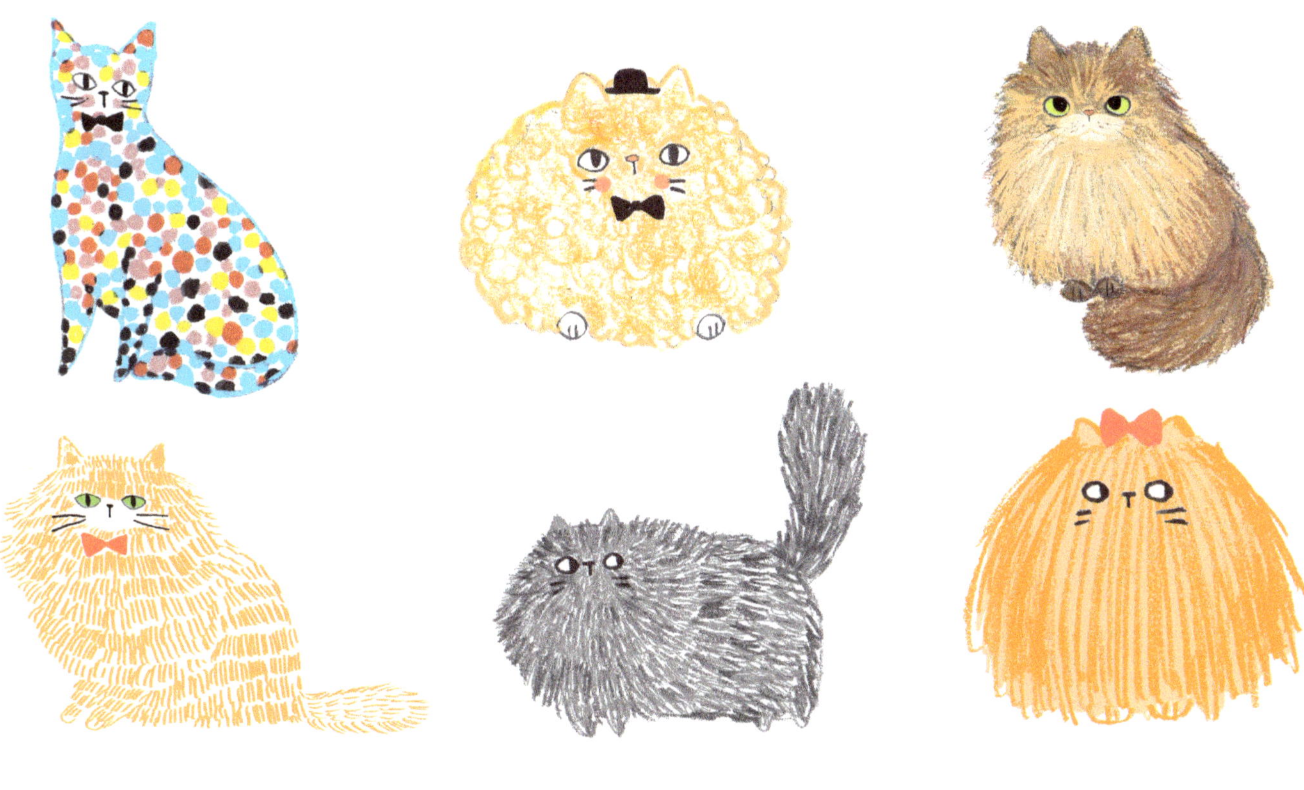

THE COLOR WHEEL

Color can help bring your drawings to life! A color wheel is useful for understanding relationships between colors. Use the color wheel when you want to find the purrfect color schemes for your drawings.

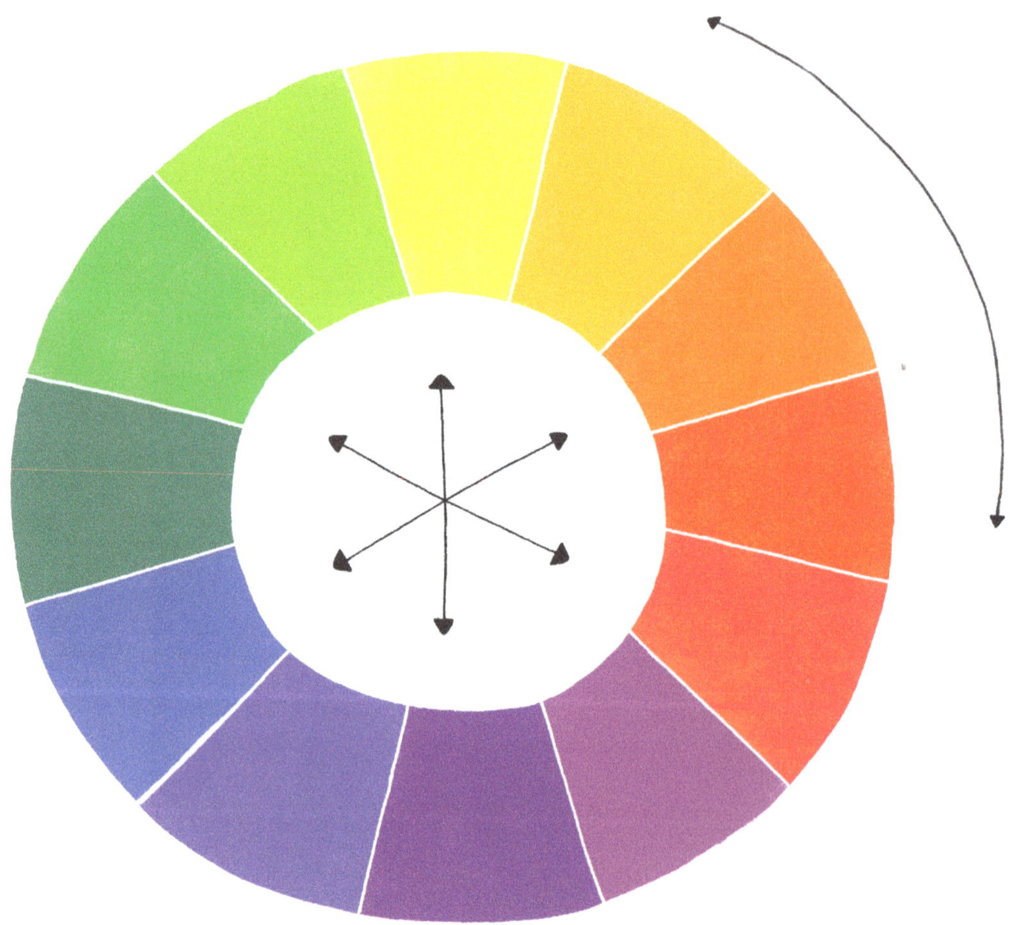

There are three **primary colors**: red, yellow, and blue. These colors cannot be created by mixing other colors. Mixing two primary colors produces a **secondary color**: orange, green, and purple. Mixing a primary color with a secondary color produces a **tertiary color**: red-orange, red-purple, yellow-orange, yellow-green, blue-green, and blue-purple. Red, orange, and yellow are "warm" colors; green, blue, and purple are "cool" colors.

Colors directly across from one another, like yellow and purple, blue and orange, and green and red are **complementary** (see arrows inside color wheel). Together, these colors will make your artwork bright and bold. Colors next to each other, such as yellow-orange and orange are **analogous** (see arrow on the outside of the color wheel). These colors look harmonious and pleasing to the eye.

Color in the artwork below using the 60-30-10 rule: a color rule of decorating that you can apply to coloring. Color in 60% of the art using a primary color, which serves as a backdrop. Next, color in 30% of the art in a secondary color. For the remaining 10%, select a few bright pops of vibrant color.

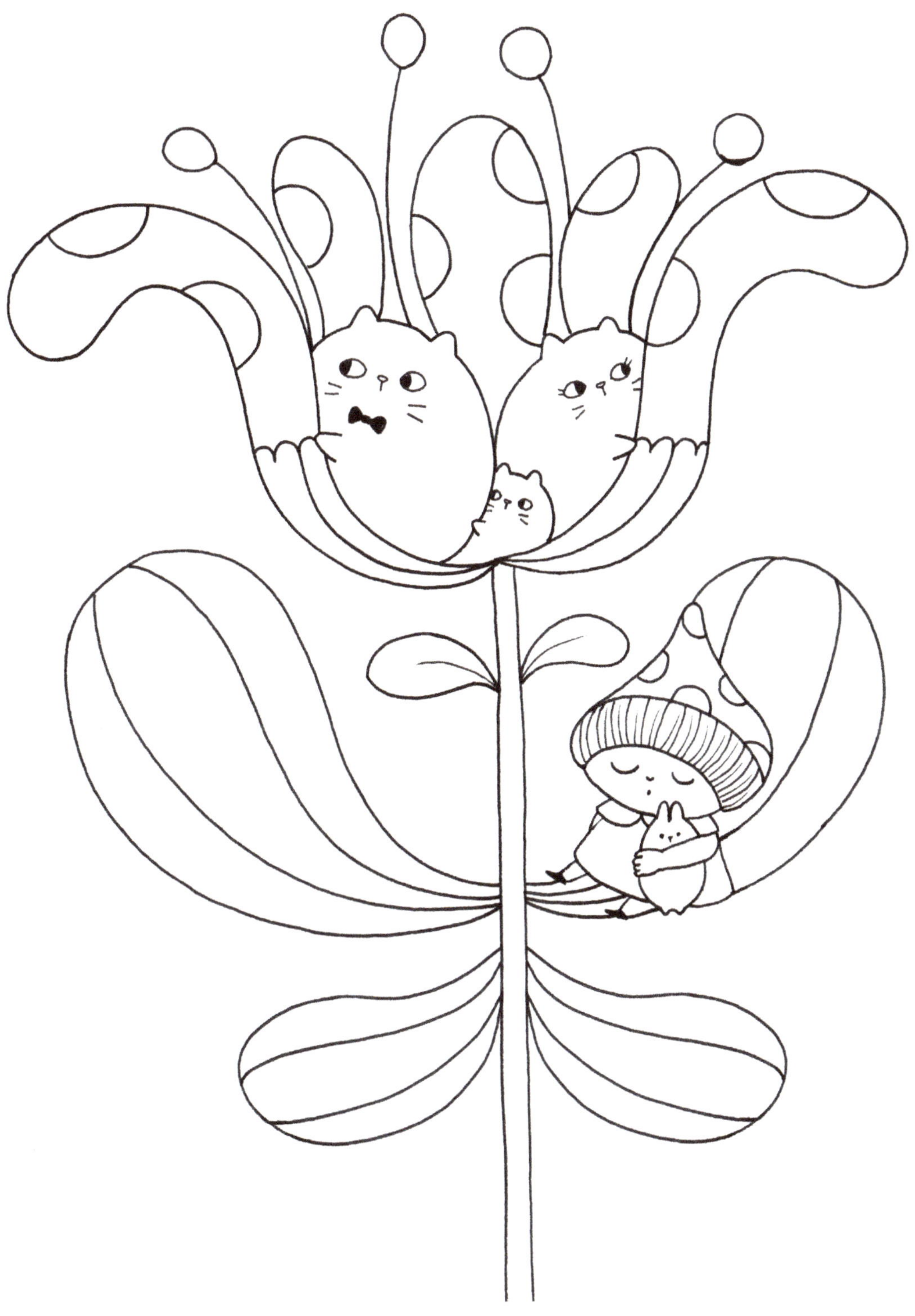

Colors can inspire different feelings, emotions, and energy. They also are an effective way to influence the tone of your drawings. For example, gray is a great color choice for a too-cool cat, whereas orange and yellow might look better on a silly, mischievous cat. How might you use the colors below to communicate the mood of a drawing or doodle?

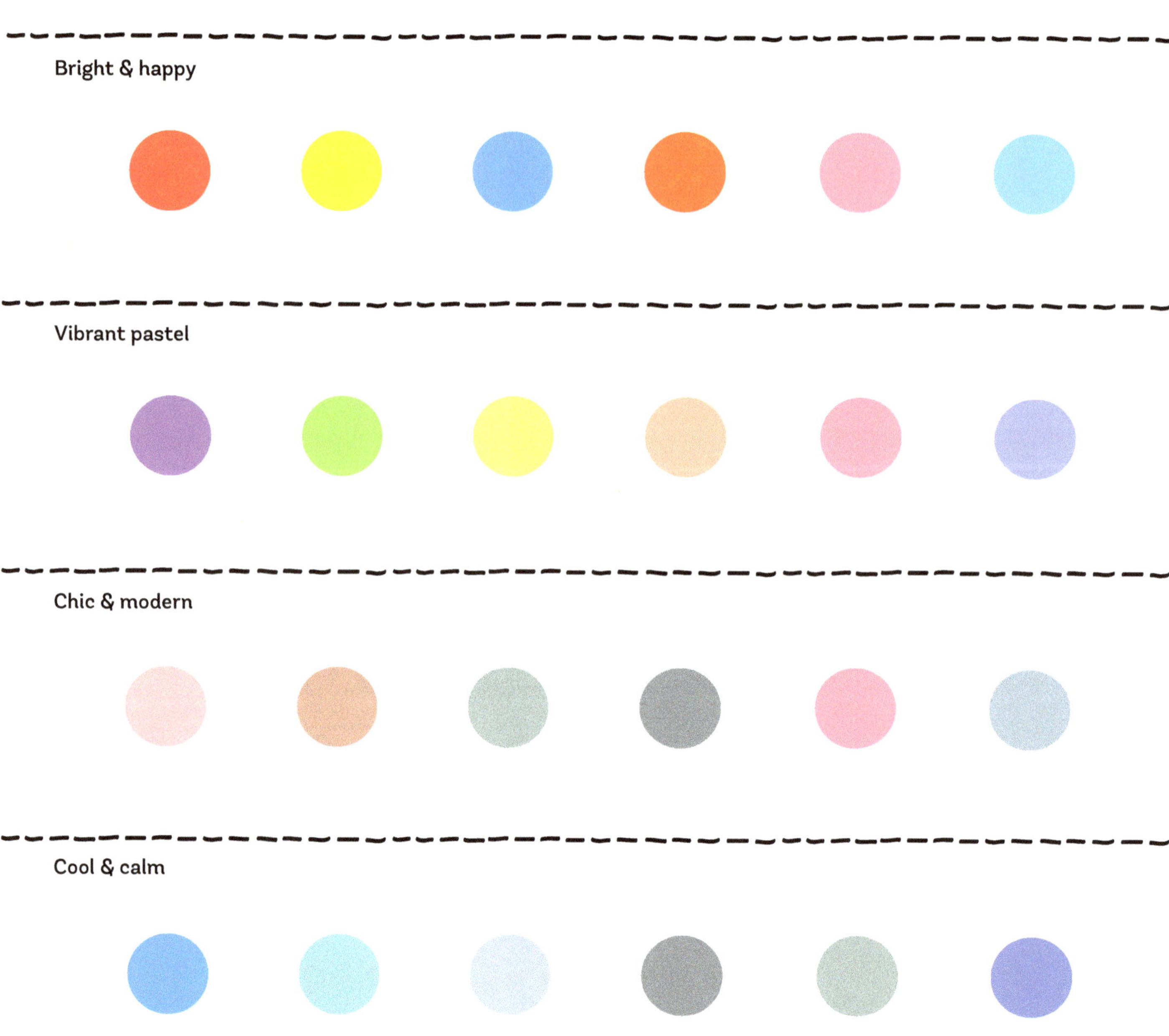

Bright & happy

Vibrant pastel

Chic & modern

Cool & calm

Use any of the colors shown on the opposite page to color in the artwork below. Will you add bold and vibrant colors to the illustration, or will you use muted shades instead? Feel free to lighten or darken them as you like.

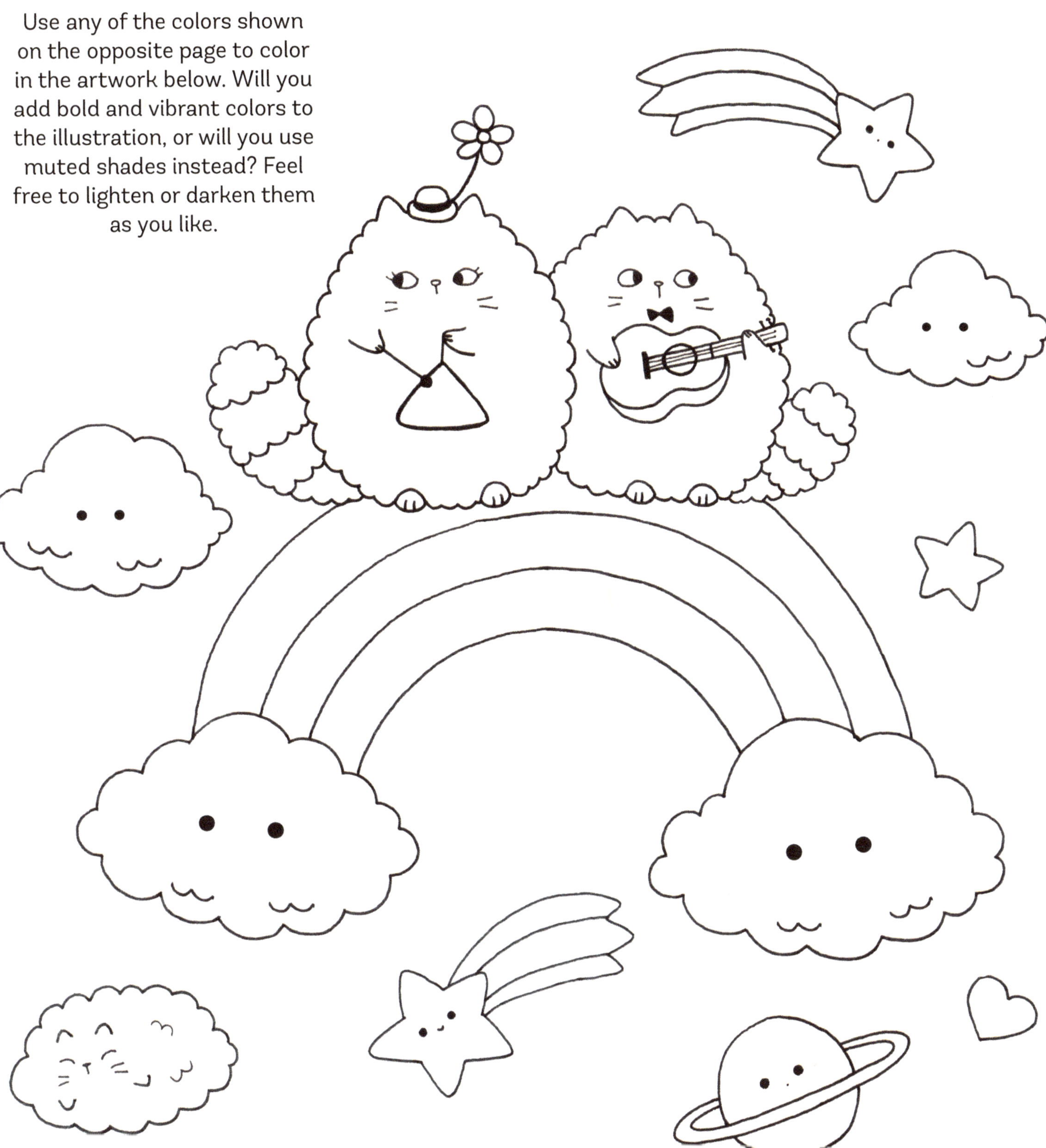

PAWSITIVELY PRETTY PASTELS

Pastels are lighter shades of colors that are made by mixing white into darker colors. They are softer and make for soothing drawings. They also add extra cuteness!

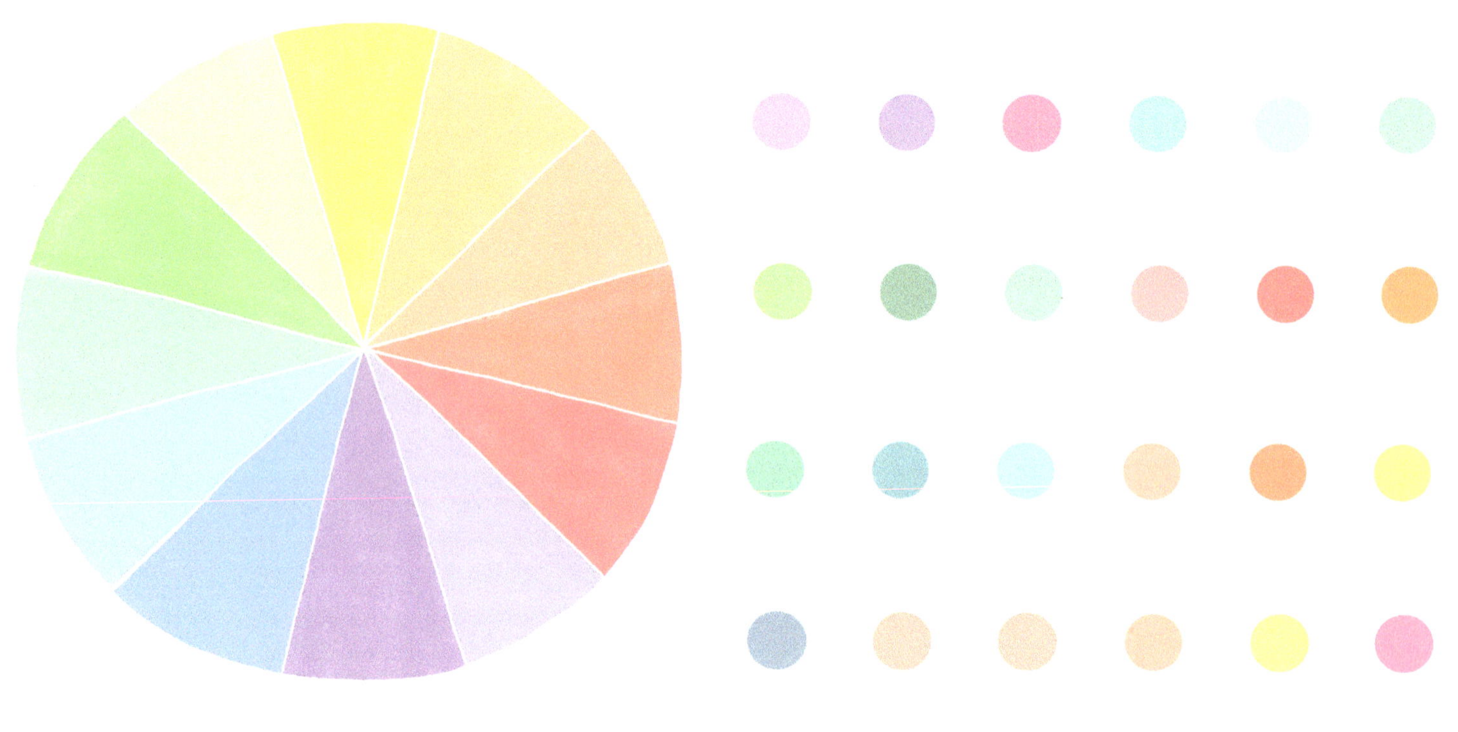

Select some favorite colors and color them into the empty circles with colored pencil. Then use a white colored pencil to make your own pastel color combinations. Use any of your favorite combinations to color in the artwork on the opposite page.

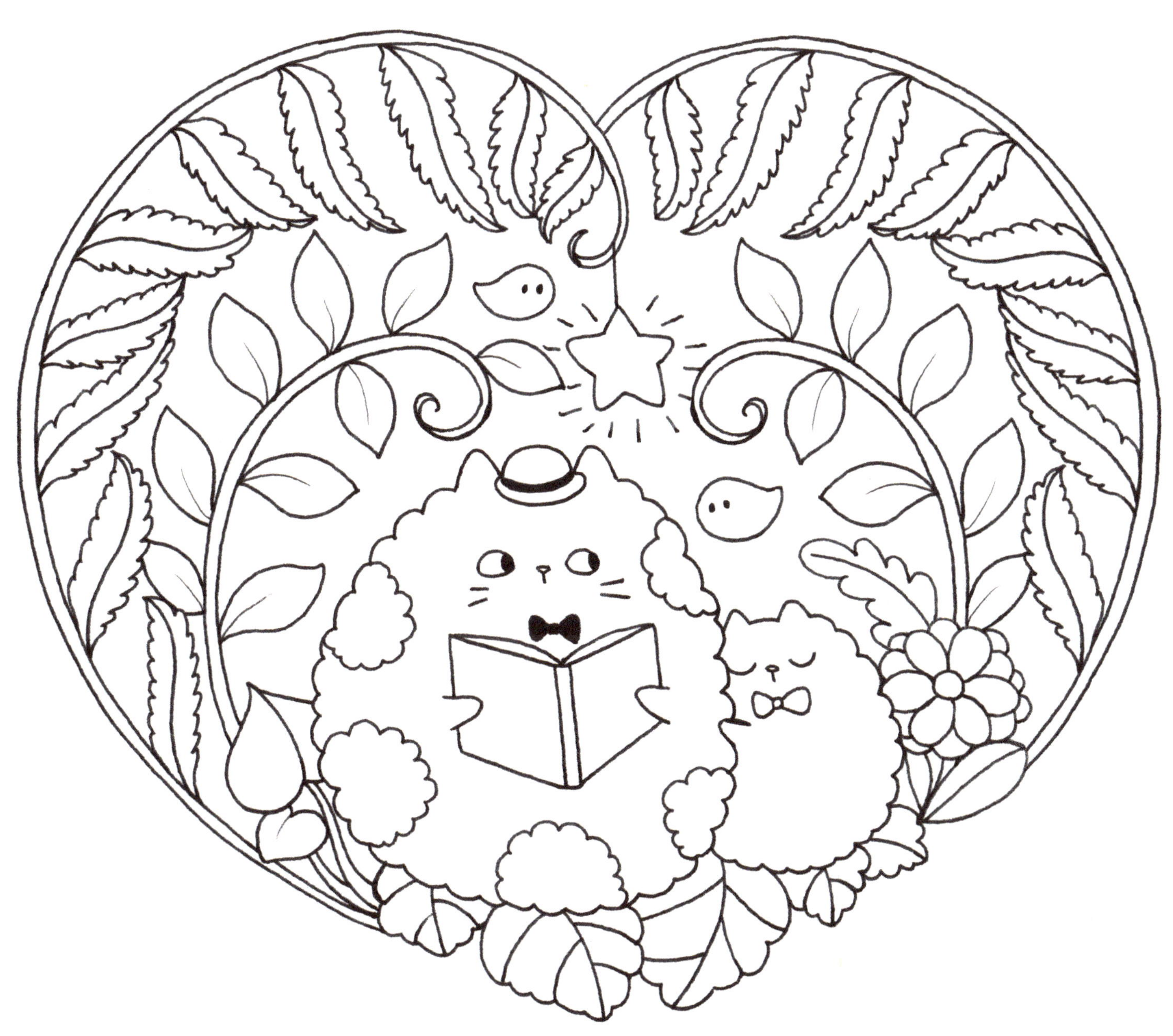

PATTERNS

In addition to adding color to your feline friends, you can also use simple shapes to create cute patterns. And what could be cuter than a pink-and-purple striped cat?

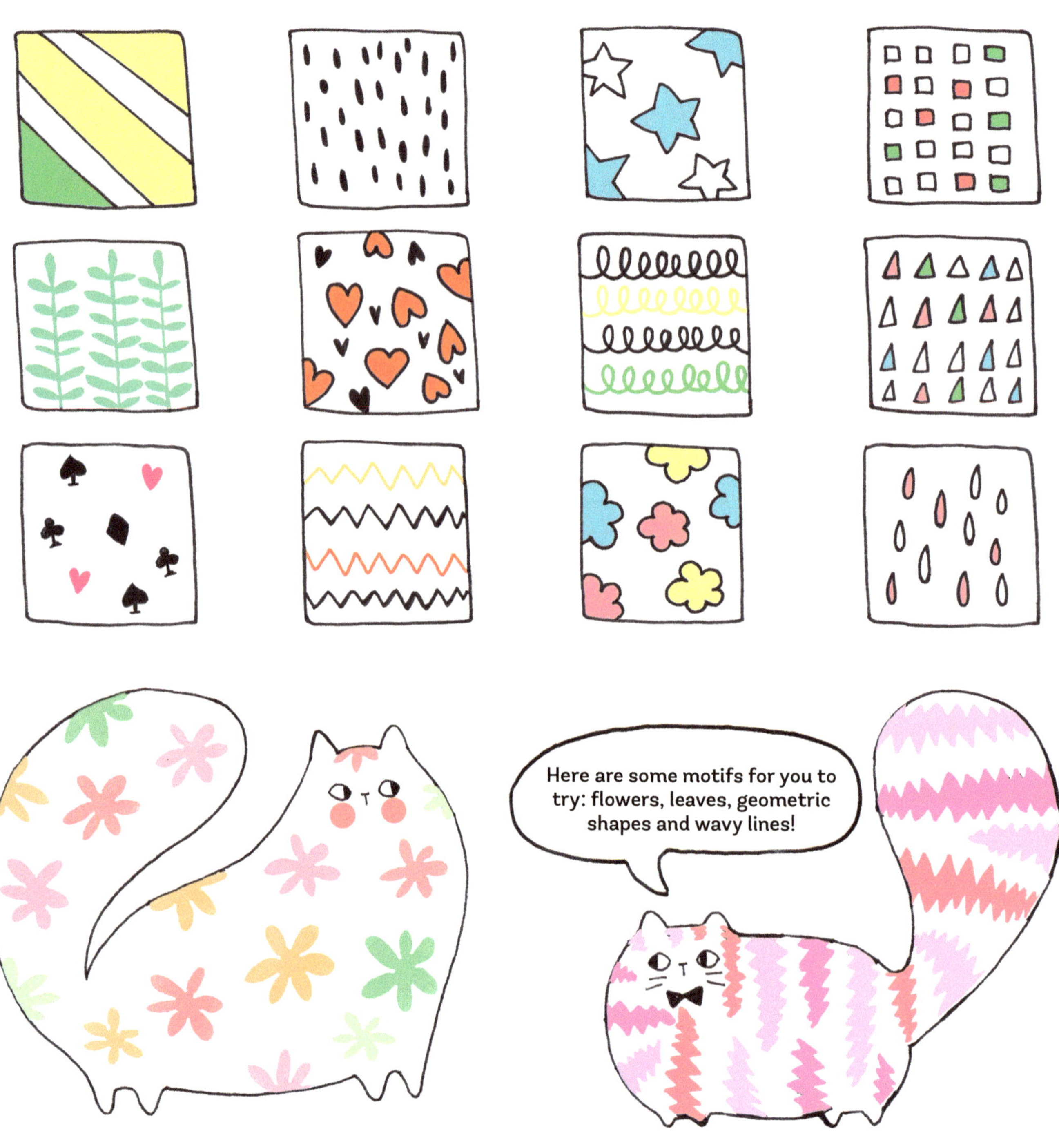

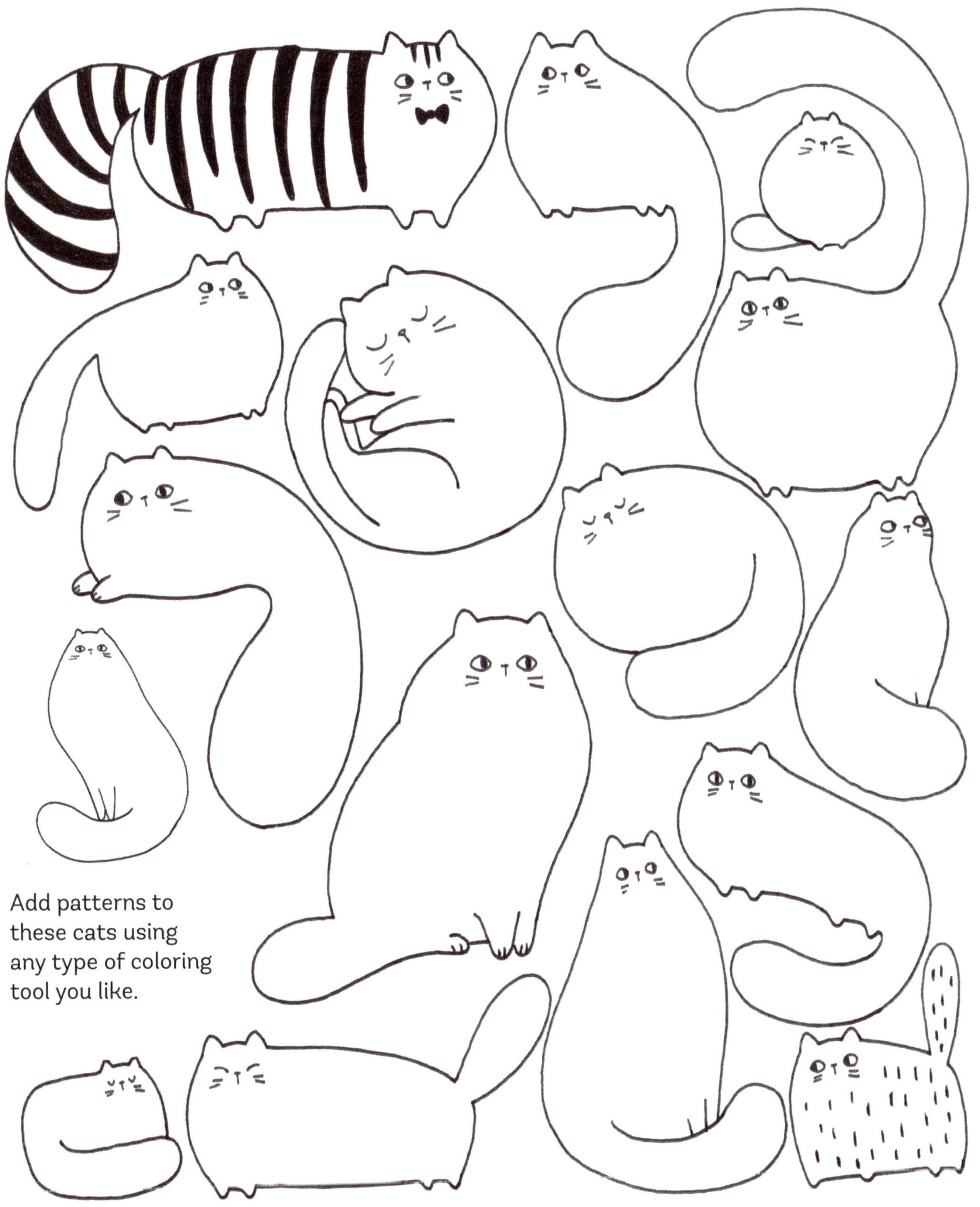

Add patterns to
these cats using
any type of coloring
tool you like.

My drawing lessons are very simple. I will give you some tips to get you started in these first few pages. Then simply follow the step-by-step drawings as you continue to move through the book!

PERSIAN

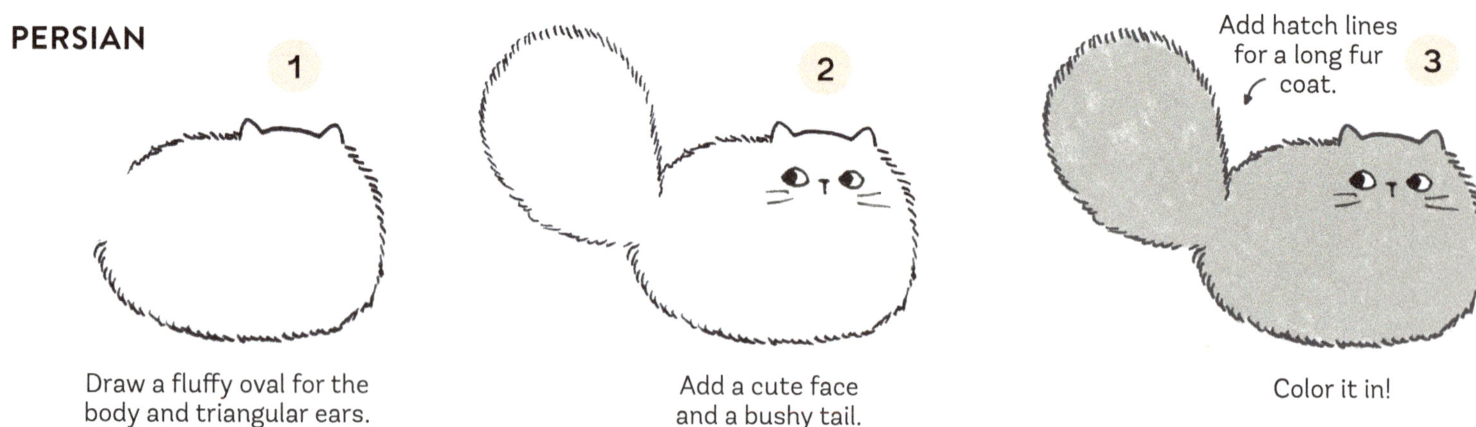

Draw a fluffy oval for the body and triangular ears.

Add a cute face and a bushy tail.

Color it in!

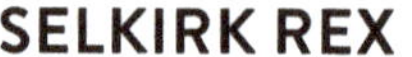

SELKIRK REX

1

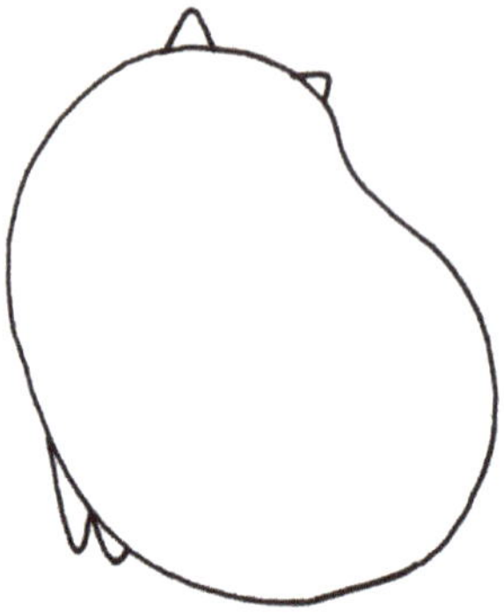

Outline a bean shape for the body. Add triangles for ears and legs.

2

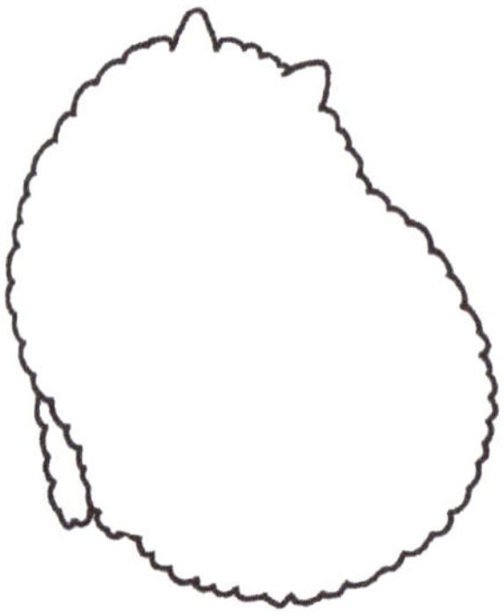

Go over the outline with scalloped lines to create fluff.

3

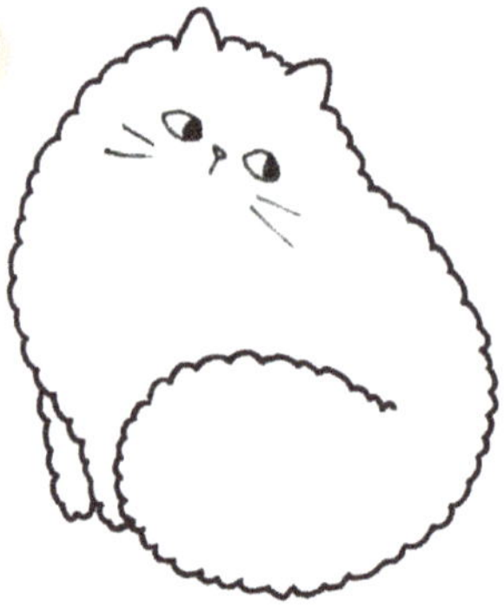

Add a fluffy oval tail and cute face.

4

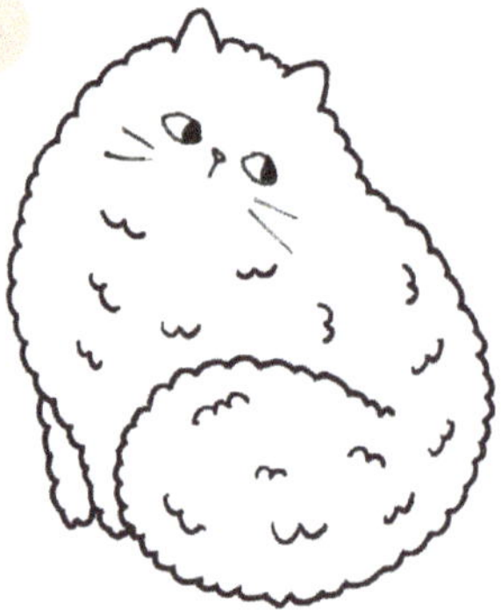

Add fluffy fur.

5

Add color!

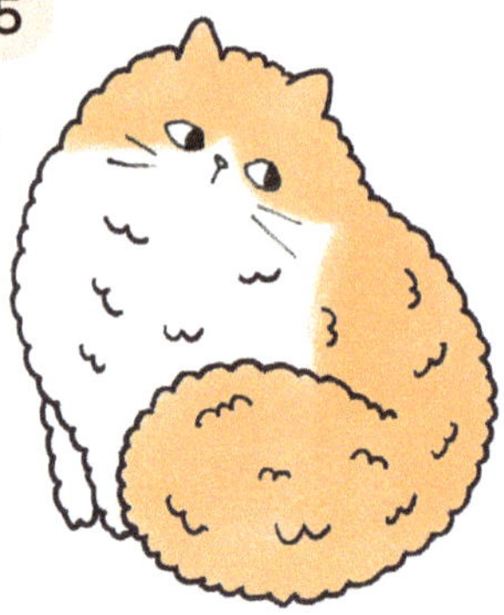

JAPANESE BOBTAIL

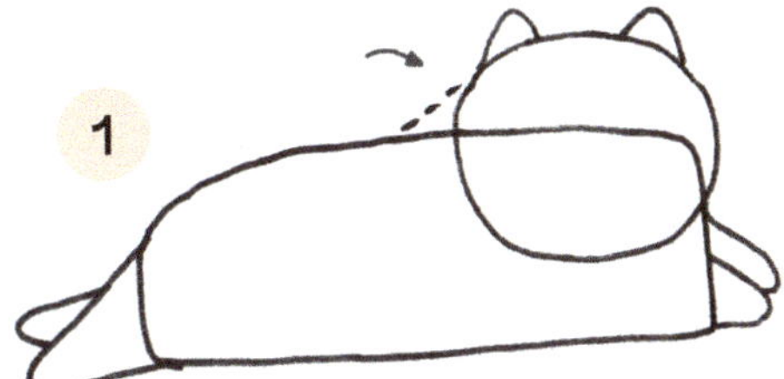

Use a circle and long rectangle
to create the body. Then add
triangles for ears and legs.

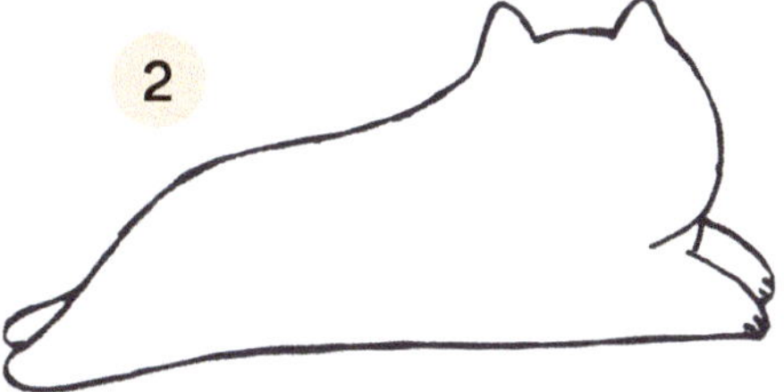

Trace the outline and erase
any unused sketch lines.

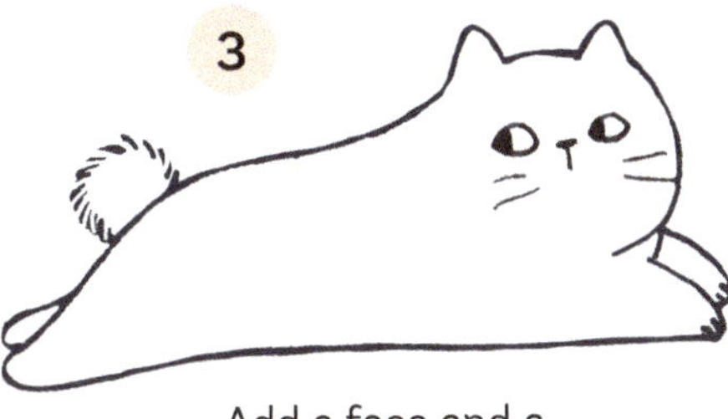

Add a face and a
fluffy circle tail.

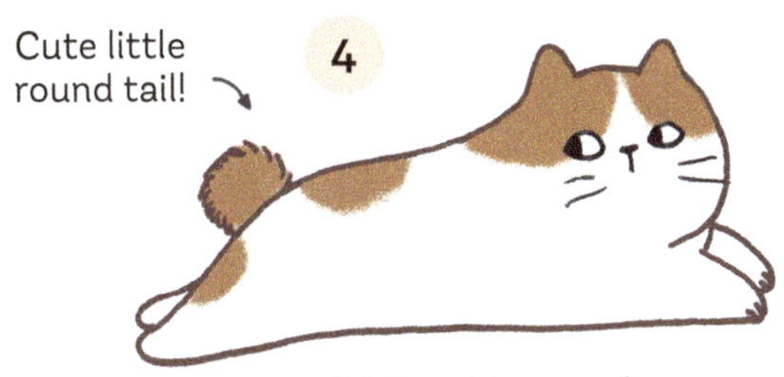

Add markings and
color it in!

ABYSSINIAN

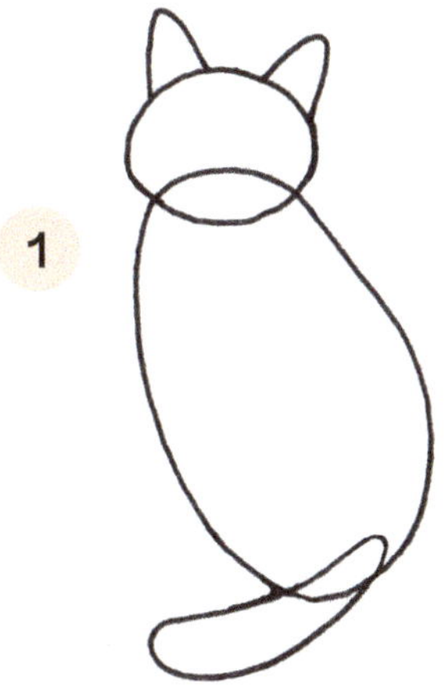

Draw a circle and oval for
the body. Then add a curvy
tail and triangular ears.

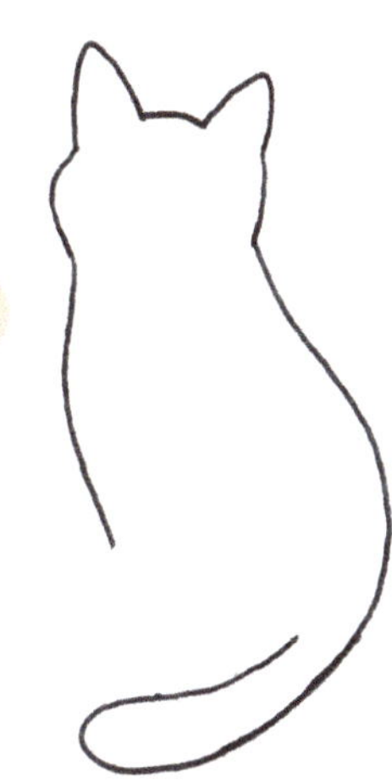

Trace the body
outline and erase
any sketch lines.

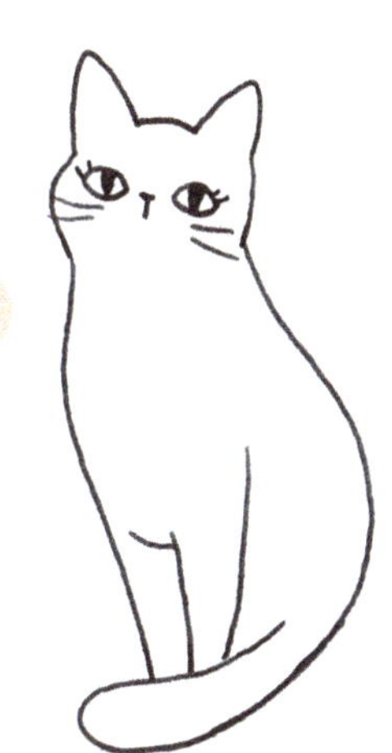

Add long legs, big
almond-shaped eyes,
nose, and whiskers.

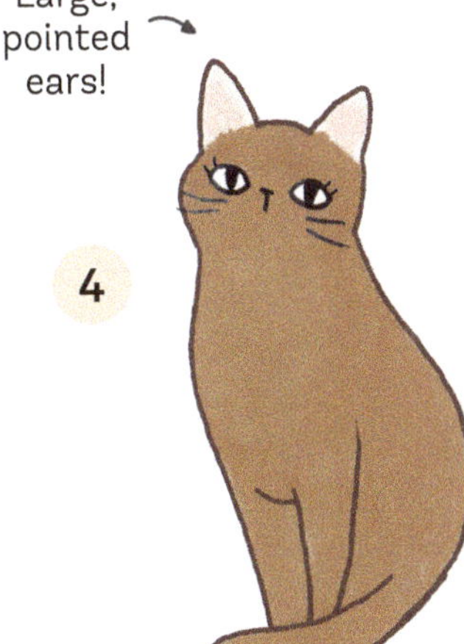

Finish with color!

RAGDOLL

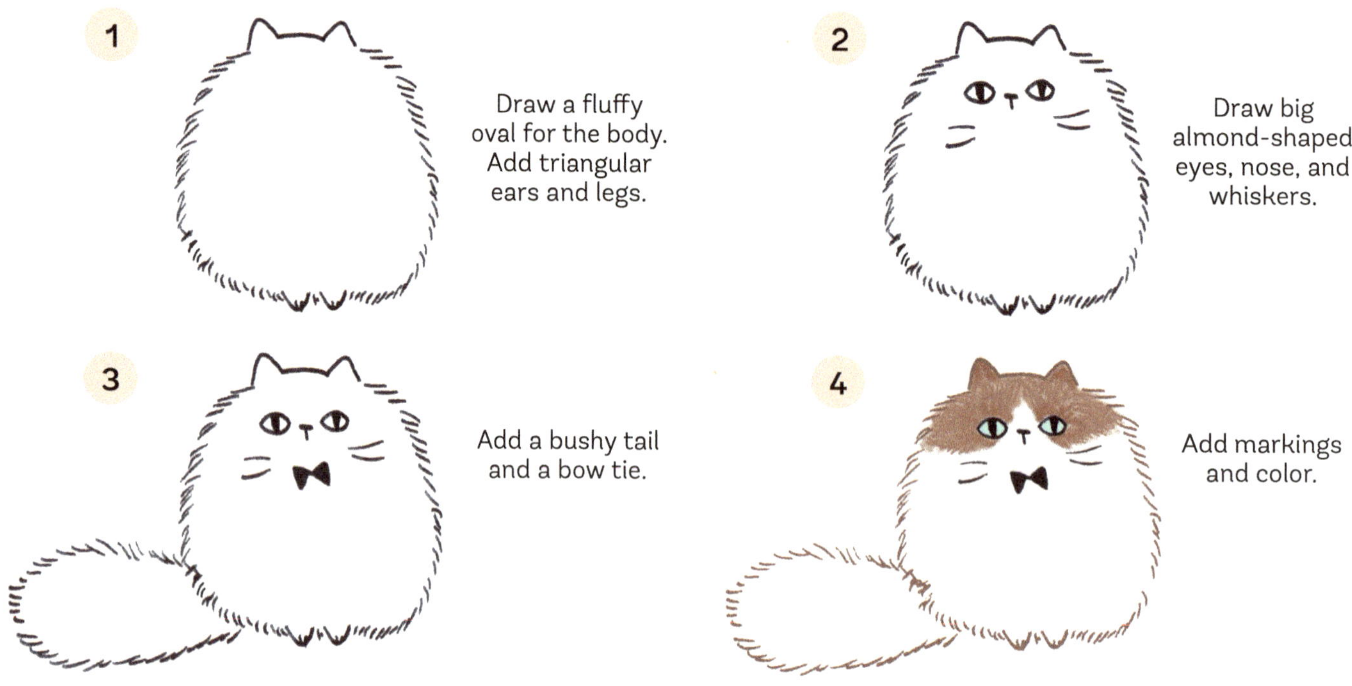

1 — Draw a fluffy oval for the body. Add triangular ears and legs.

2 — Draw big almond-shaped eyes, nose, and whiskers.

3 — Add a bushy tail and a bow tie.

4 — Add markings and color.

QUICK TIPS

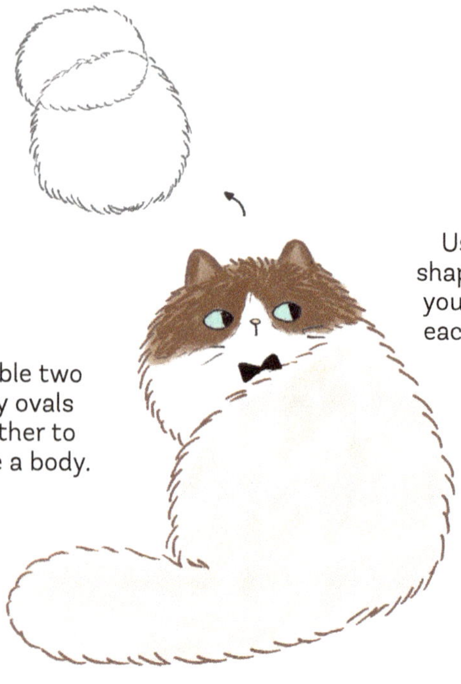

Scribble two fluffy ovals together to create a body.

Use simple shapes to start your drawings each time. It's easy!

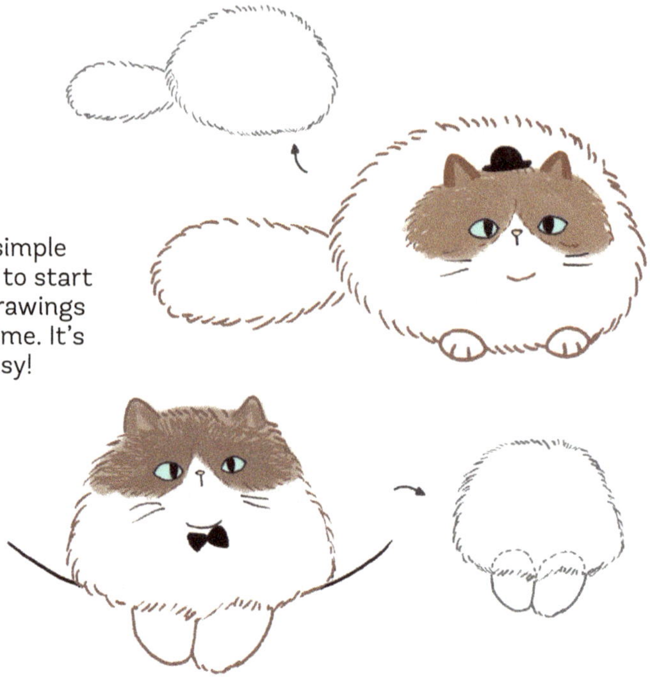

Fill the page with ragdolls. Practice drawing different poses by varying body shapes.
Why not try a fluffy rectangle to start your drawing?

BRITISH SHORTHAIR

1 Draw an oval first; then draw a curvy tail. Add triangular ears.

2 Add a cute face.

3 Draw a bow tie.

4 Add color.

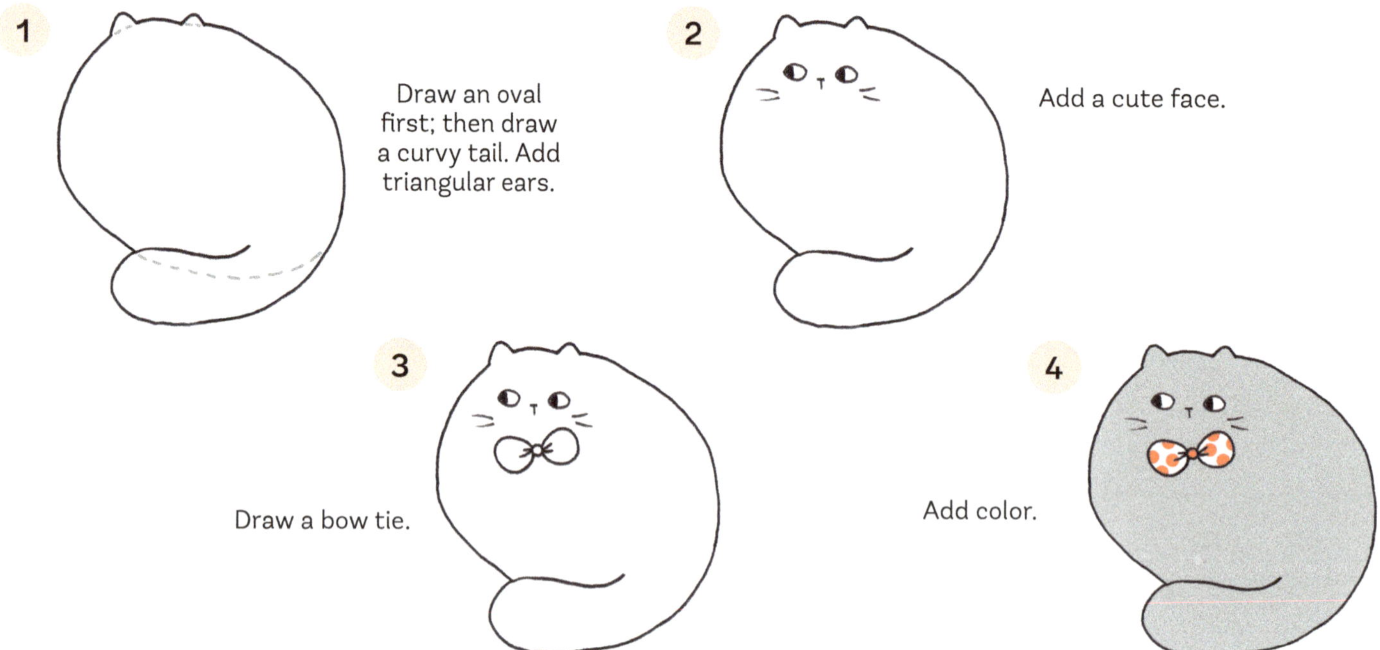

QUICK TIPS

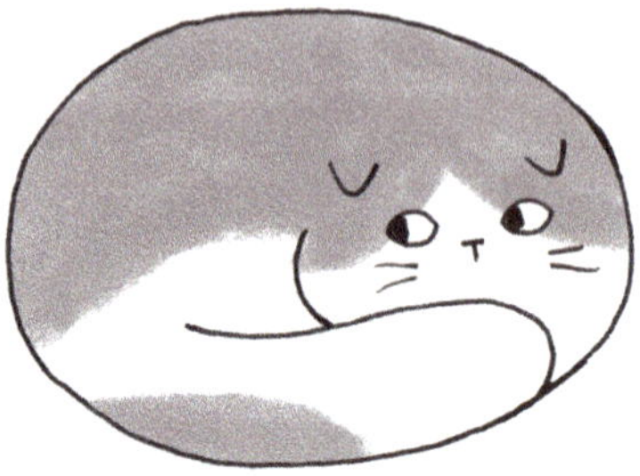

Turn it into a Scottish Fold by changing the ears to folded ones.

Start with a bean-shaped body.

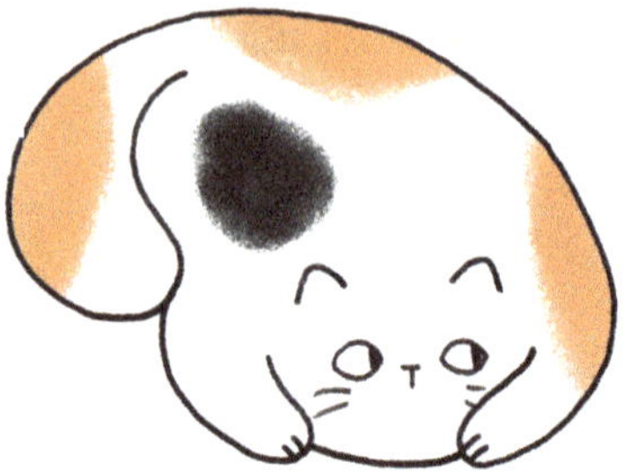

Try experimenting with different patterns to create different breeds.

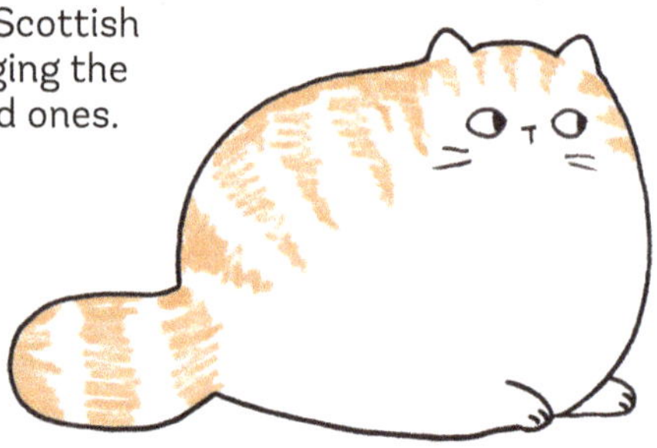

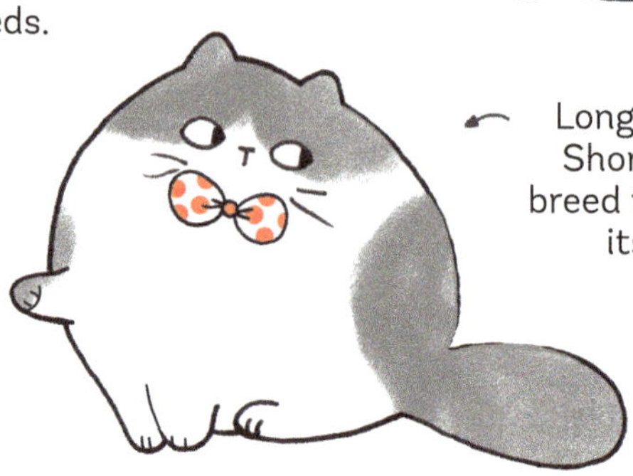

Long live the British Shorthair: a hearty breed that can live into its late teens!

Turn these simple shapes into British Shorthairs or Scottish Folds.

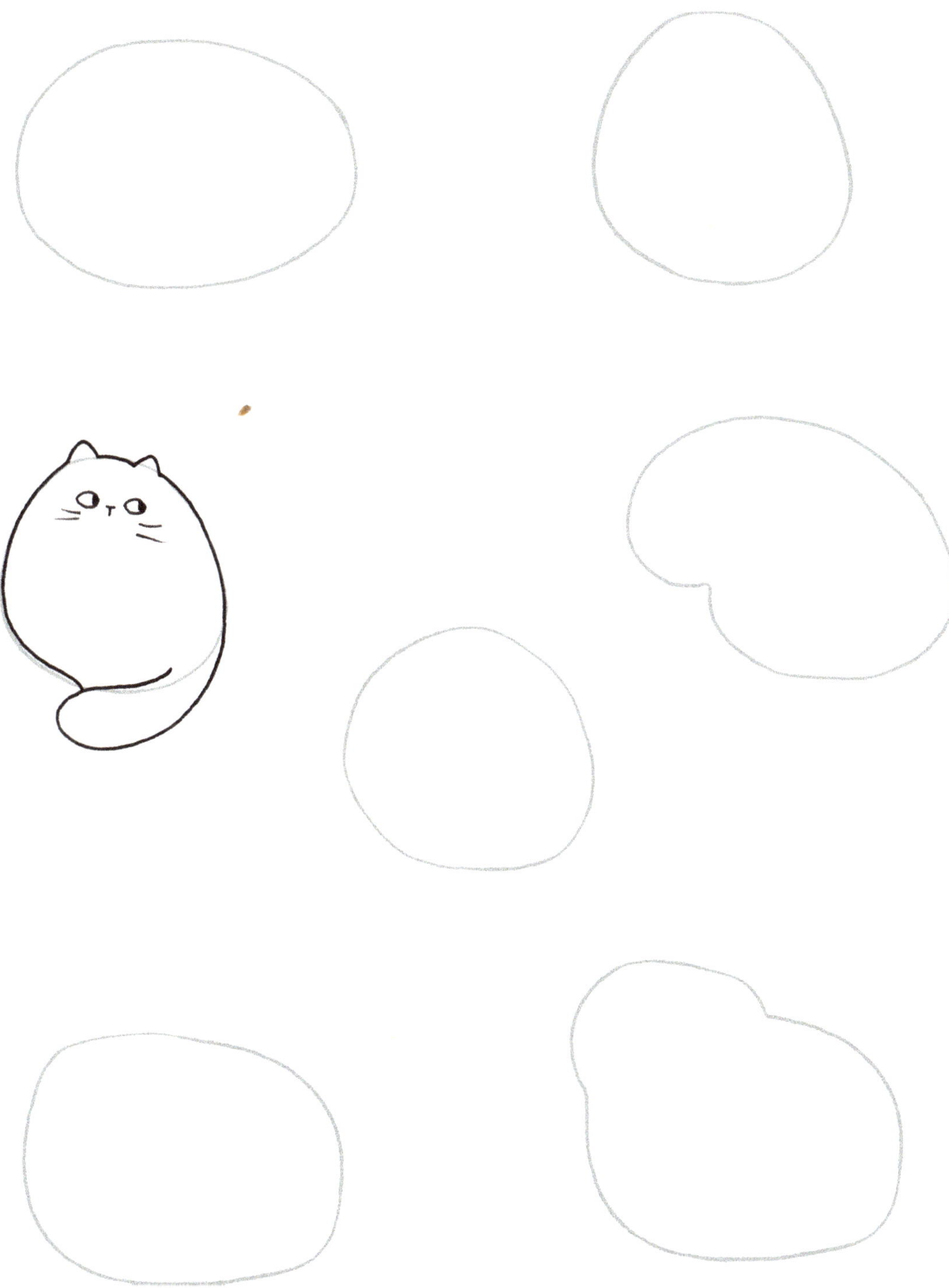

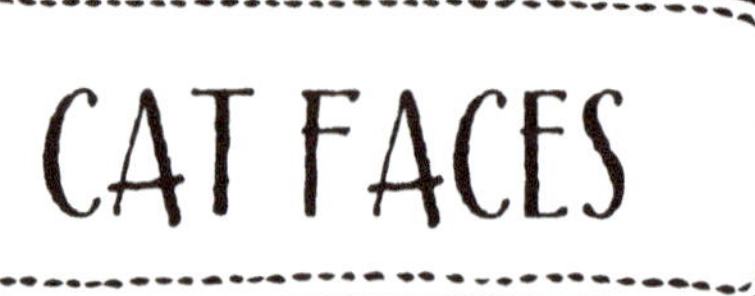

As any cat person can tell you, a feline's body language and facial expression can tell a lot about its mood. Complete the cat drawings on these pages by adding expressions, colors, and markings.

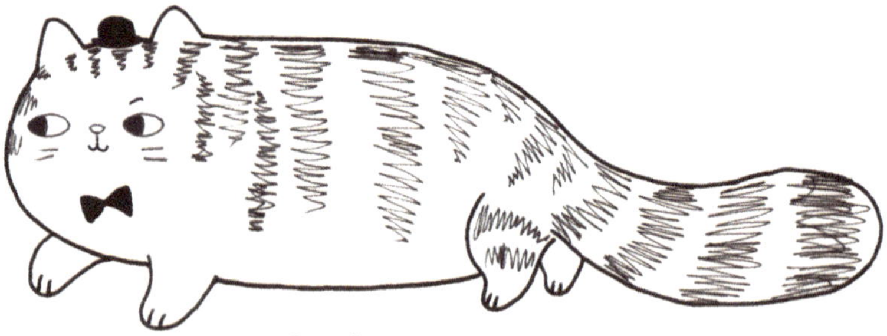

Sneaky

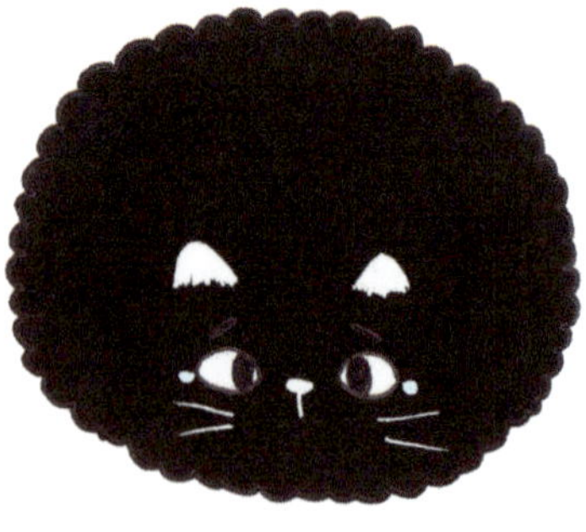

Scared

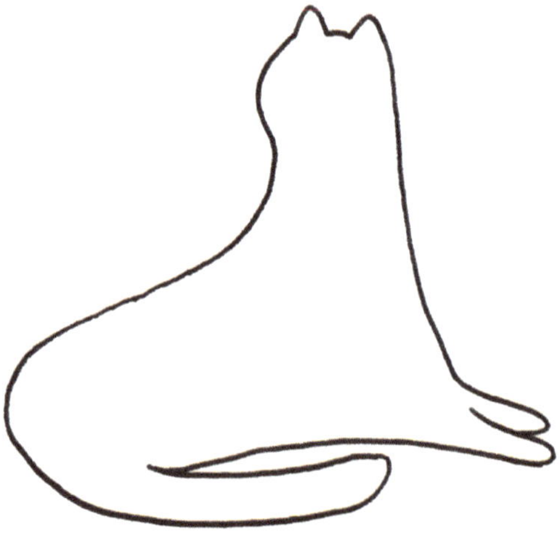

Relaxed

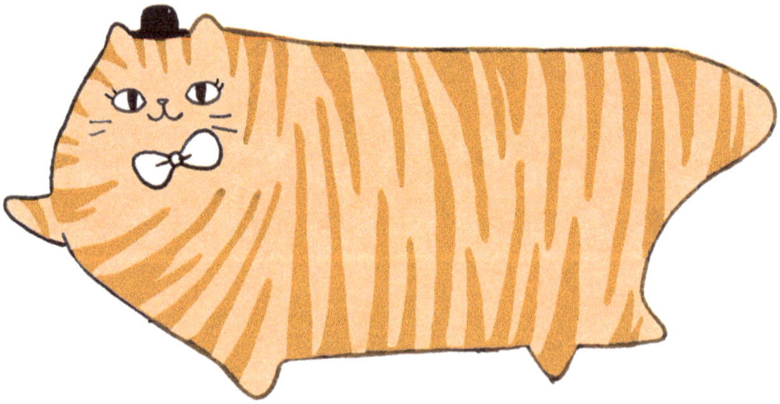

Confident

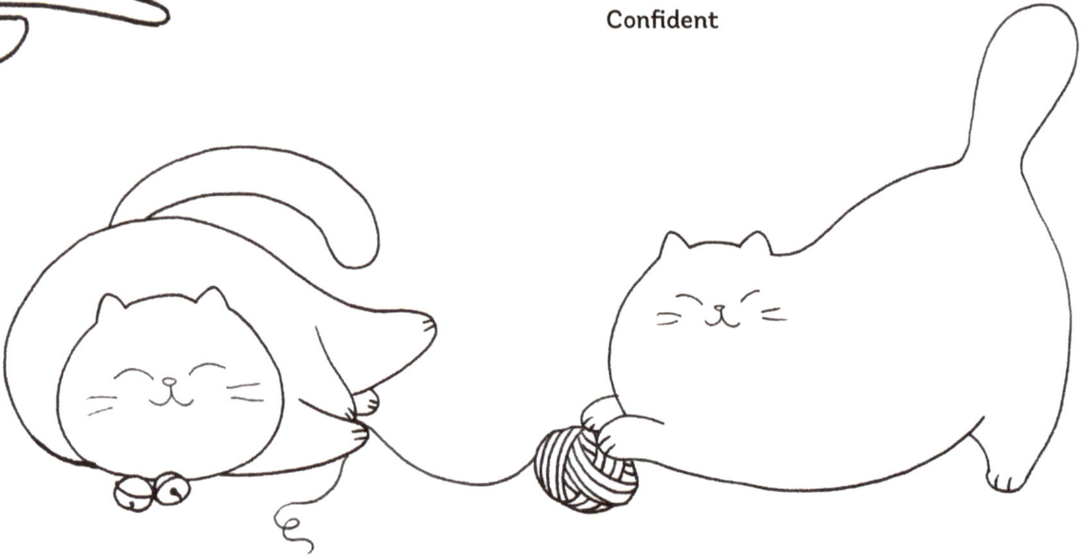

Cheerful and Playful

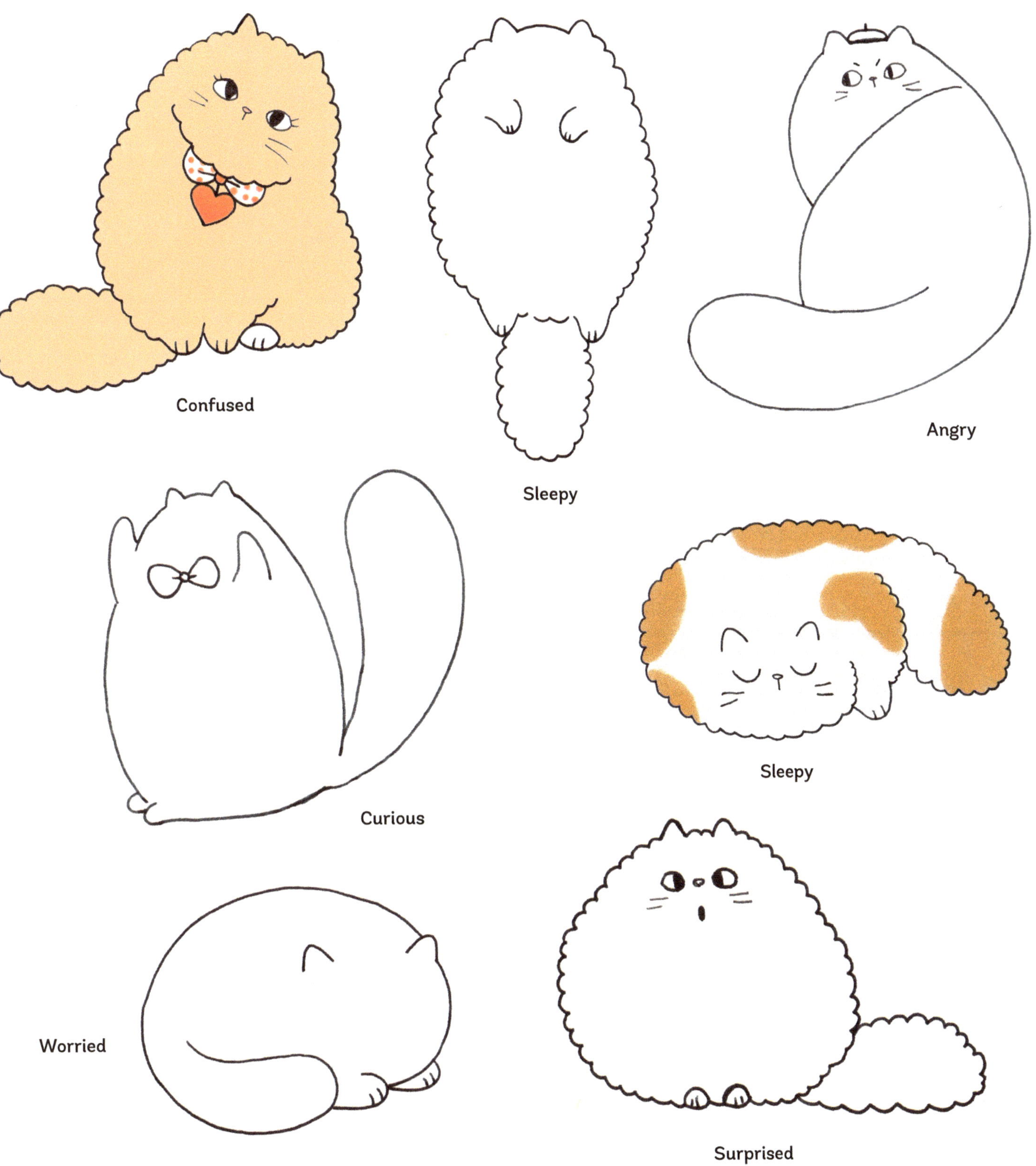

Confused

Sleepy

Angry

Curious

Sleepy

Worried

Surprised

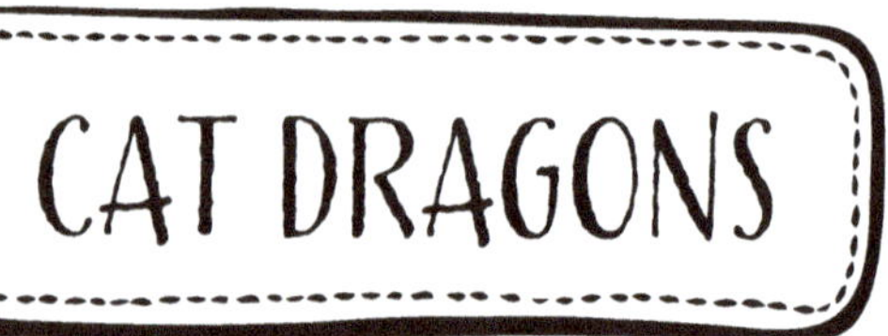
CAT DRAGONS

Follow along with each step to draw these mythical cat creatures.

SLEEPY DRAGON

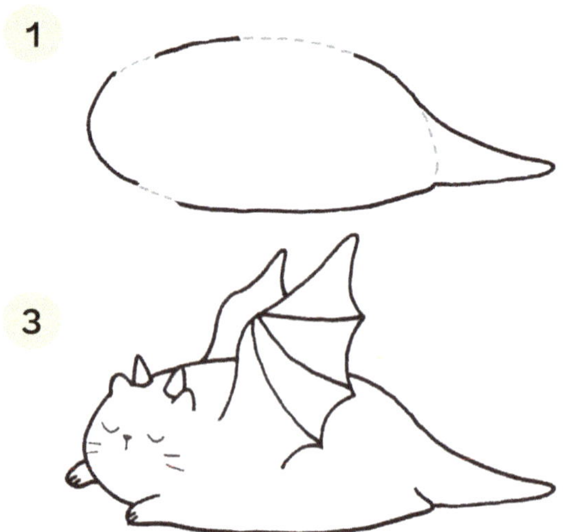

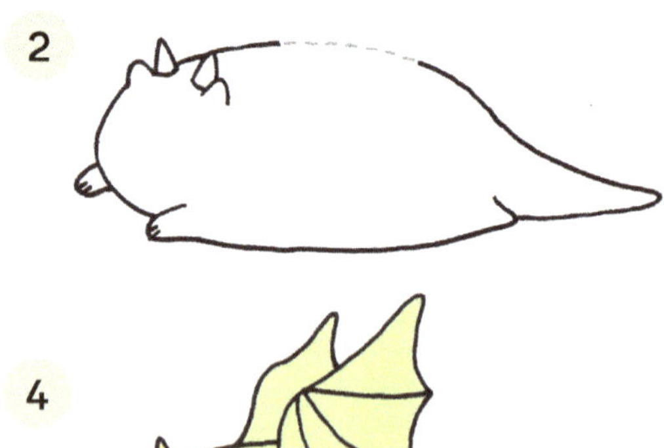

FLYING DRAGON

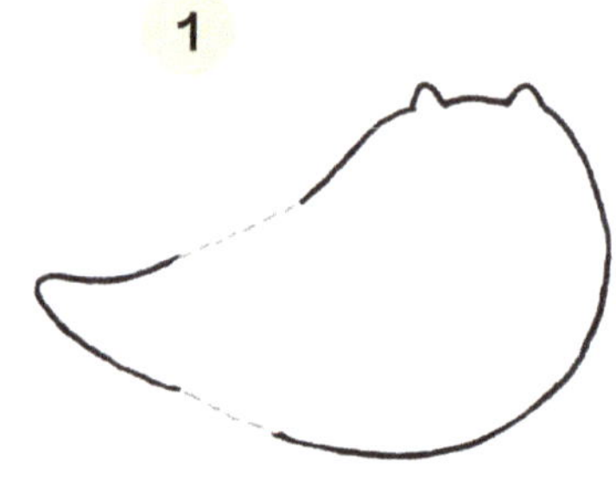

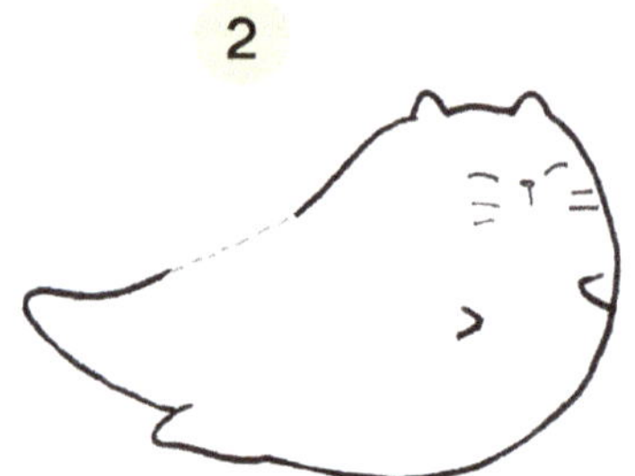

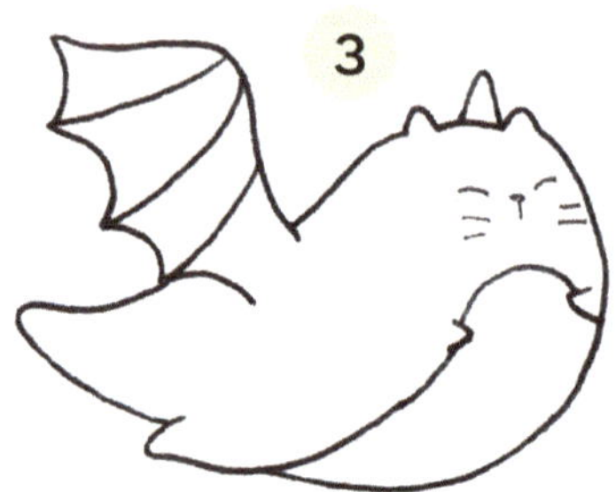

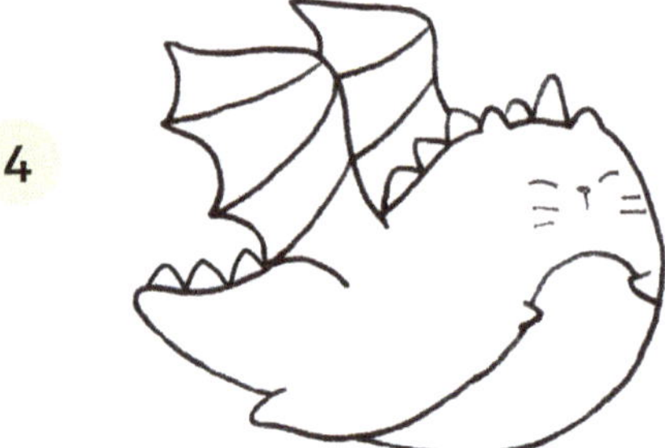

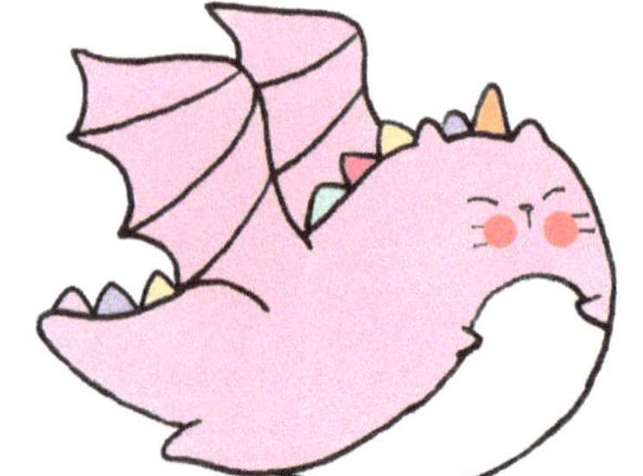

CUDDLY DRAGON

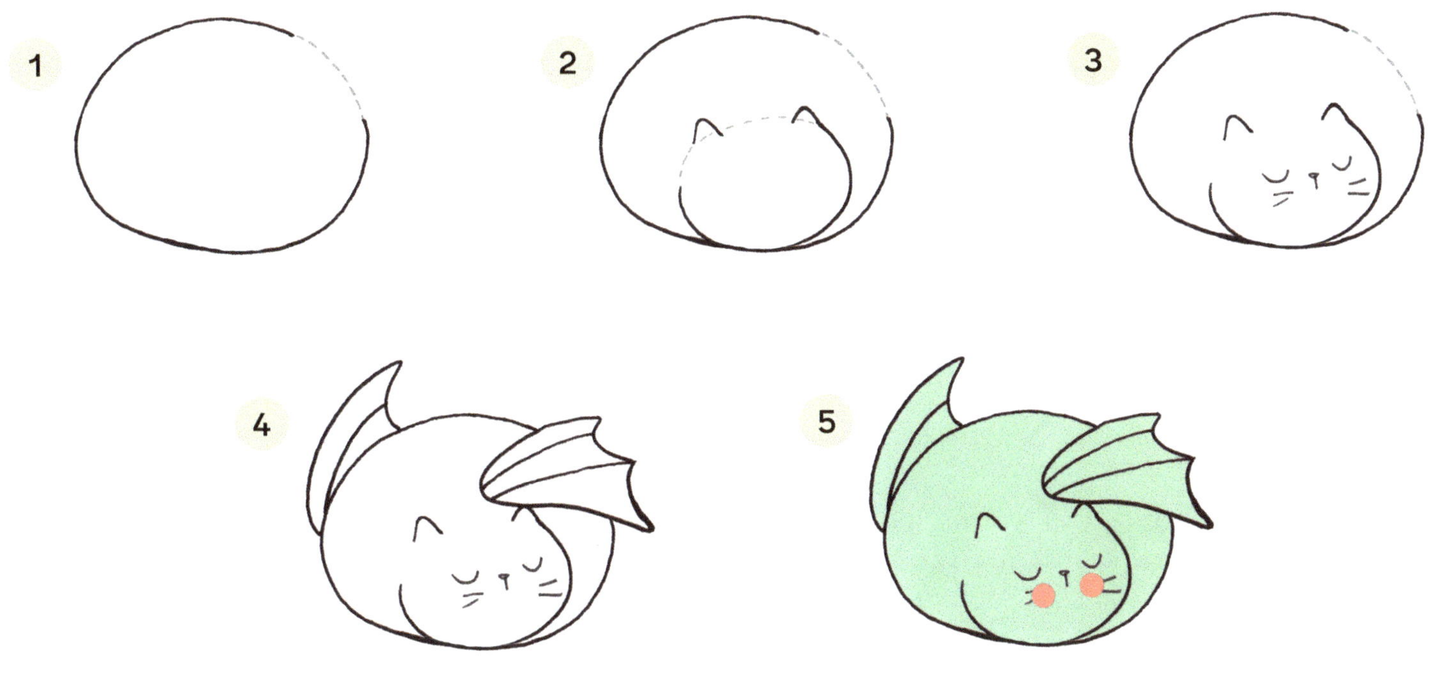

Draw some more cat dragons below.

OUT-OF-THIS-WORLD CATS

Follow along with each step to draw these otherworldly cats!

GHOST CAT

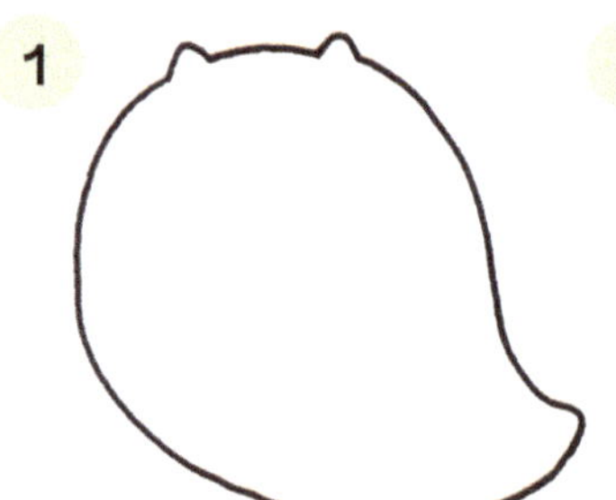
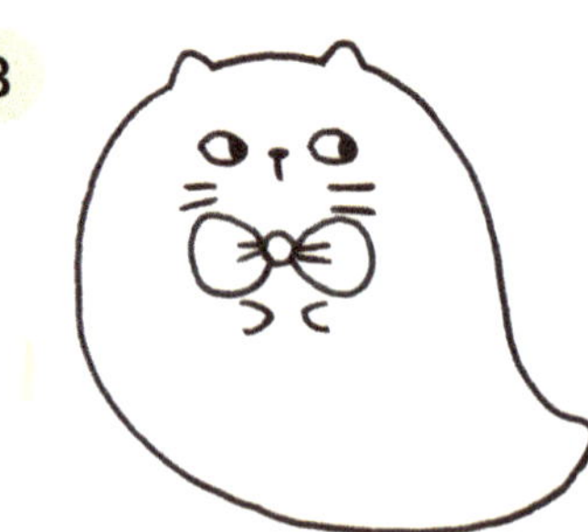
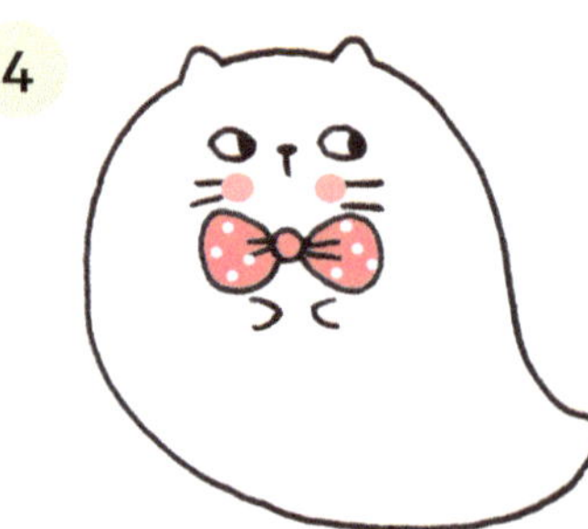

UNICORN CAT

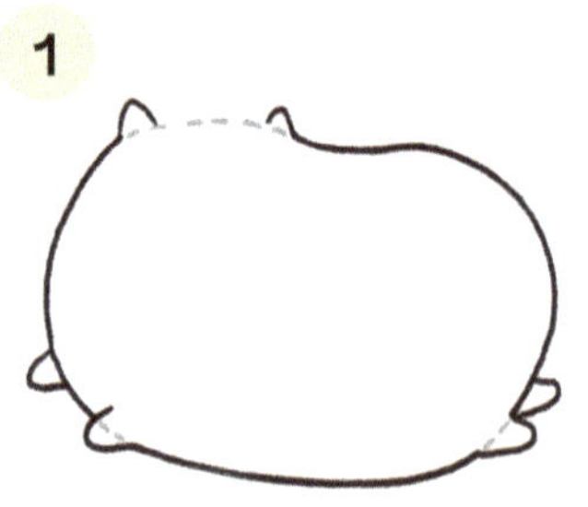
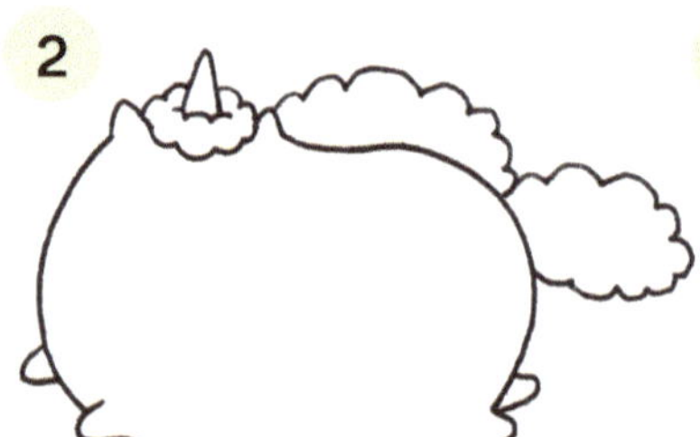
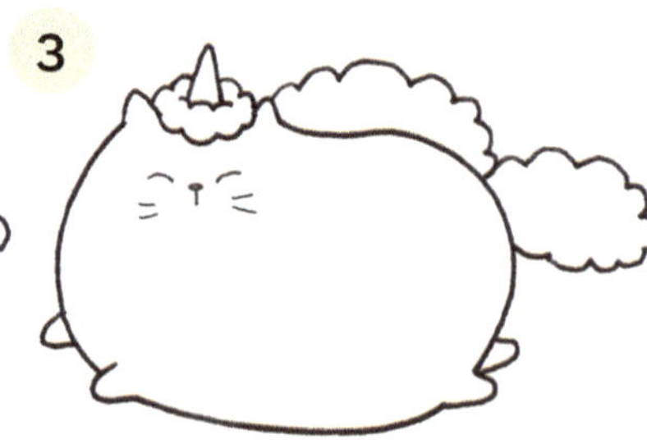
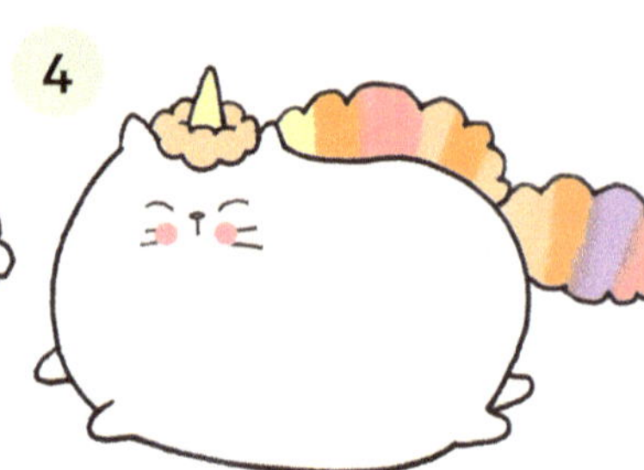

ANGEL CAT

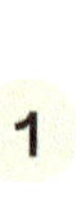
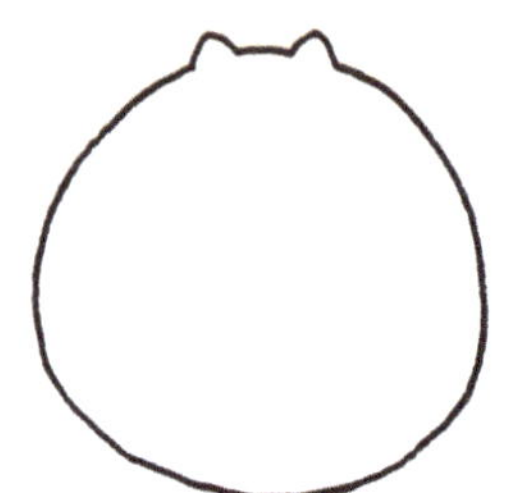
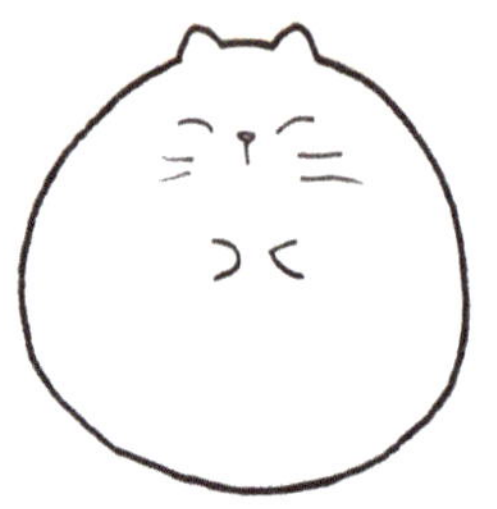
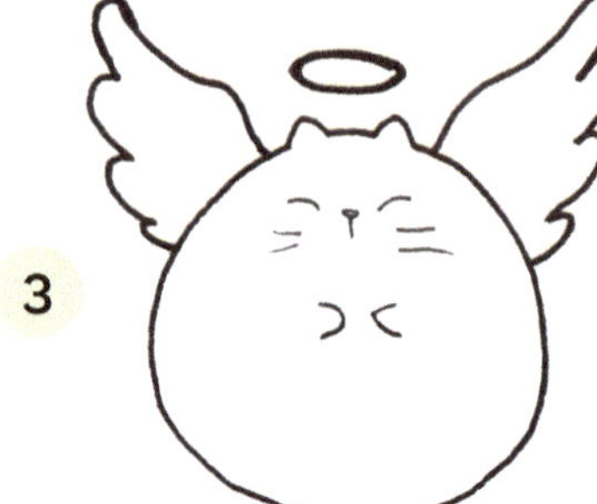
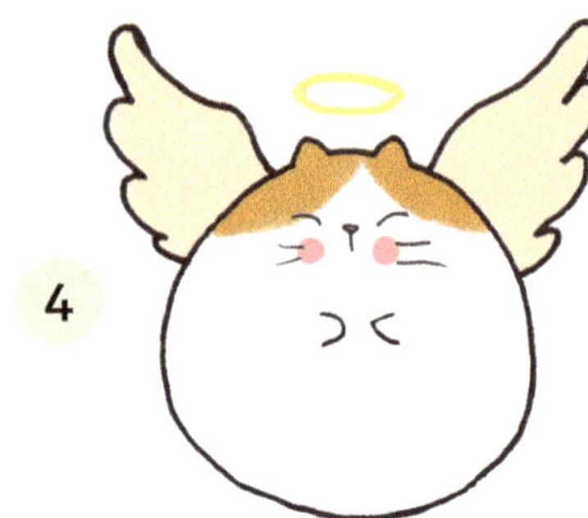

Add color to these magical cats!

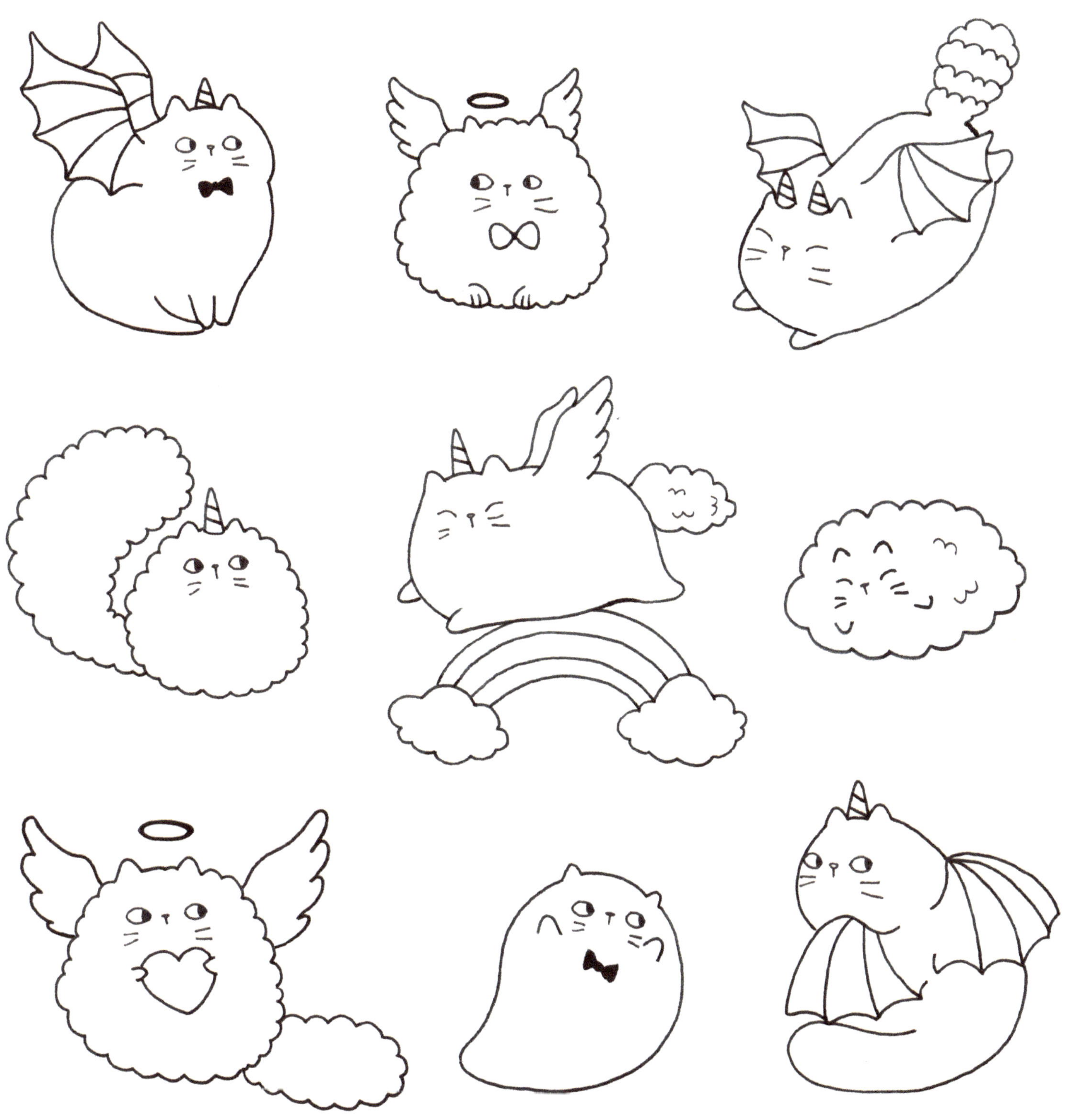

Even cats follow the zodiac!

WHAT'S YOUR SIGN?

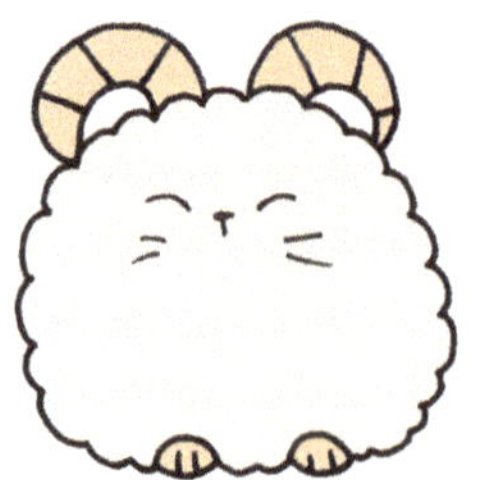

ARIES
March 21 – April 19
Warm, lovable, honest

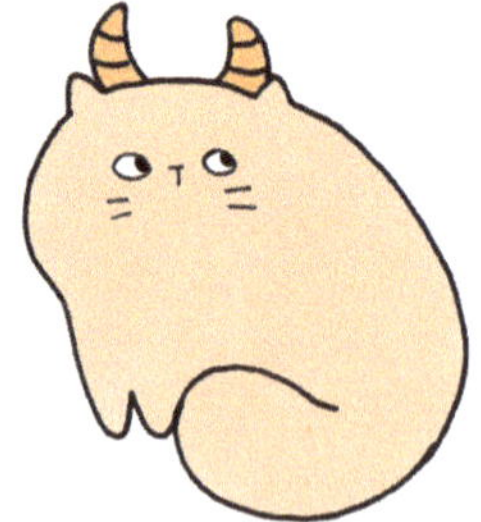

TAURUS
April 20 – May 20
Resilient and stubborn

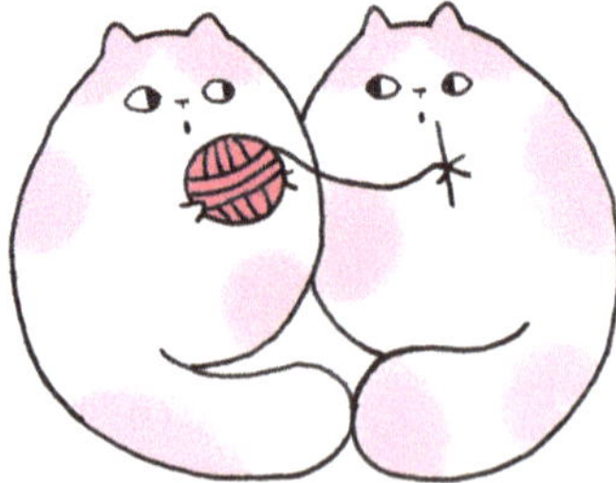

GEMINI
May 21 – June 20
Communicative and
charismatic

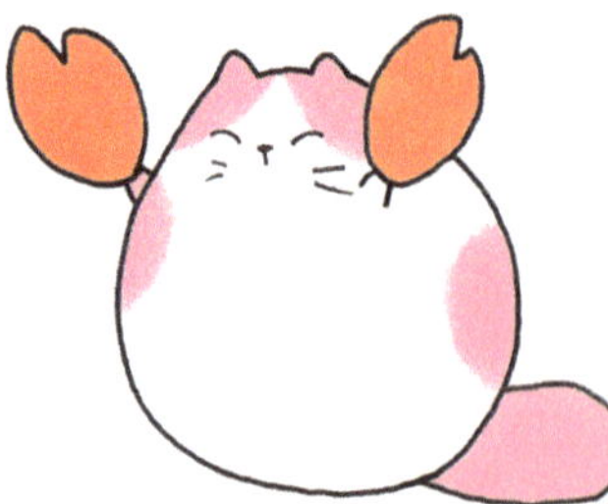

CANCER
June 21 – July 22
Outgoing and social

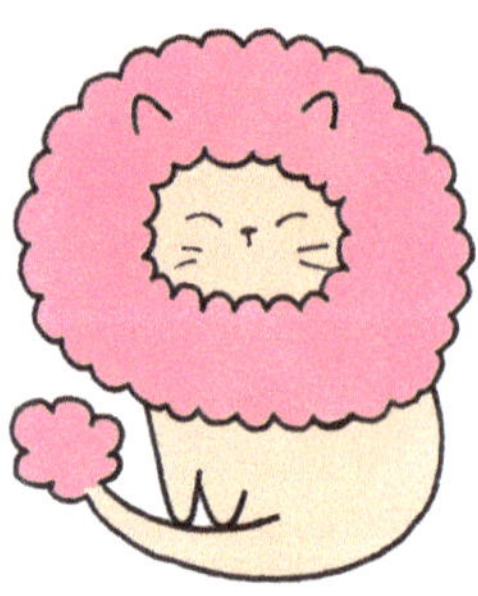

LEO
July 23 – August 22
Passionate and loyal

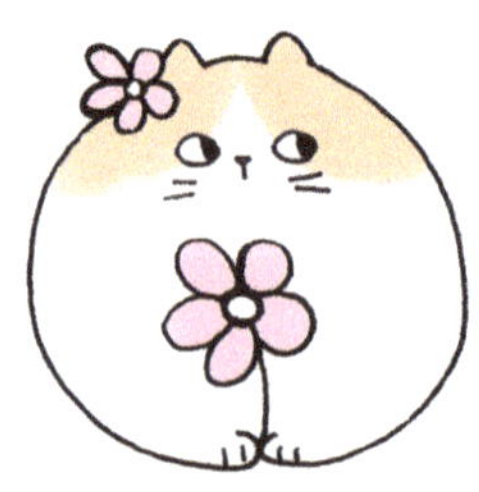

VIRGO
August 23 – September 22
Perfectionist and organized

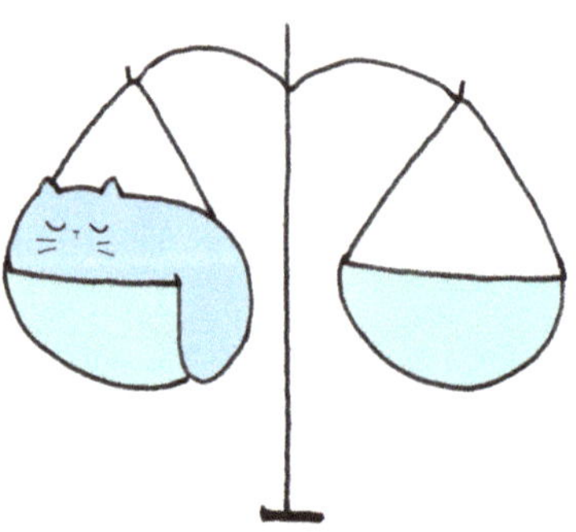

LIBRA
September 23 – October 22
Balanced and people-pleasing

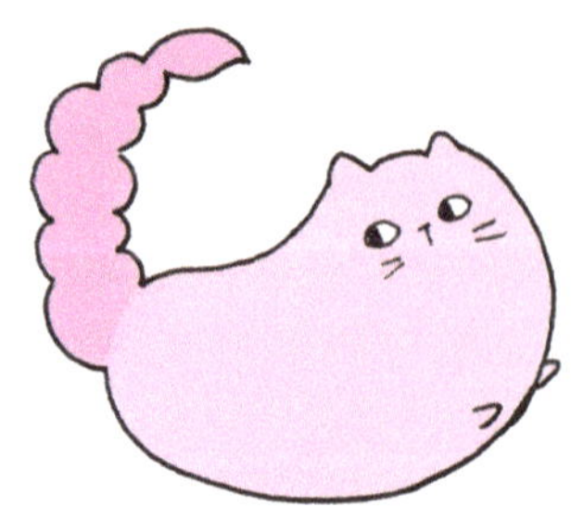

SCORPIO
October 23 – November 21
Mysterious and loyal

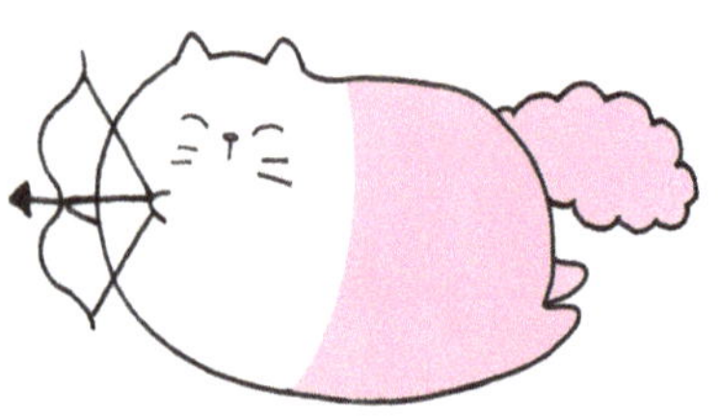

SAGITTARIUS
November 22 – December 21
Adventurous and frank

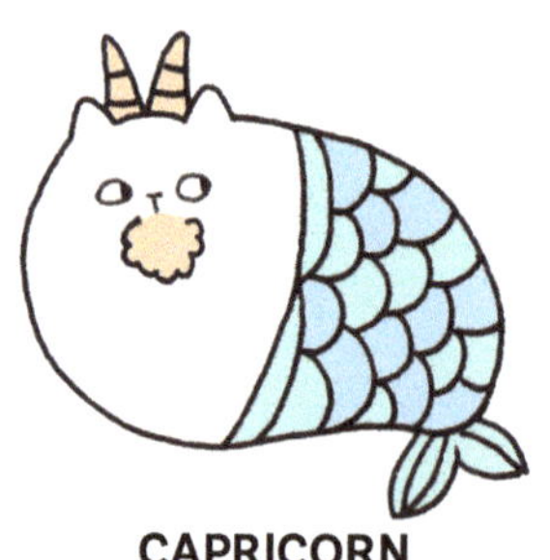

CAPRICORN
December 22 – January 19
Practical and determined

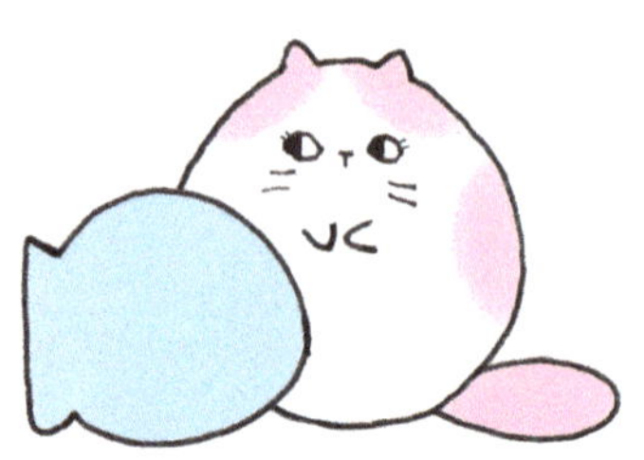

AQUARIUS
January 20 – February 18
Assertive and complex

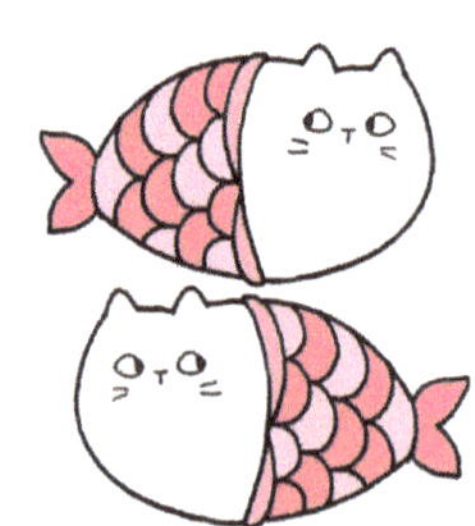

PISCES
February 19 – March 20
Compassionate and creative

ARIES

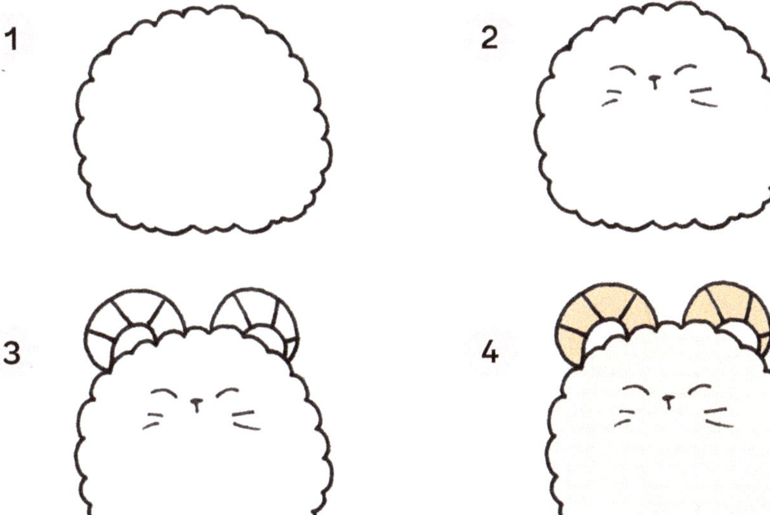

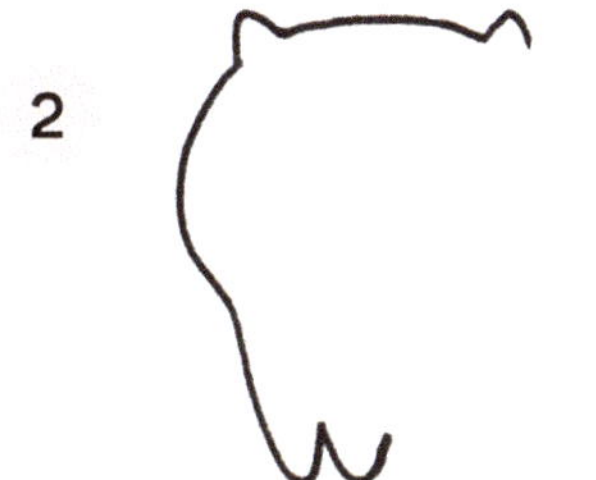

TAURUS

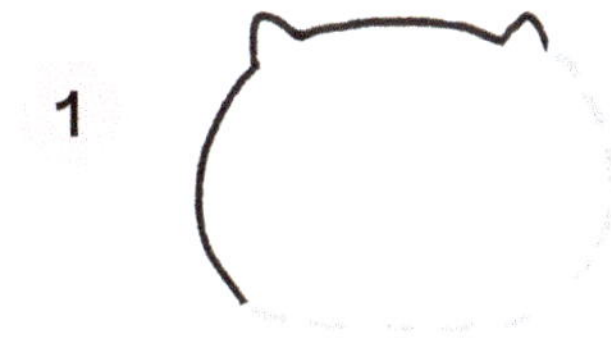

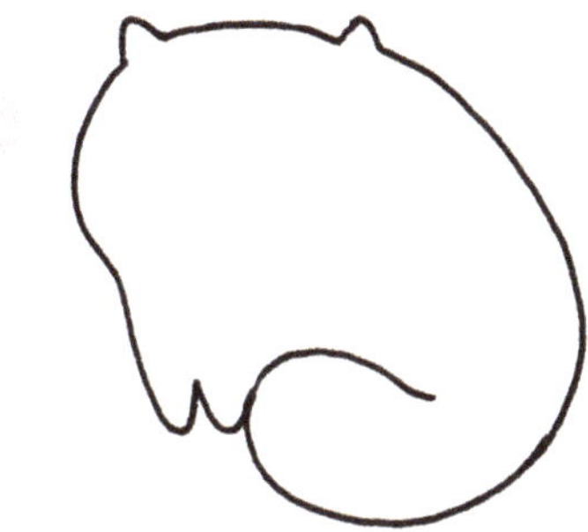

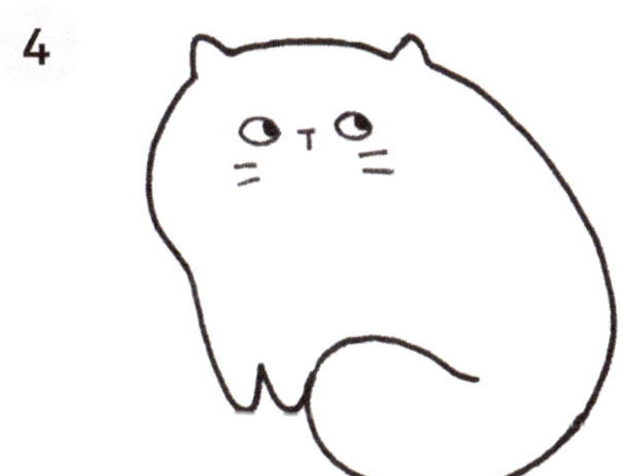

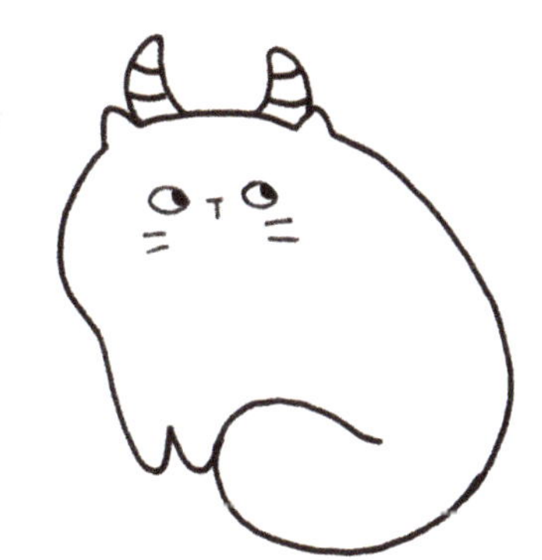

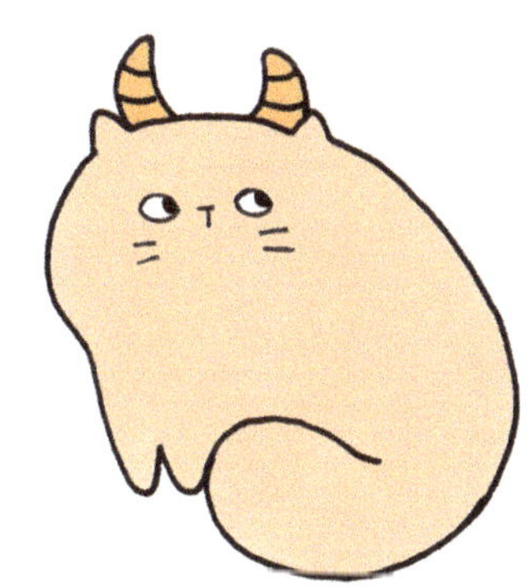

CANCER

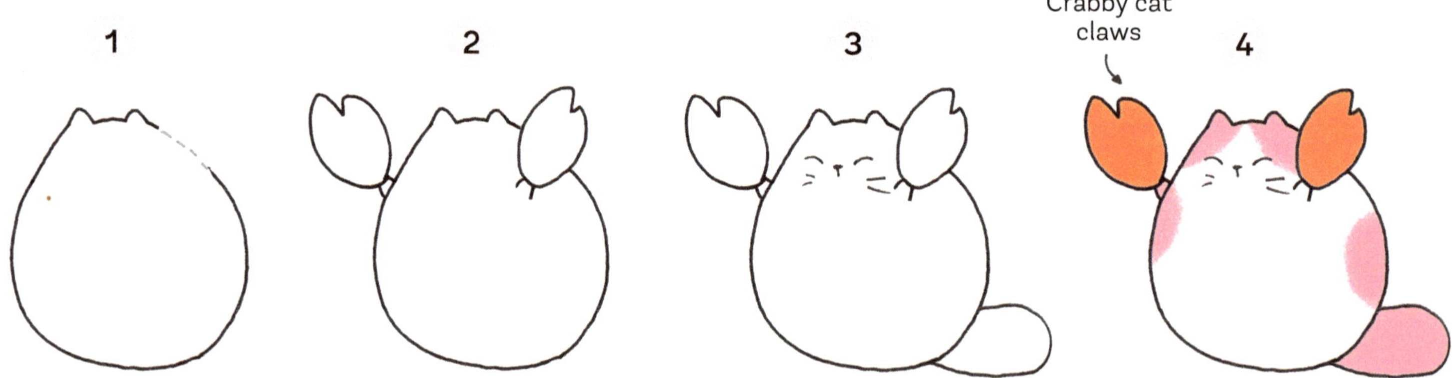

LEO

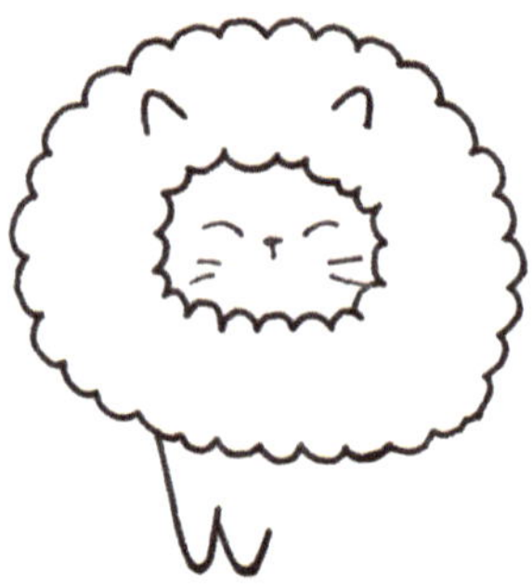

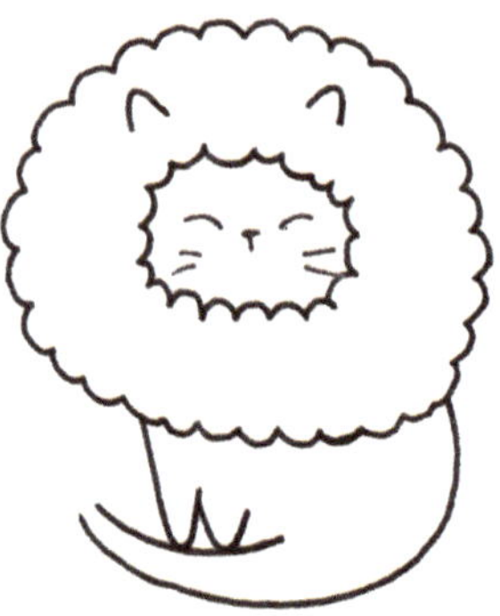

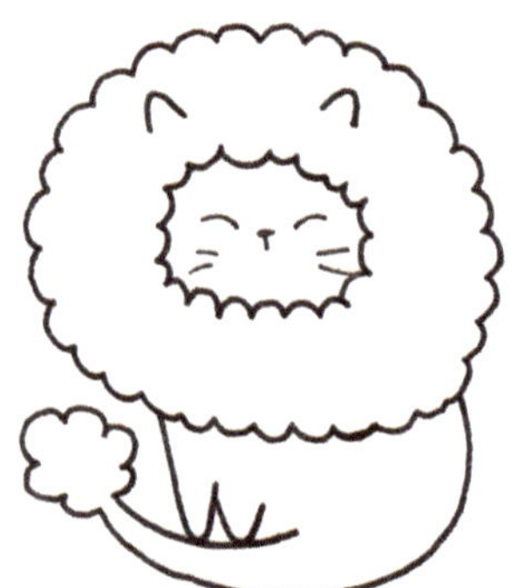

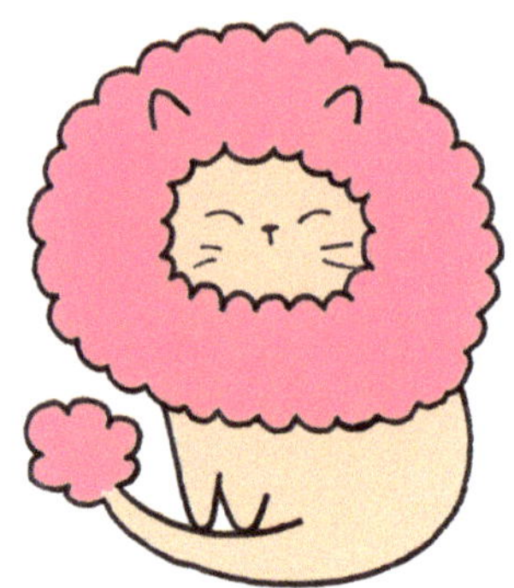

SAGITTARIUS

1
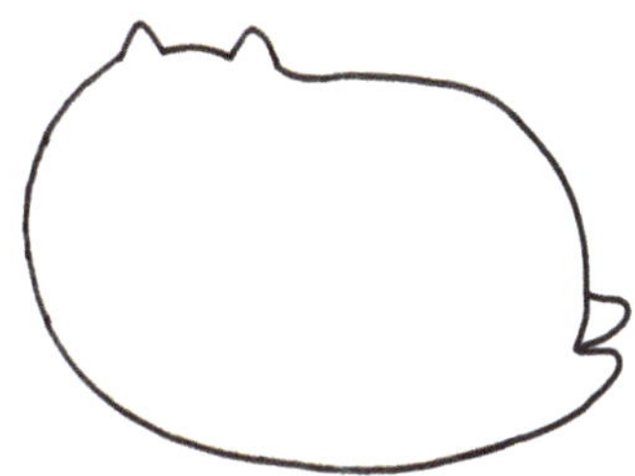

2
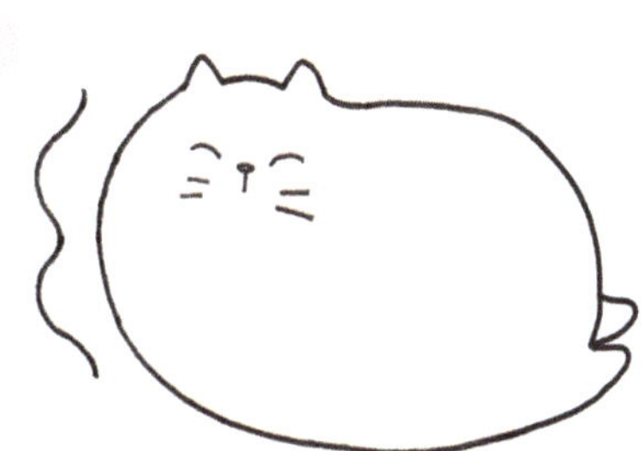

3
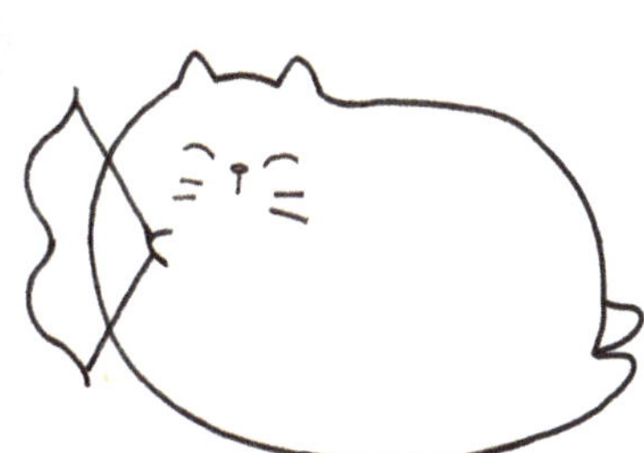

4
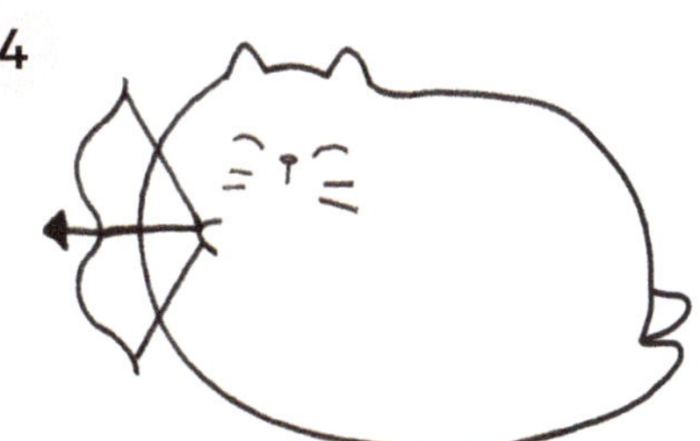

5
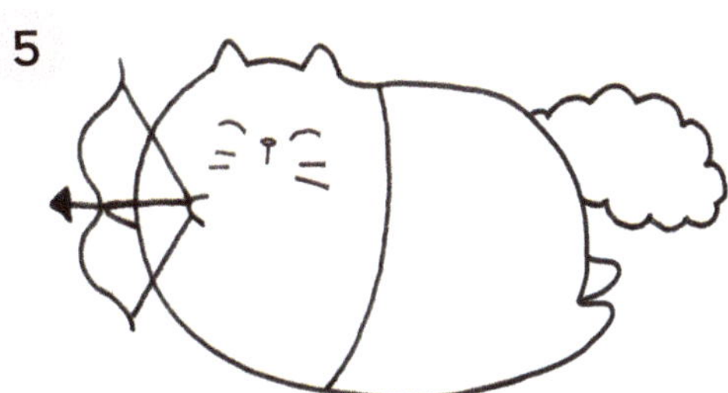

6
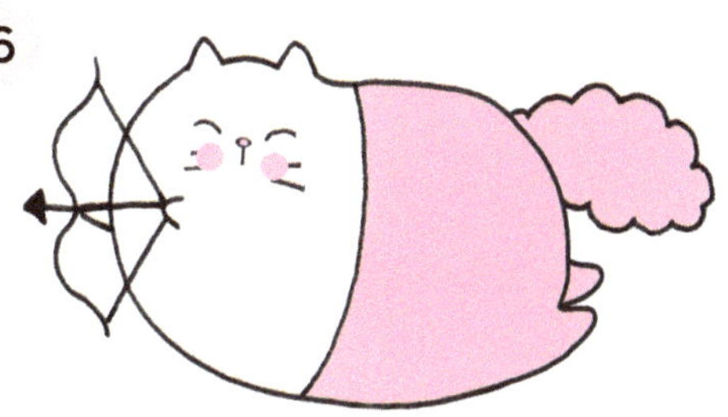

CAPRICORN

1
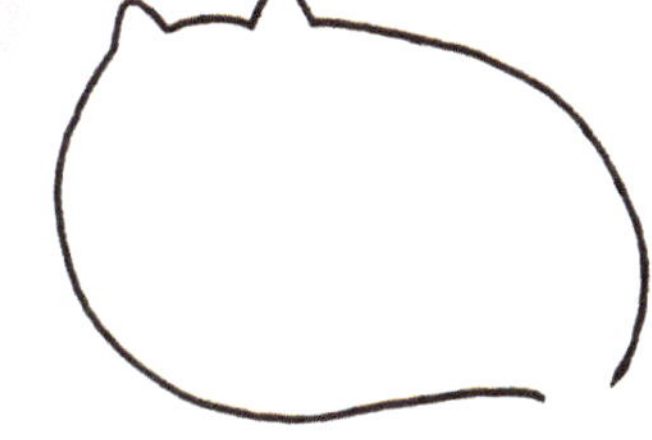

2
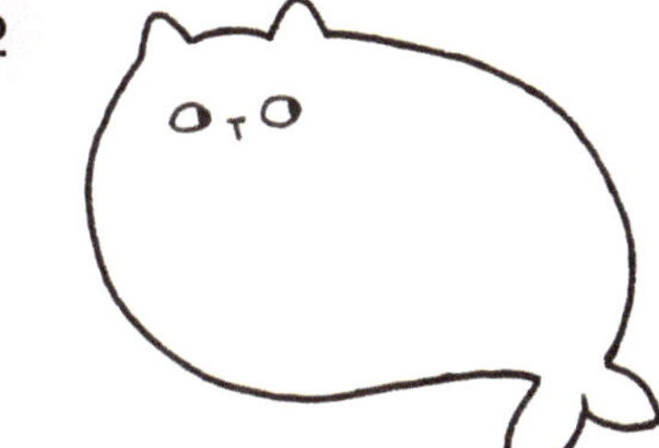

3
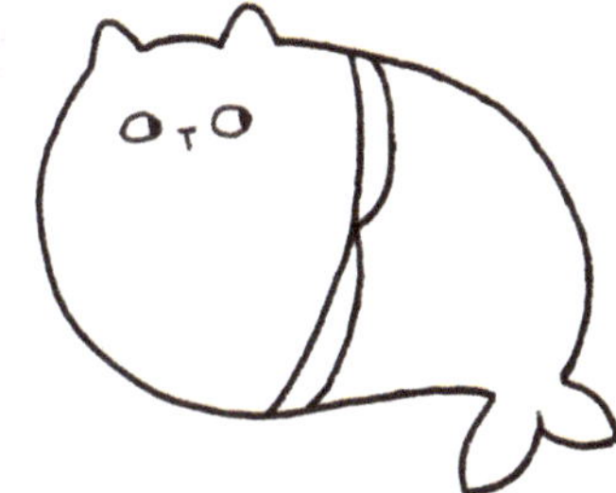

4
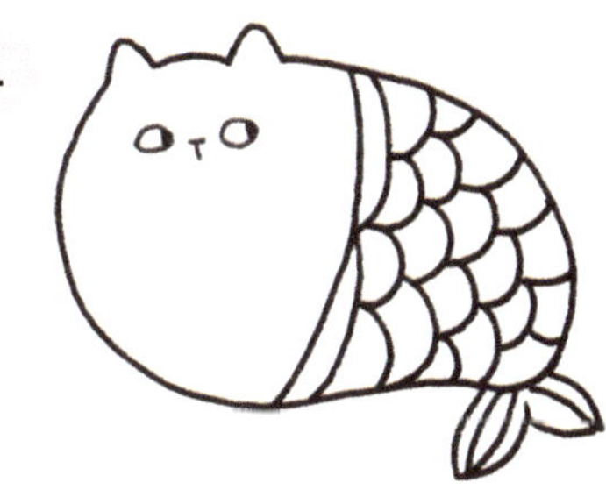

5
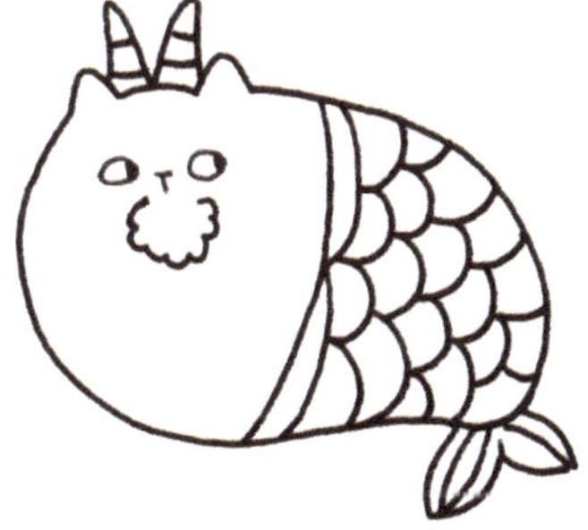

6
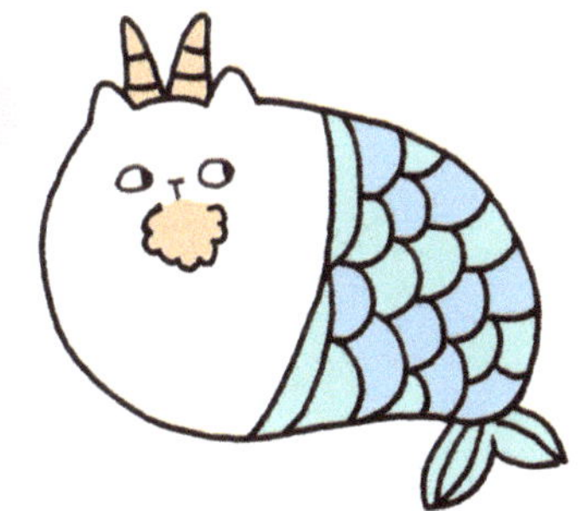

Now fill these pages with star sign cats. Don't forget to add magical color!

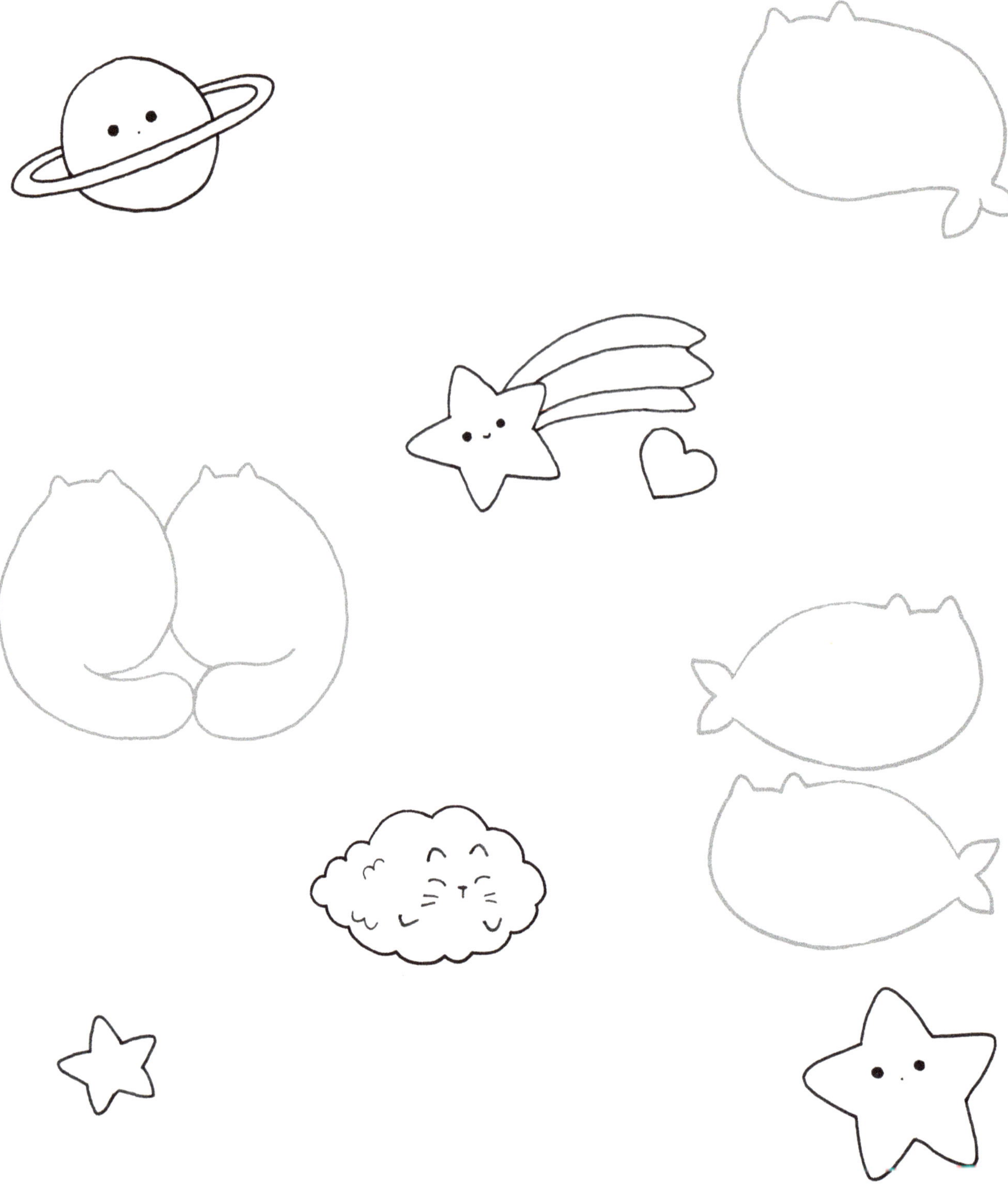

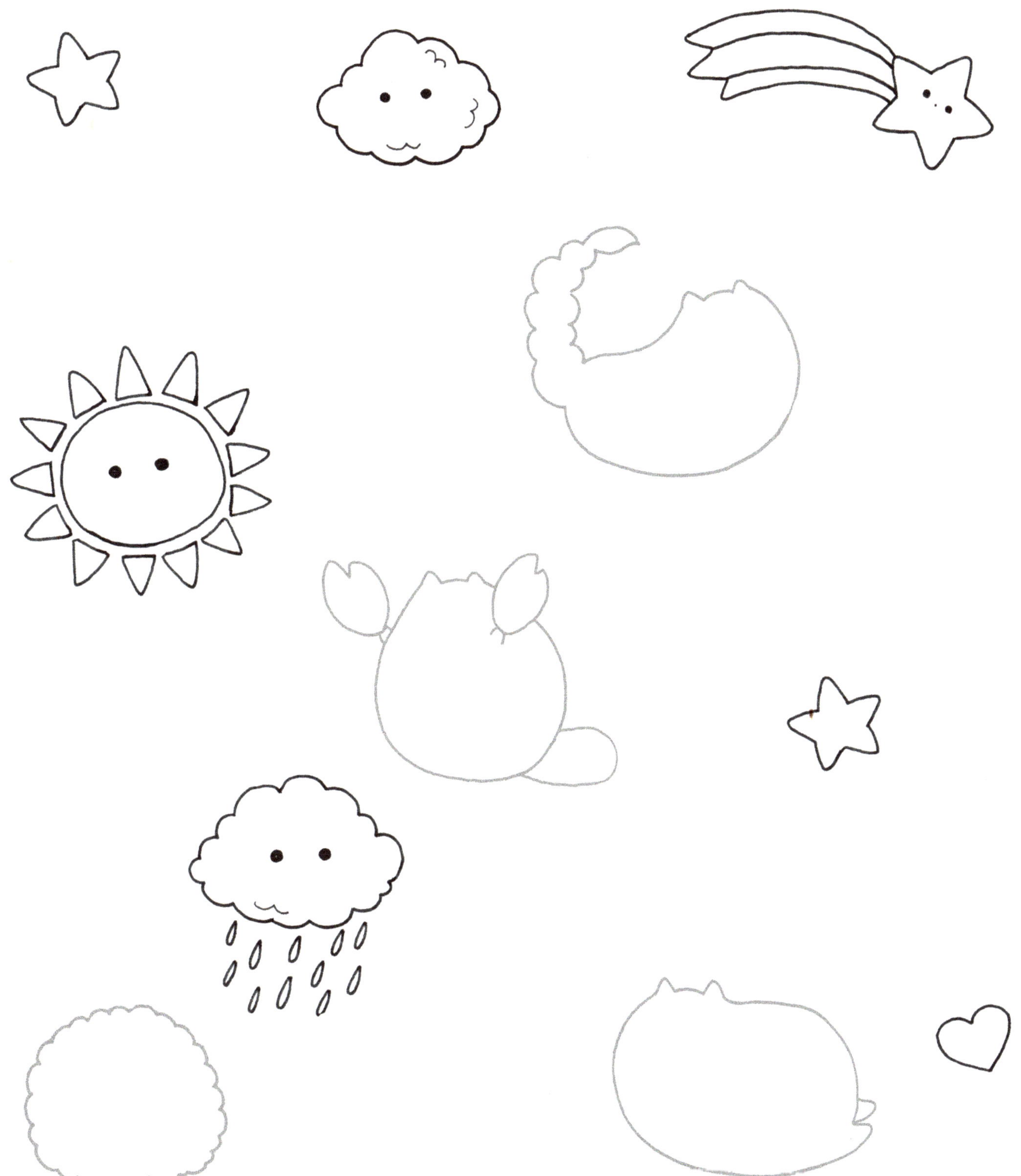

BECKONING CAT

MANEKI-NEKO

The Beckoning Cat, known as Maneki-neko in Japanese, is said to bring good luck to its owner. Traditionally, it's a calico Japanese Bobtail.

BOTH PAWS RAISED

To bring money, good fortune, and customers.

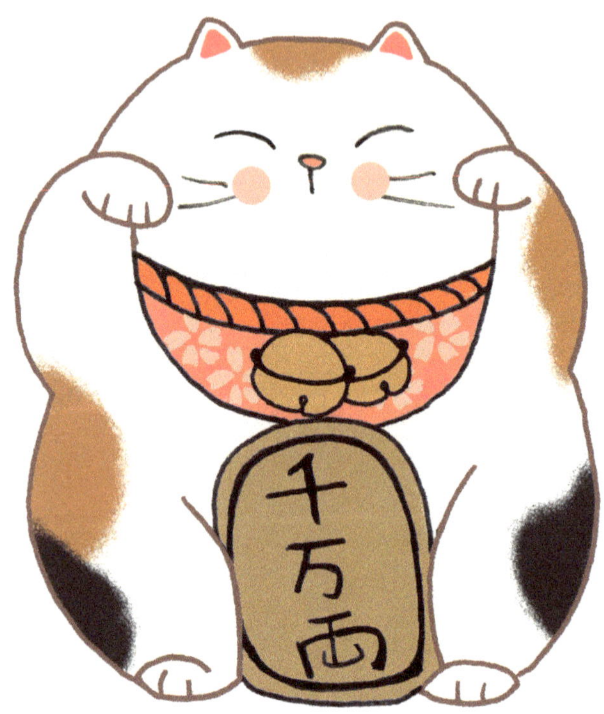

KOBAN COIN

Represents wealth that is brought to its owner.

BIB & BELL

The lucky cat is adorned with a bib and bell, the same way as it was dressed by its wealthy owner in the Edo period in Japan.

Decorate the beckoning cat. You could add a bib and bells as you like!

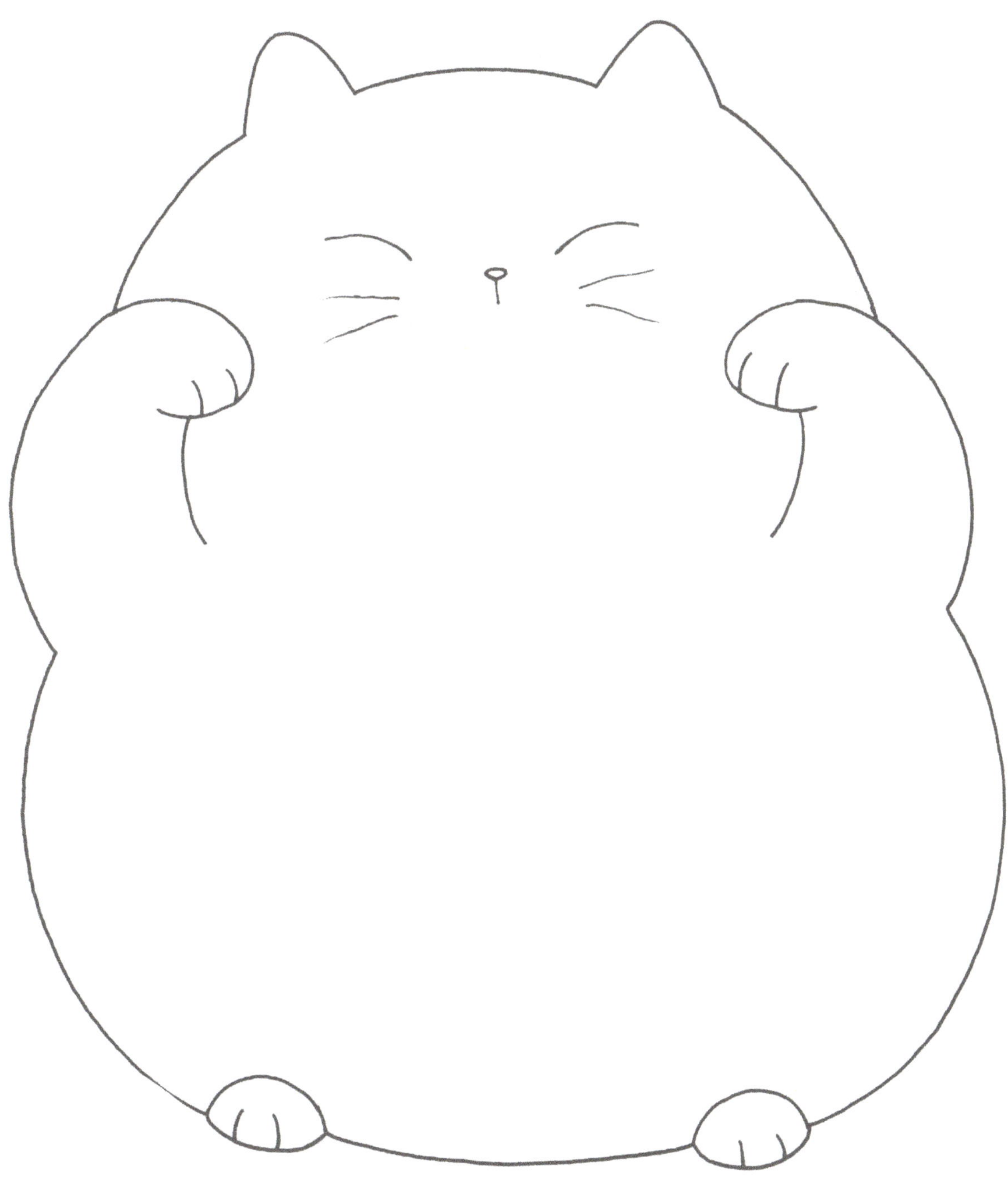

BECKONING CAT

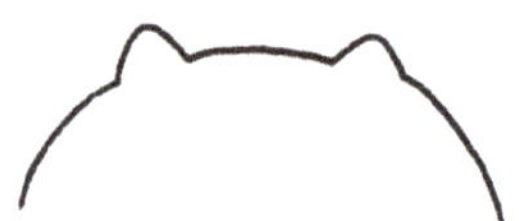

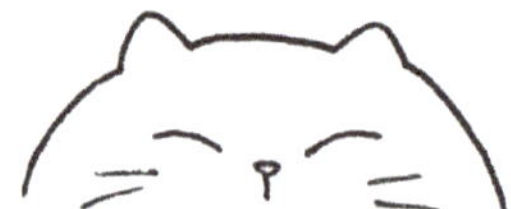

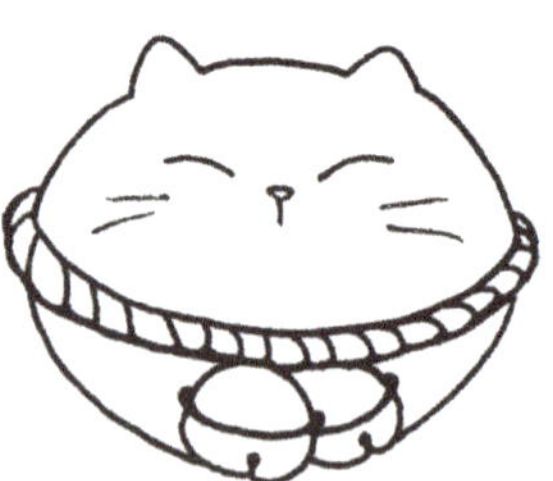

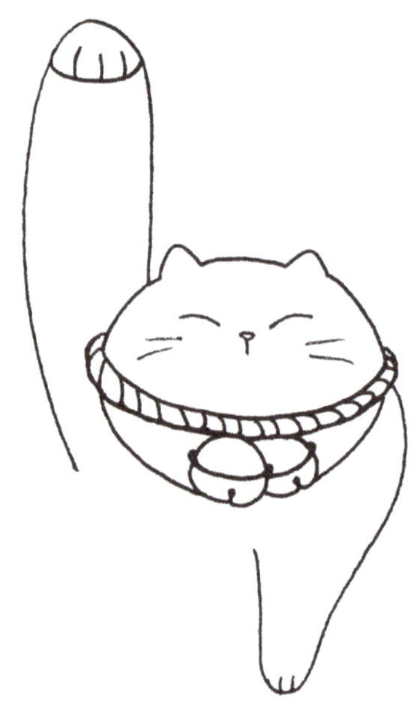

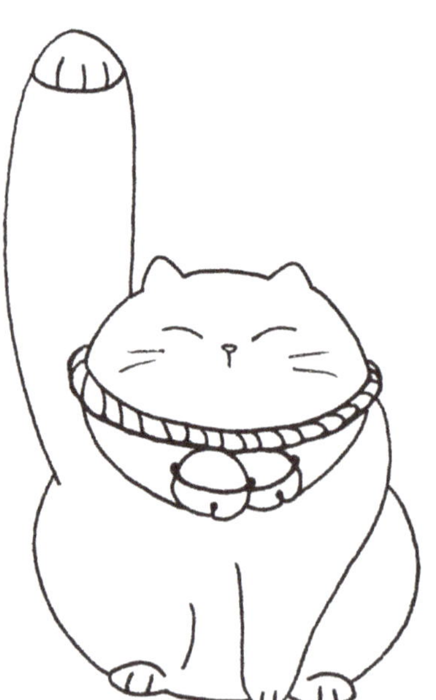

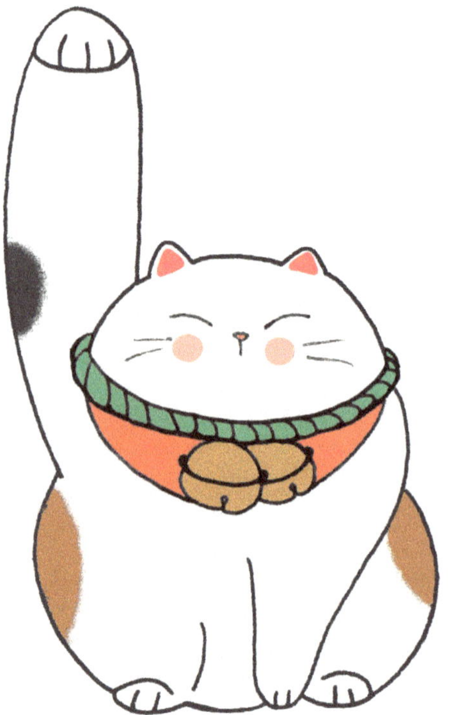

Left Paw Raised
To invite people
and customers

Carp
Symbolizes wealth

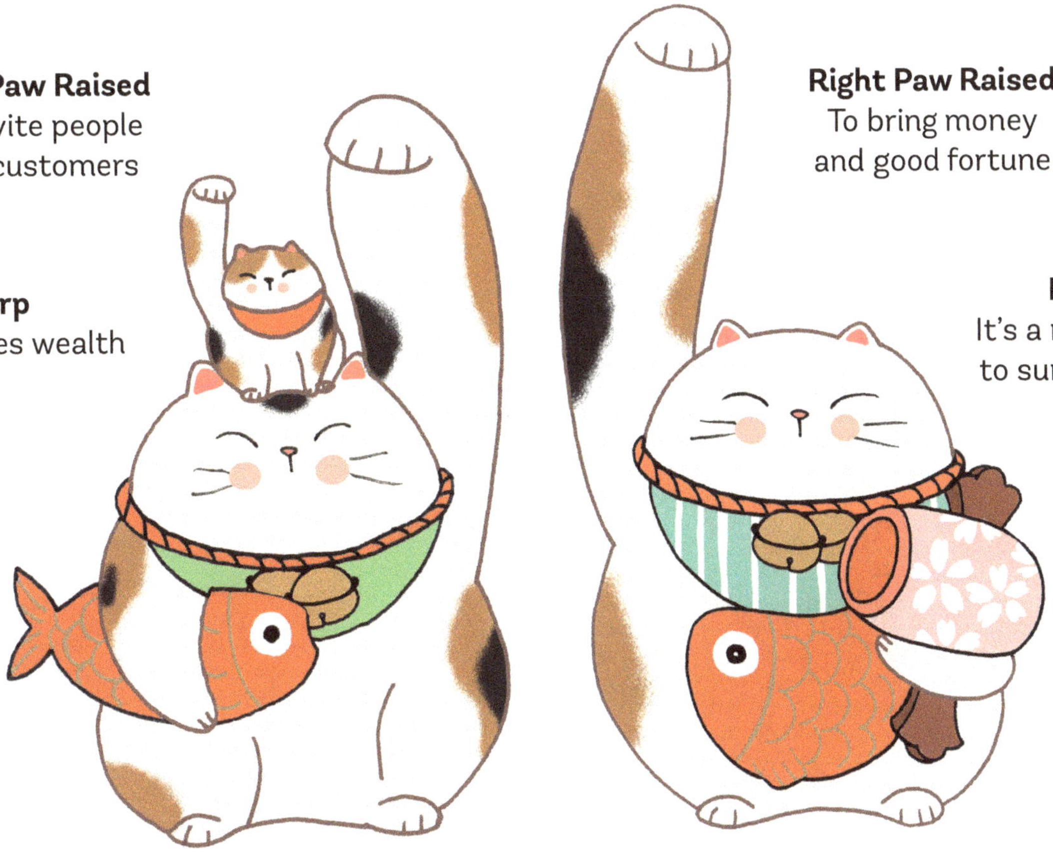

Right Paw Raised
To bring money
and good fortune

Hammer
It's a money-mallet
to summon wealth

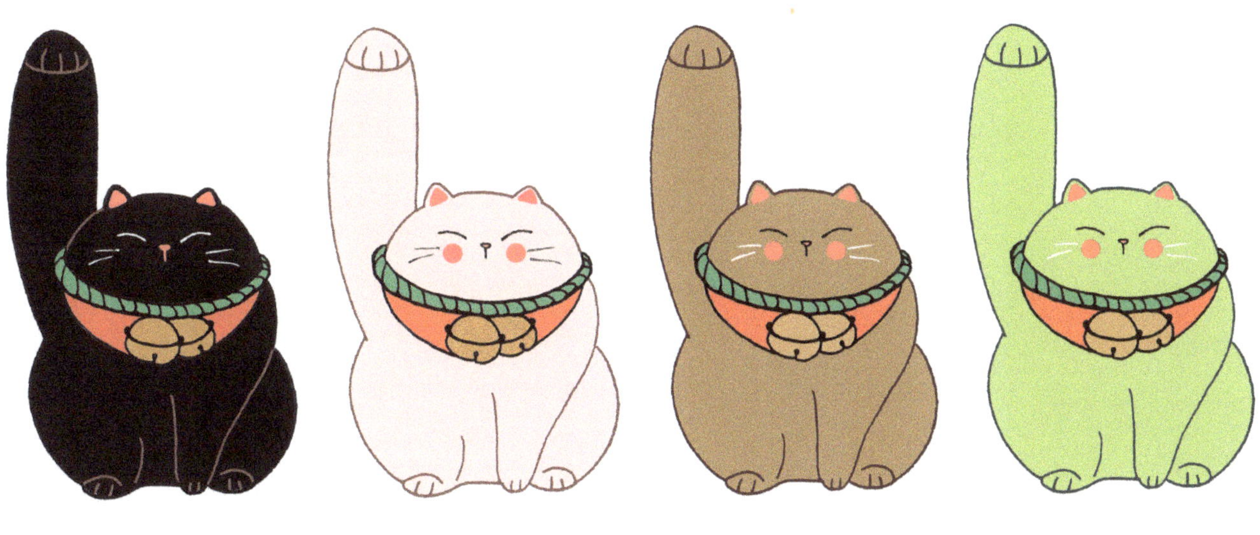

Black
To ward off evil
spirits and stalkers

Pink
To beckon love
into your life

Gold
To bring wealth
into your life

Green
To bring success
to your studies

CLOTHES & ACCESSORIES

In real life, cats are great at warming our hands and feet, so it makes perfect sense to draw cat mittens, cat socks, and a whole line of other cat accessories! Follow the steps to get started, and don't forget to add cute color and markings.

WARM MITTENS

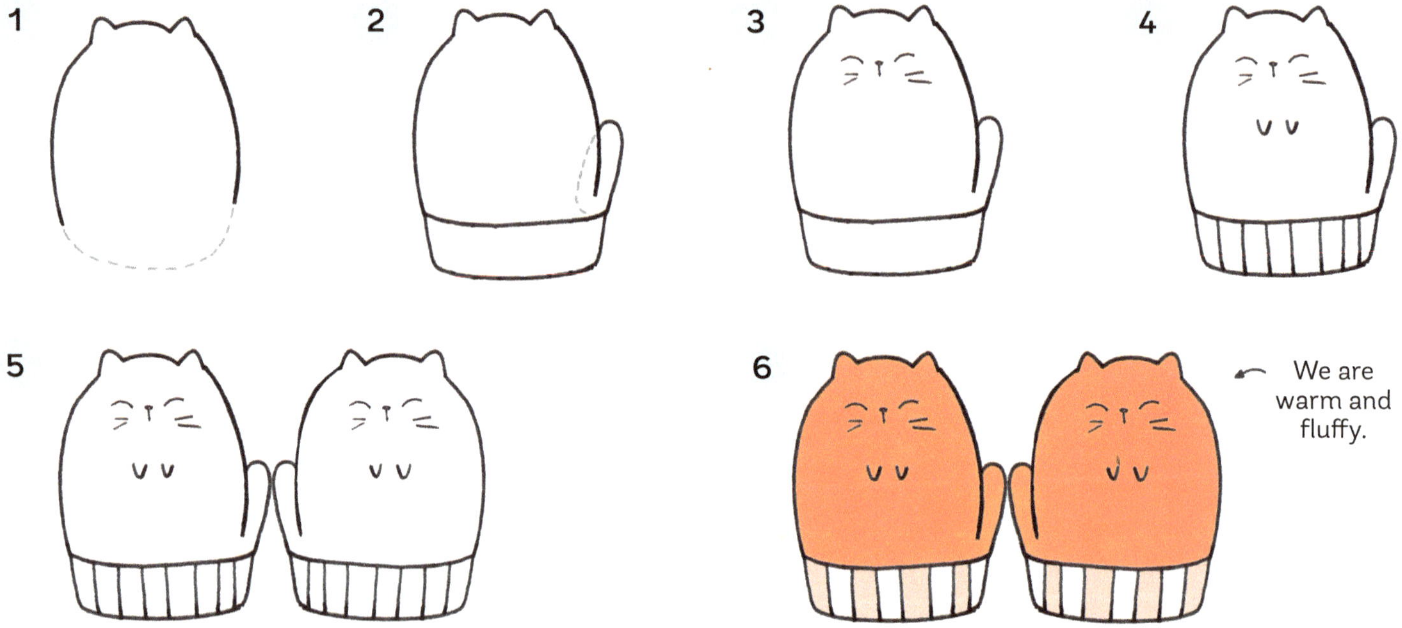

1 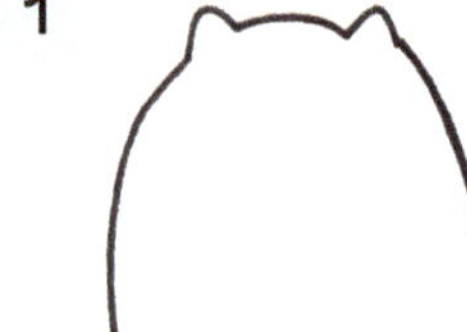

2 

3 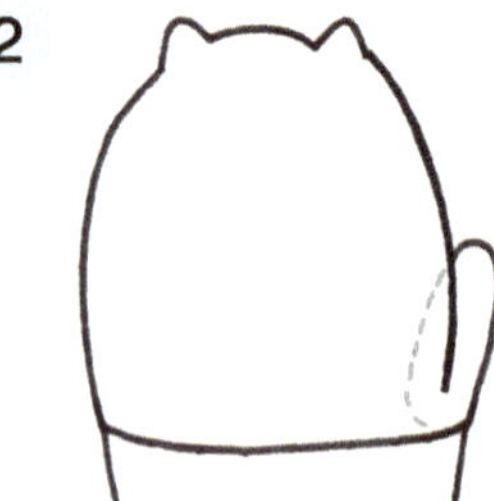

4 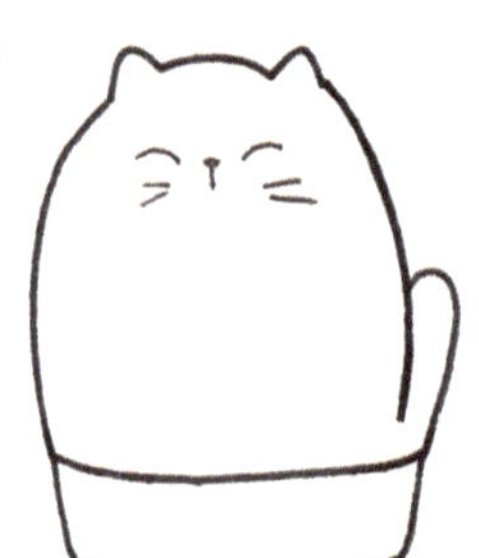

5 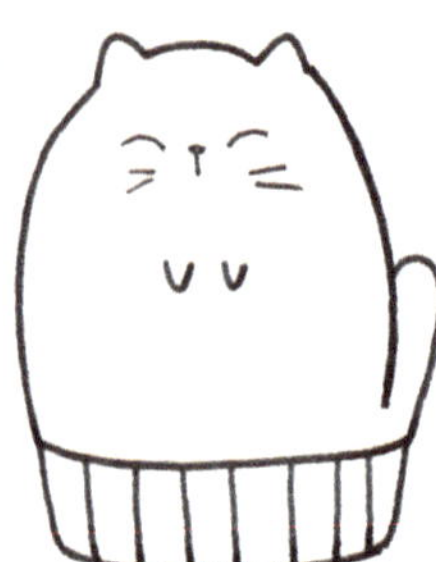

6 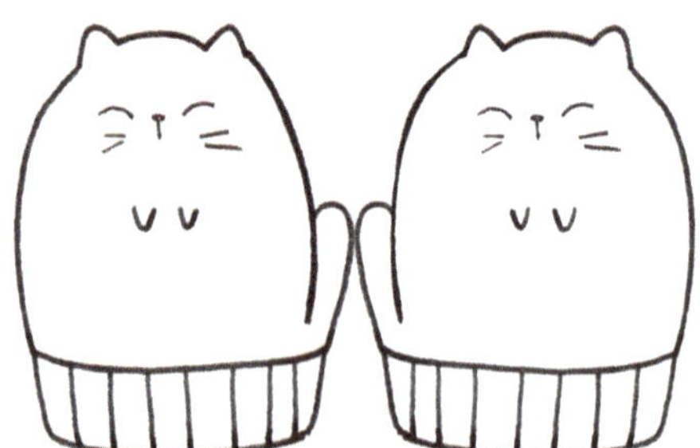

FLUFFY SOCKS

1 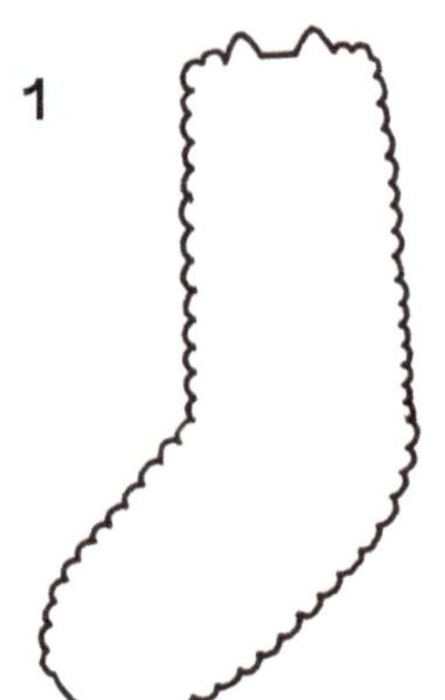

2 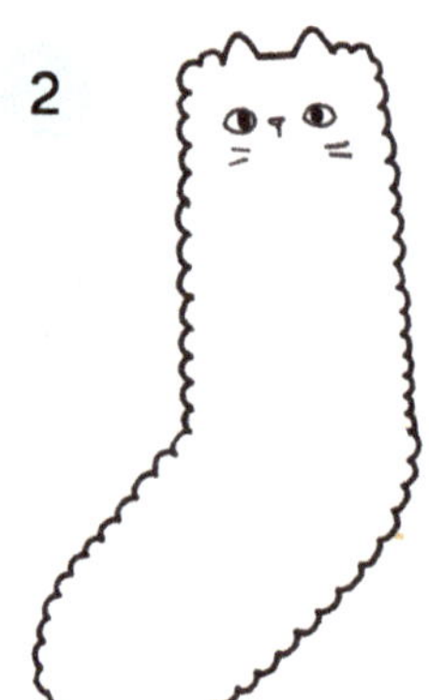

3 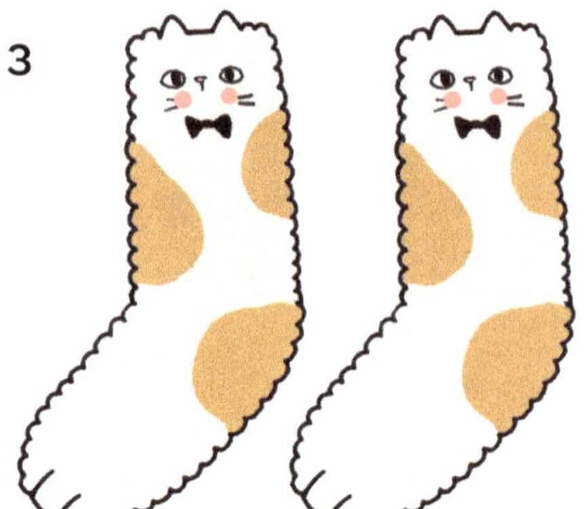

Use your color tools to
design and decorate these
accessories, and then fill
in the blank spots with
accessories of your own.

Follow the steps below to draw more cute cat accessories. Use your tools to add color!

TOASTY BEANIE

1
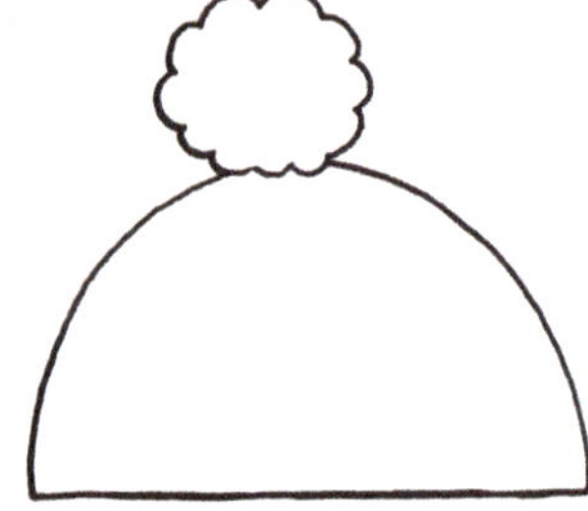

2
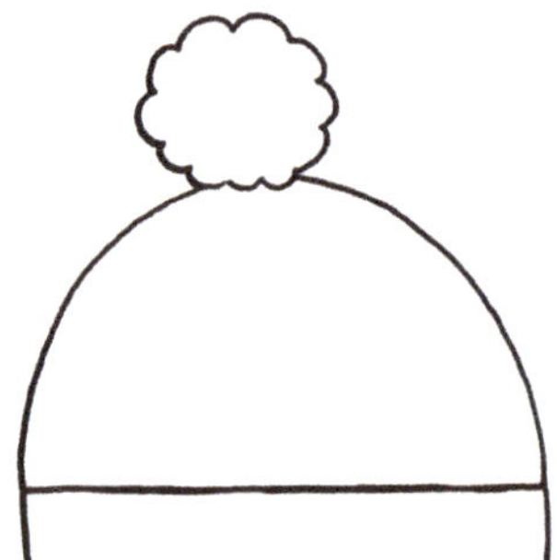

3
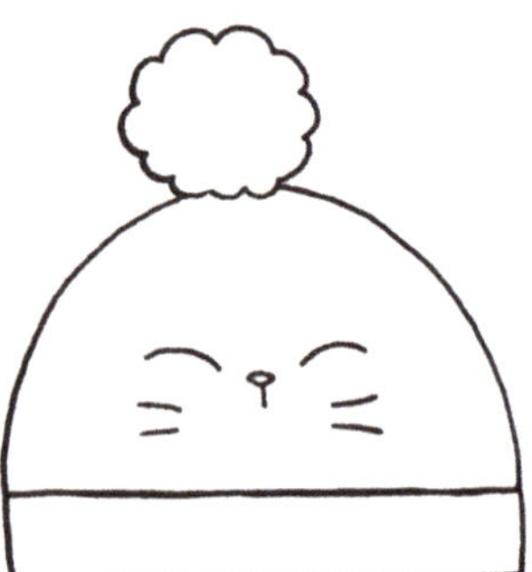

4
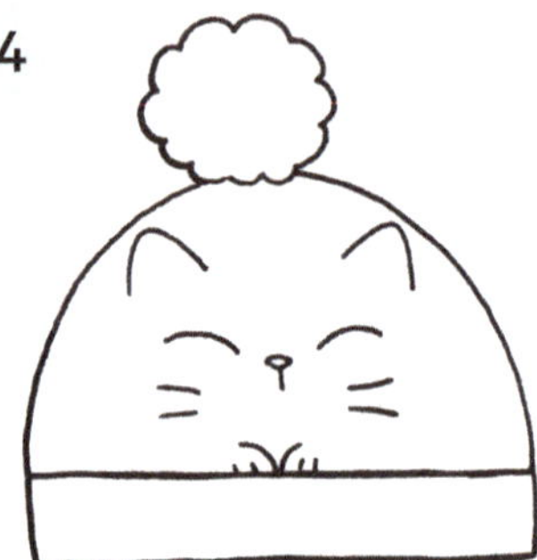

5
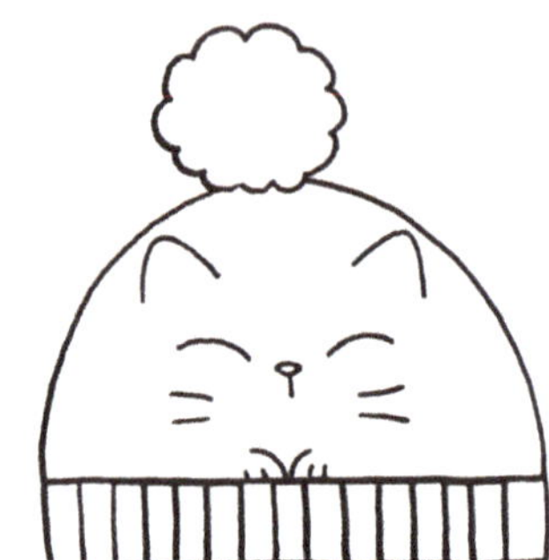

6
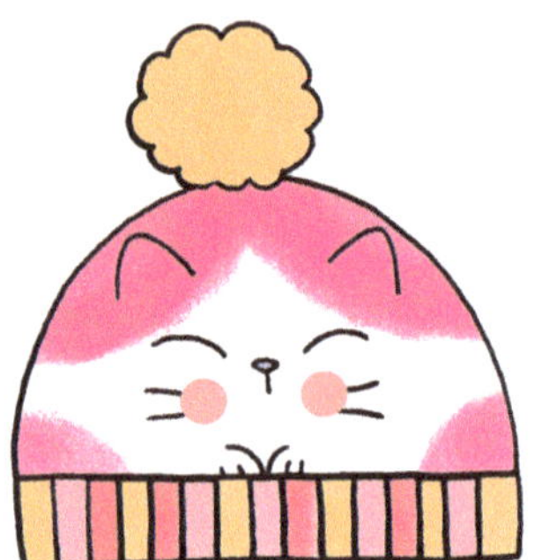

EARMUFFS

1

2
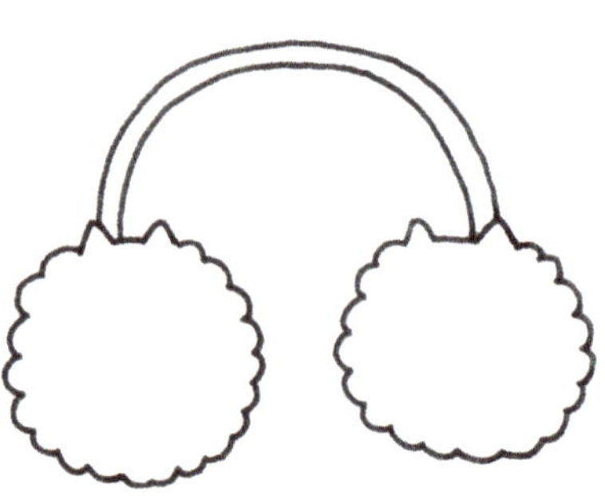

3
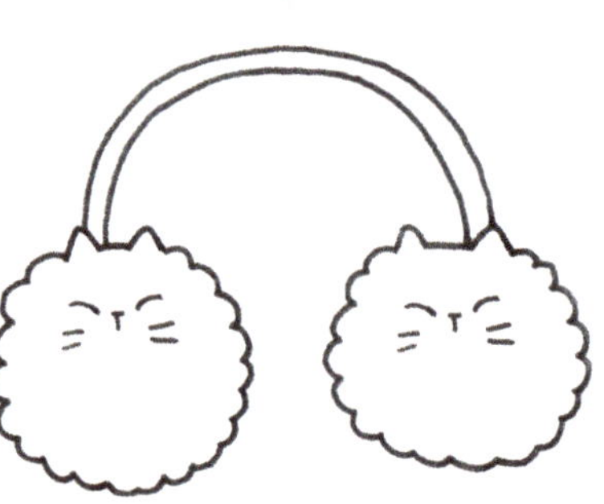

4
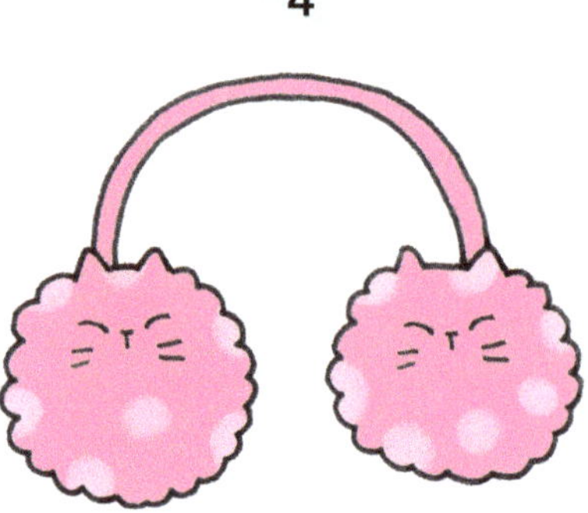

KEYCHAIN

1   2   3   4   5

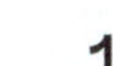 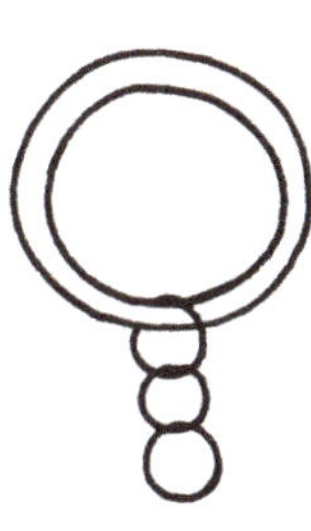 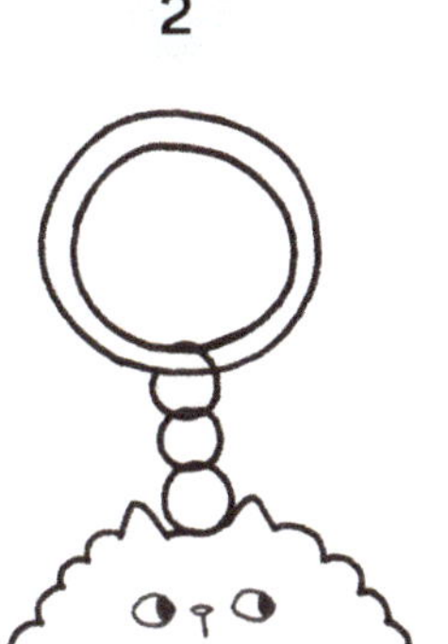 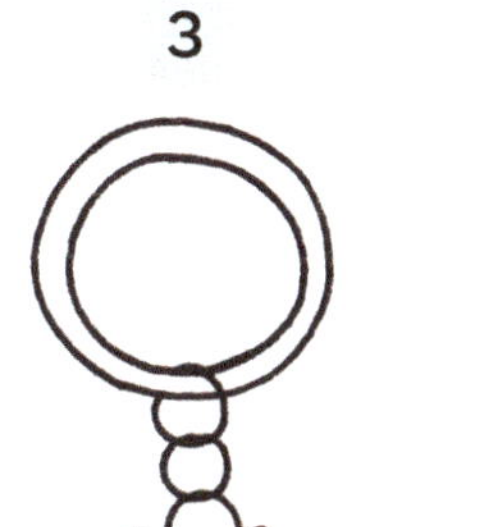 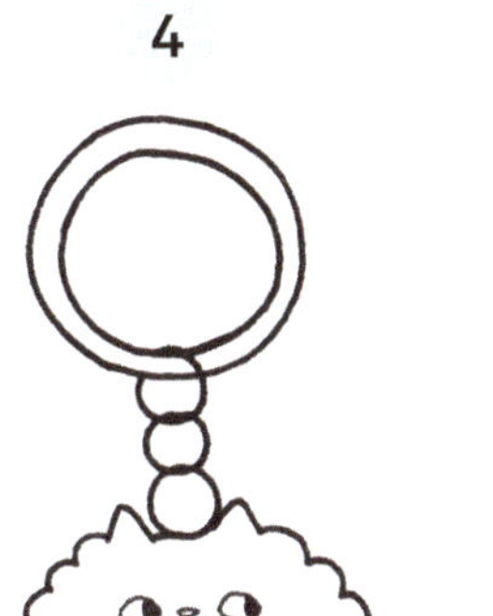 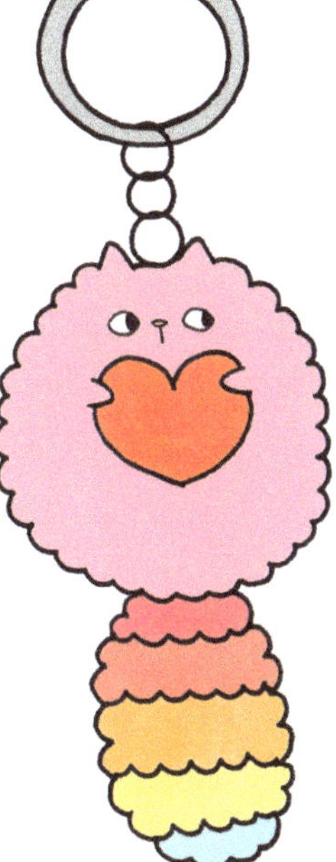

SUNGLASSES

1

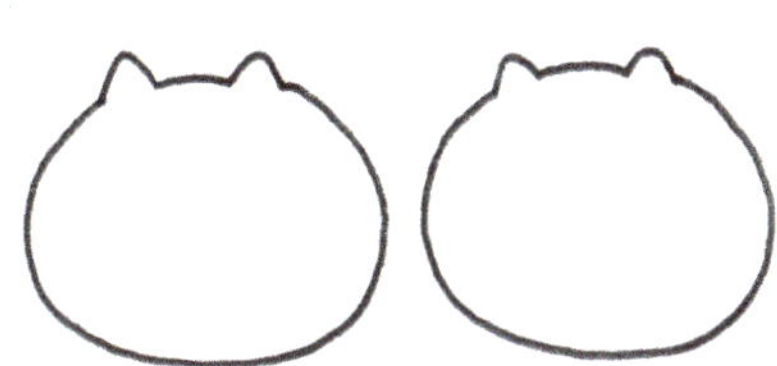

2

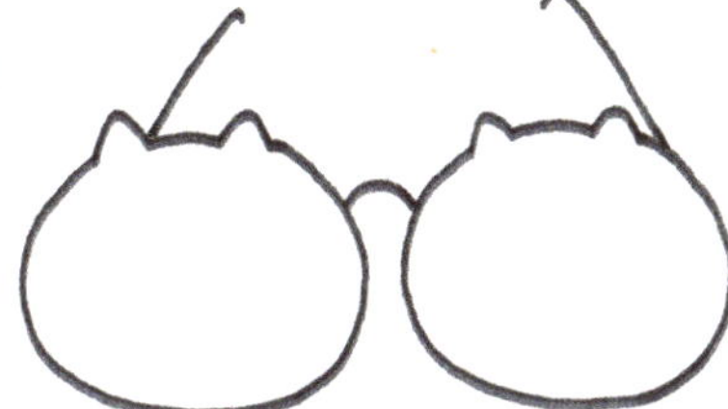

3

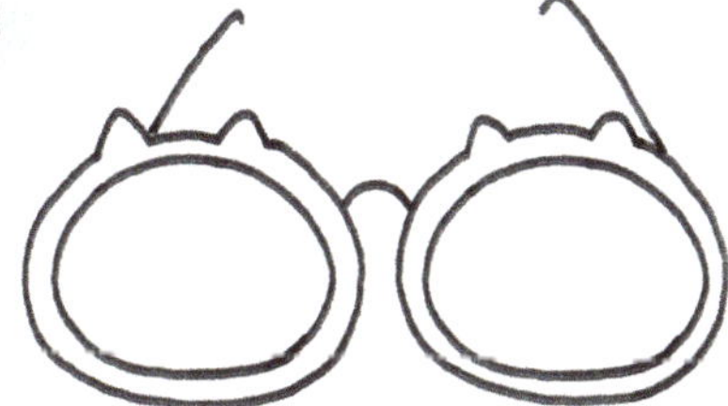

4

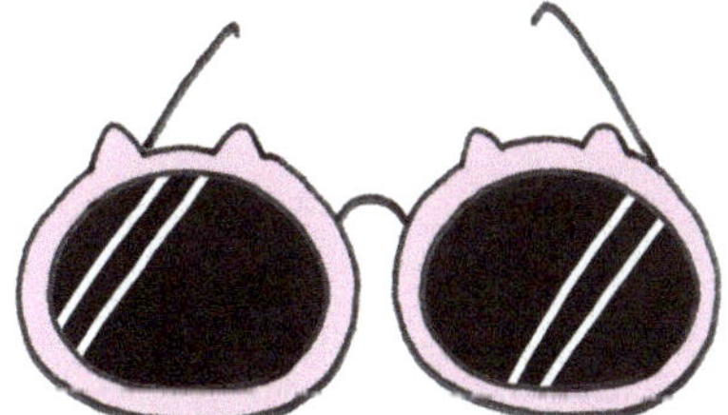

PLUSH SLIPPERS

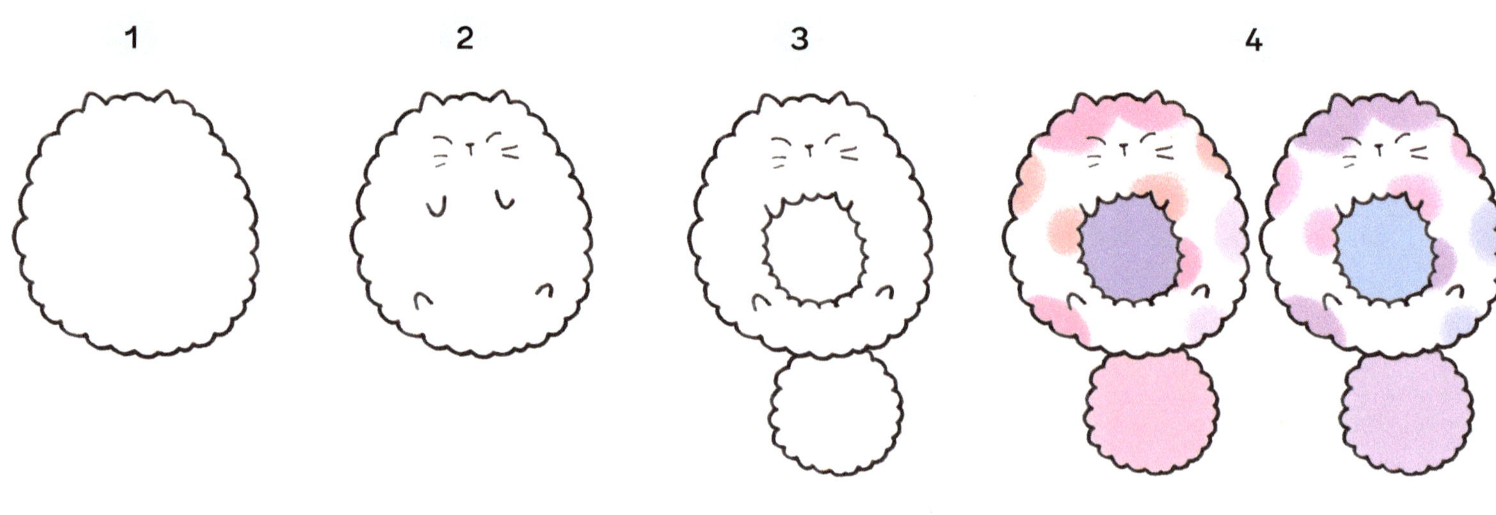

1   2   3   4

FLUFFY SANDALS

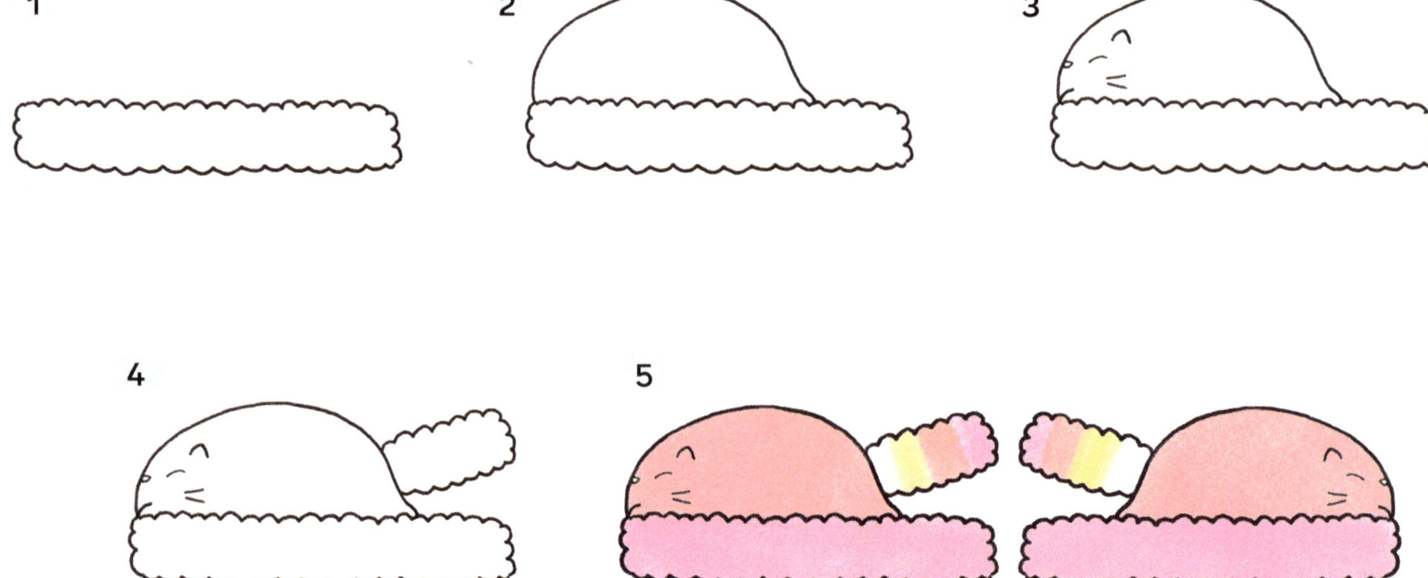

1   2   3

4   5

Your turn! Complete your fabulous feline-inspired footwear collection below.
How about a pair of cowboy boots or wellies?

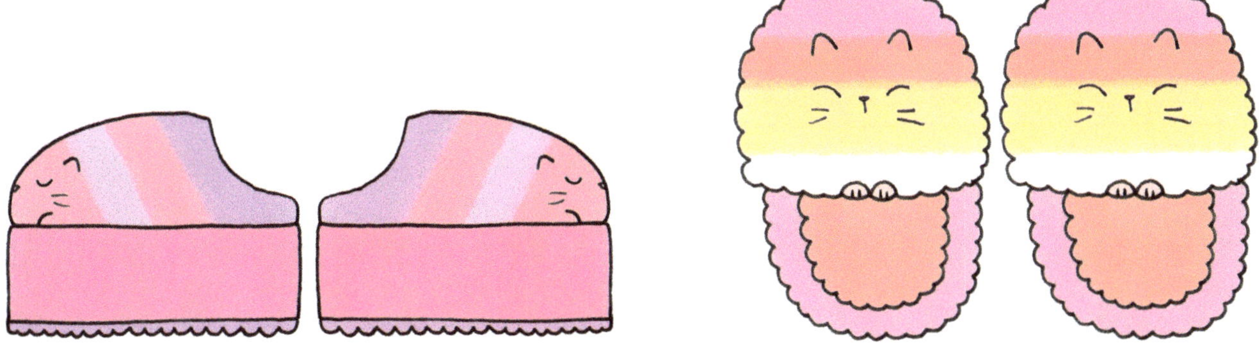

Cats can have emotional baggage too!

ANXIOUS CAT COIN PURSE

1 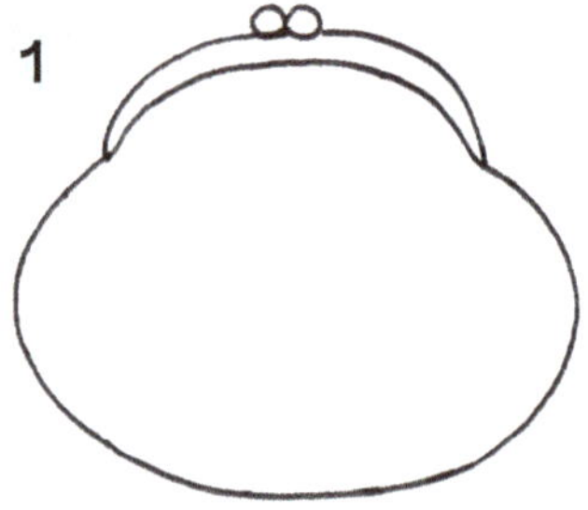 2 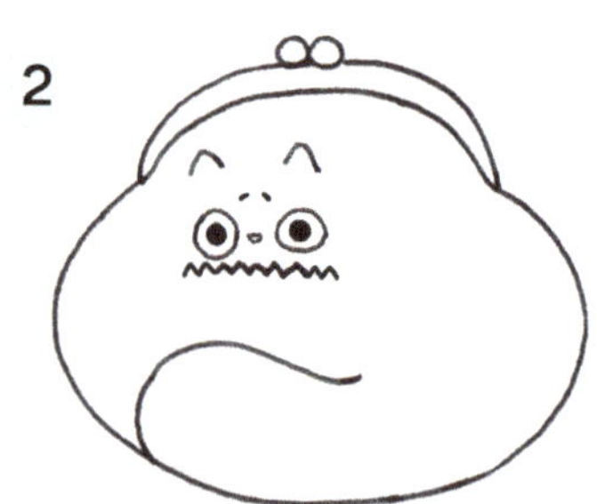 3 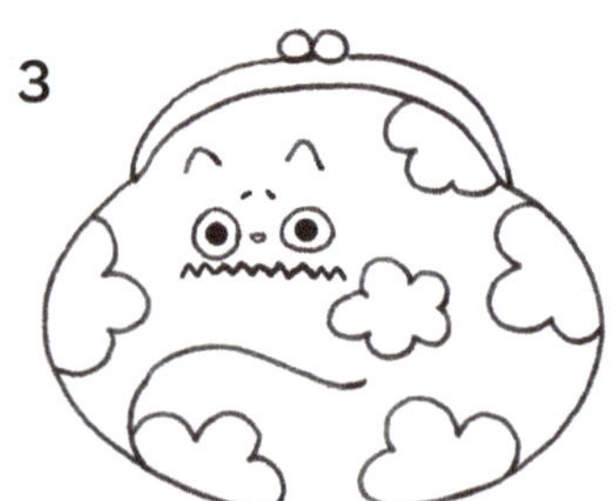 4 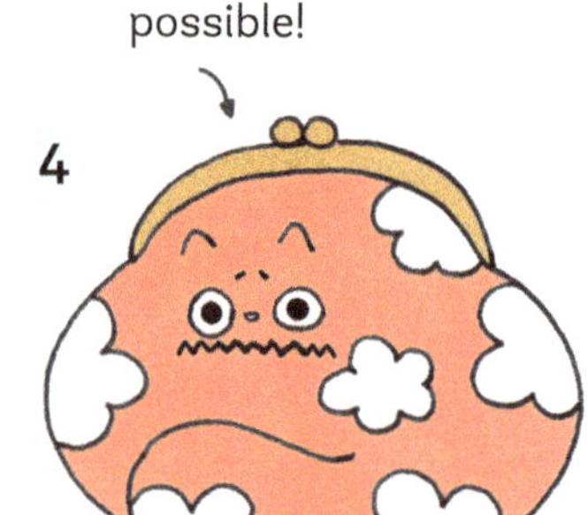

Make it as cute as possible!

WORRIED BUCKET BAG

1 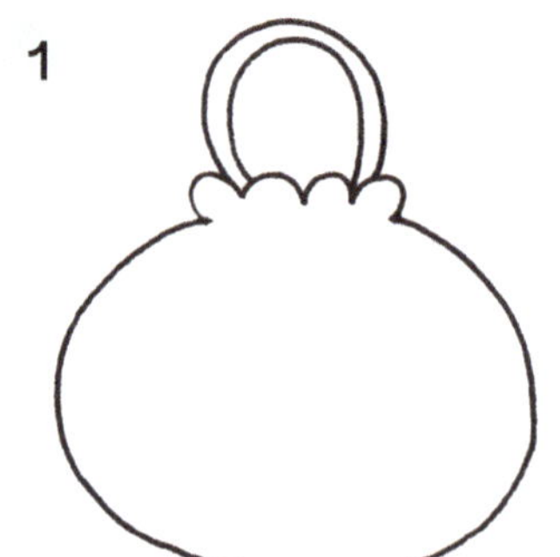 2 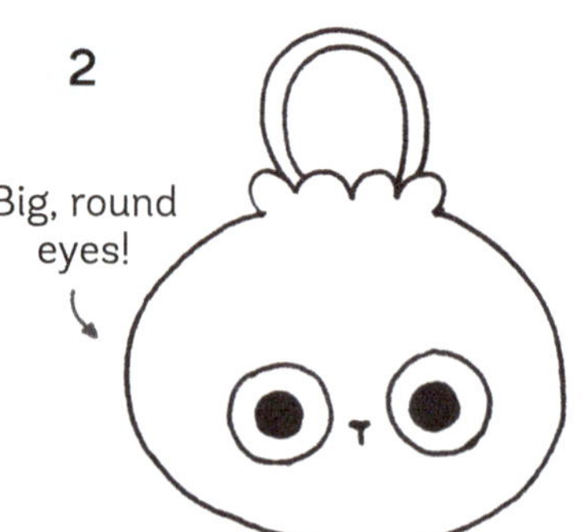 3 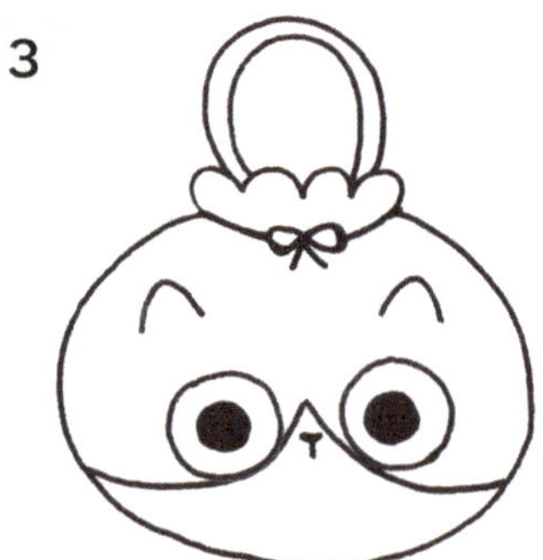 4 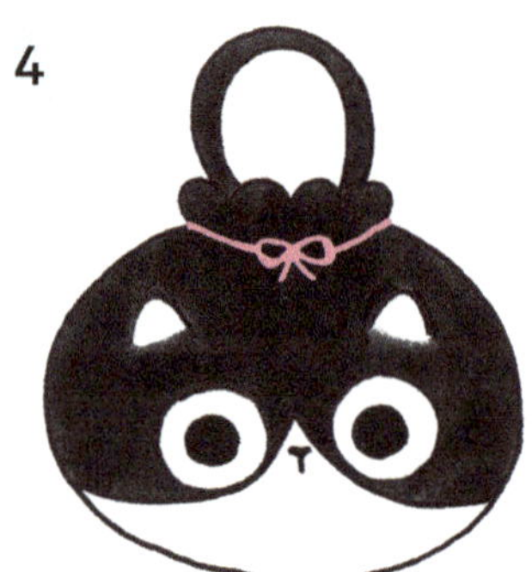

Big, round eyes!

REGRETFUL BRIEFCASE

Tears show this cat's deep regret.

1 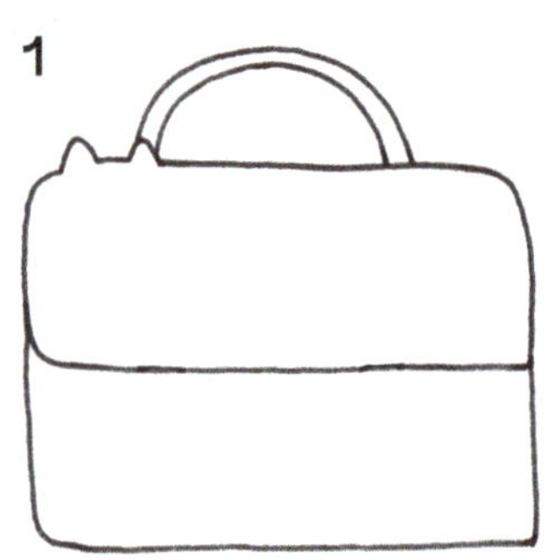 2 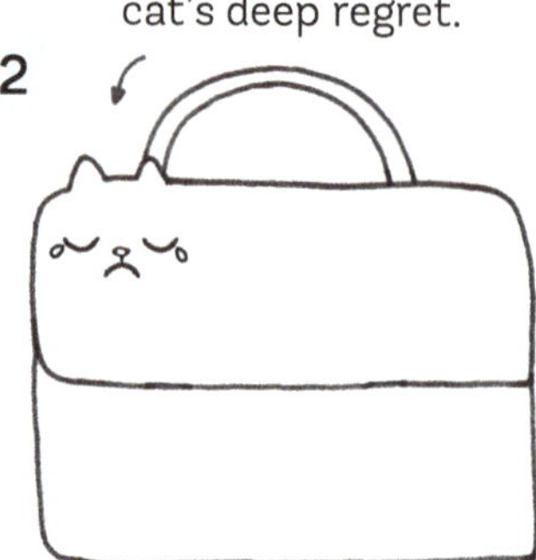 3 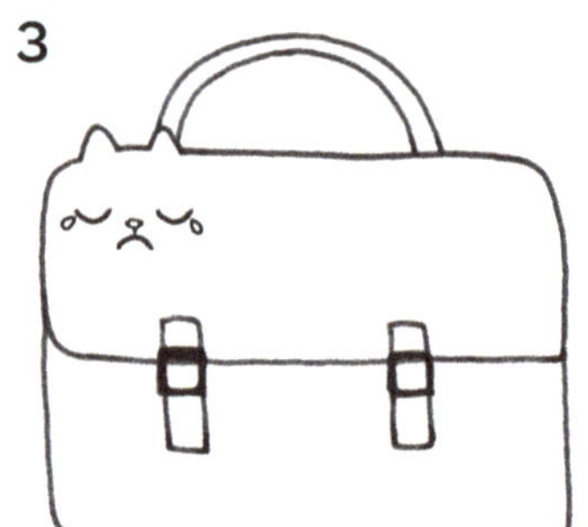 4 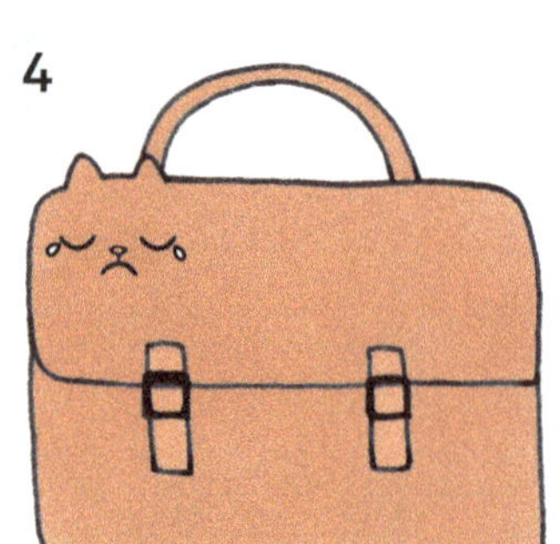

46

Draw your emotional cat baggage here. Add expressions, patterns, colors, and as many details as you like.

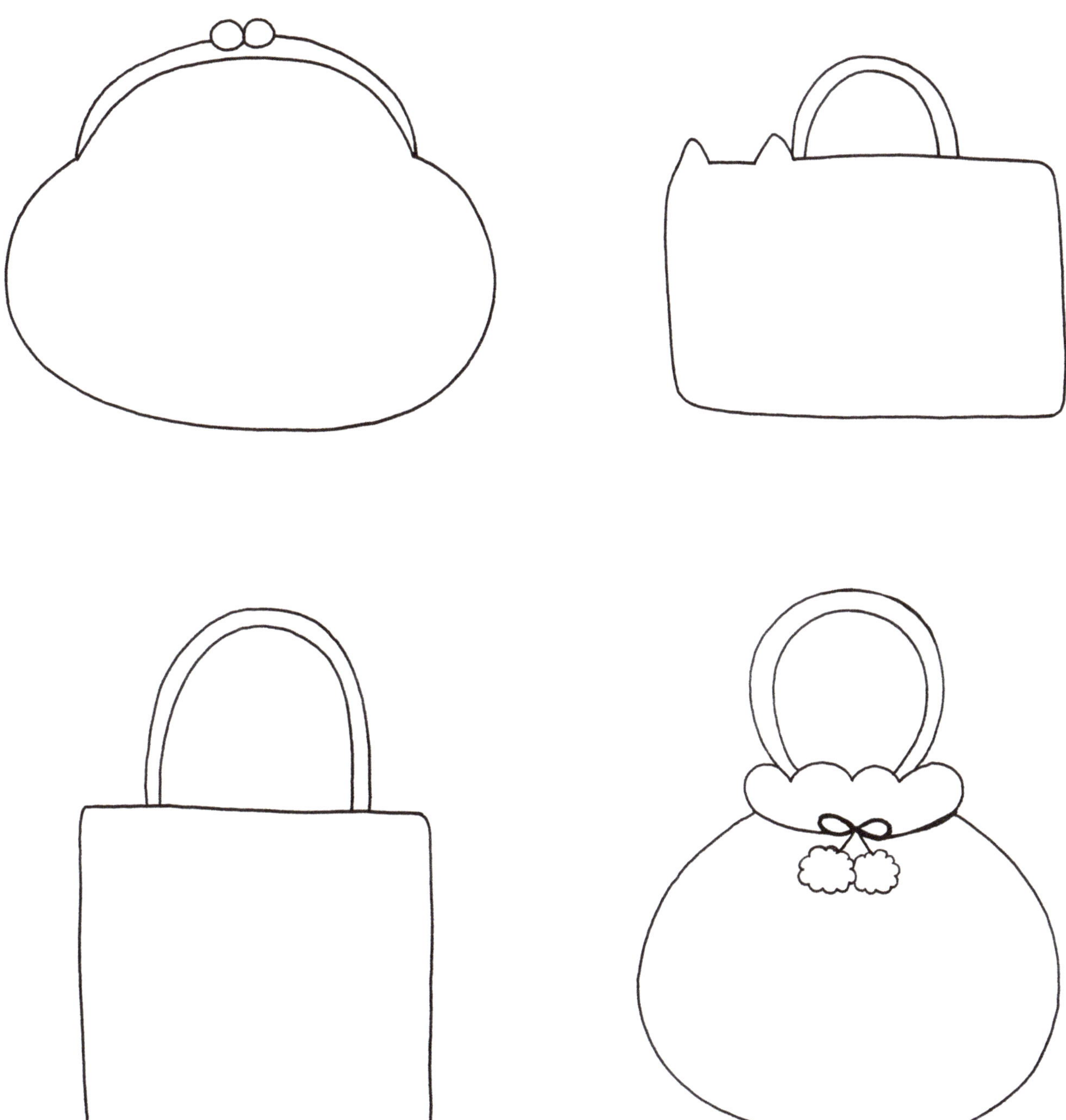

Draw cat scarves, clothes, towels, or anything else you like on these hangers.

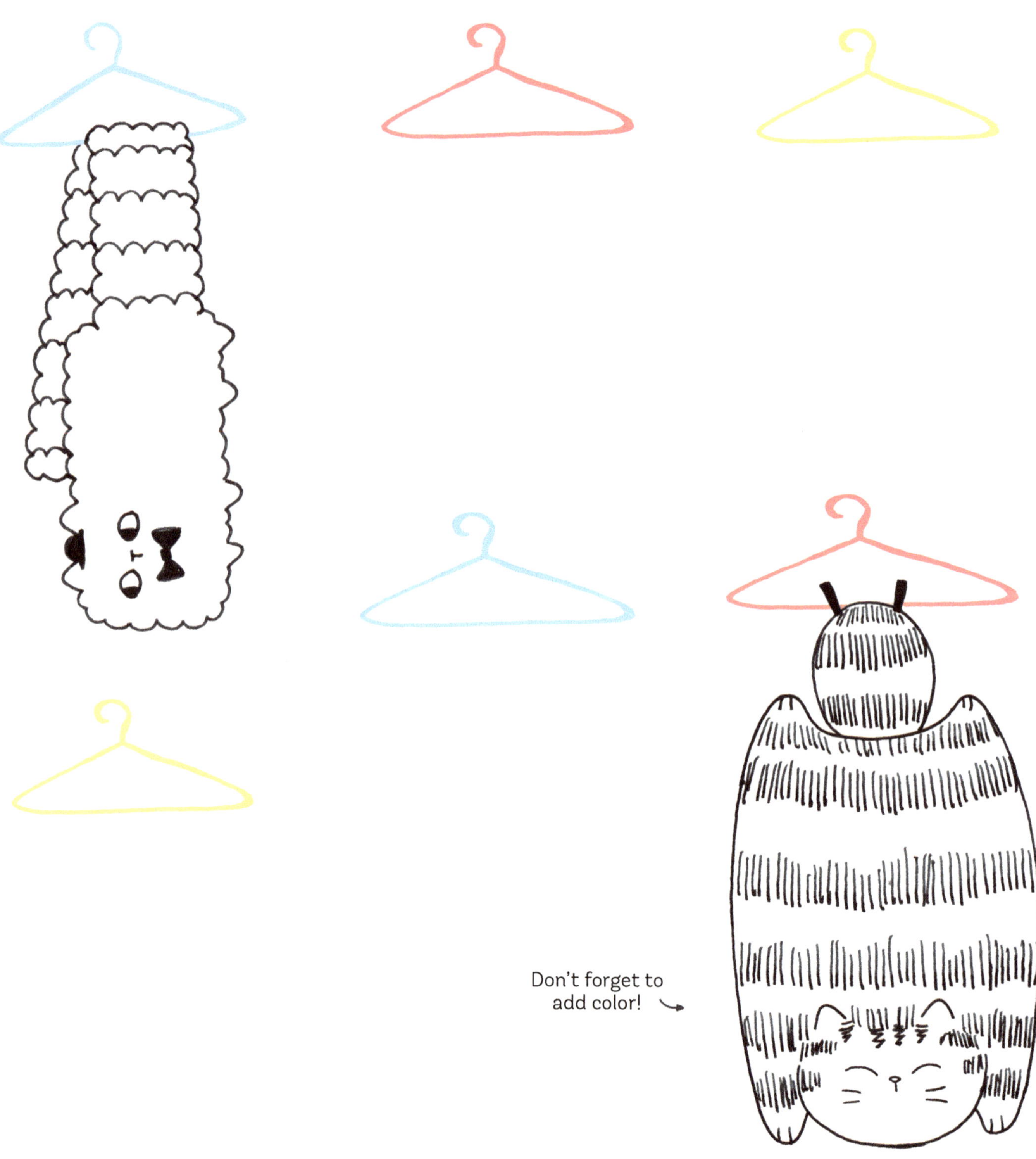

What's in your accessory collection? Doodle it here!

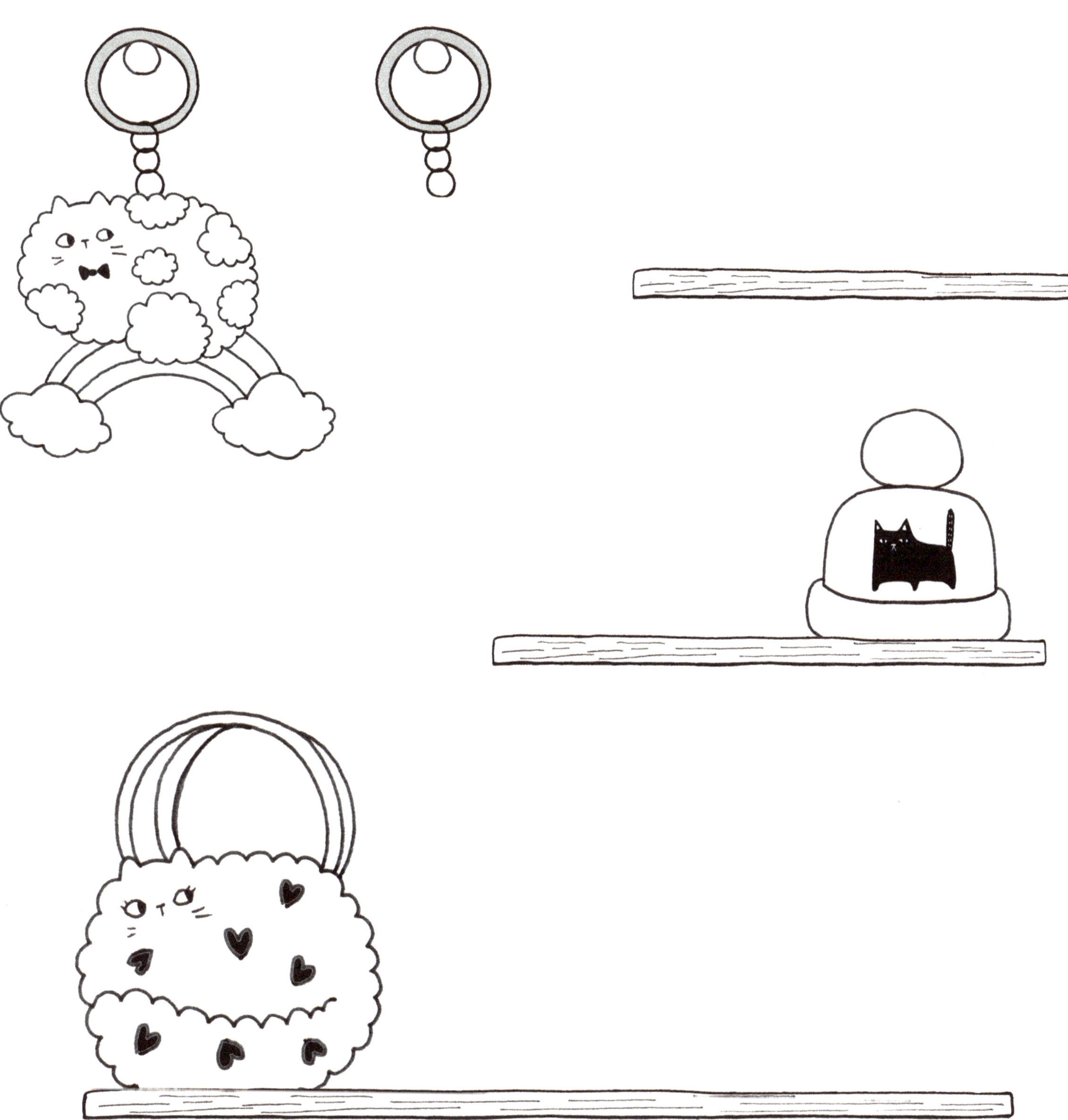

Do you have any cat-themed clothes or accessories? (I love cute clothes with cat motifs—this is my dream wardrobe!) Add bright rainbow colors to make these pieces super cute.

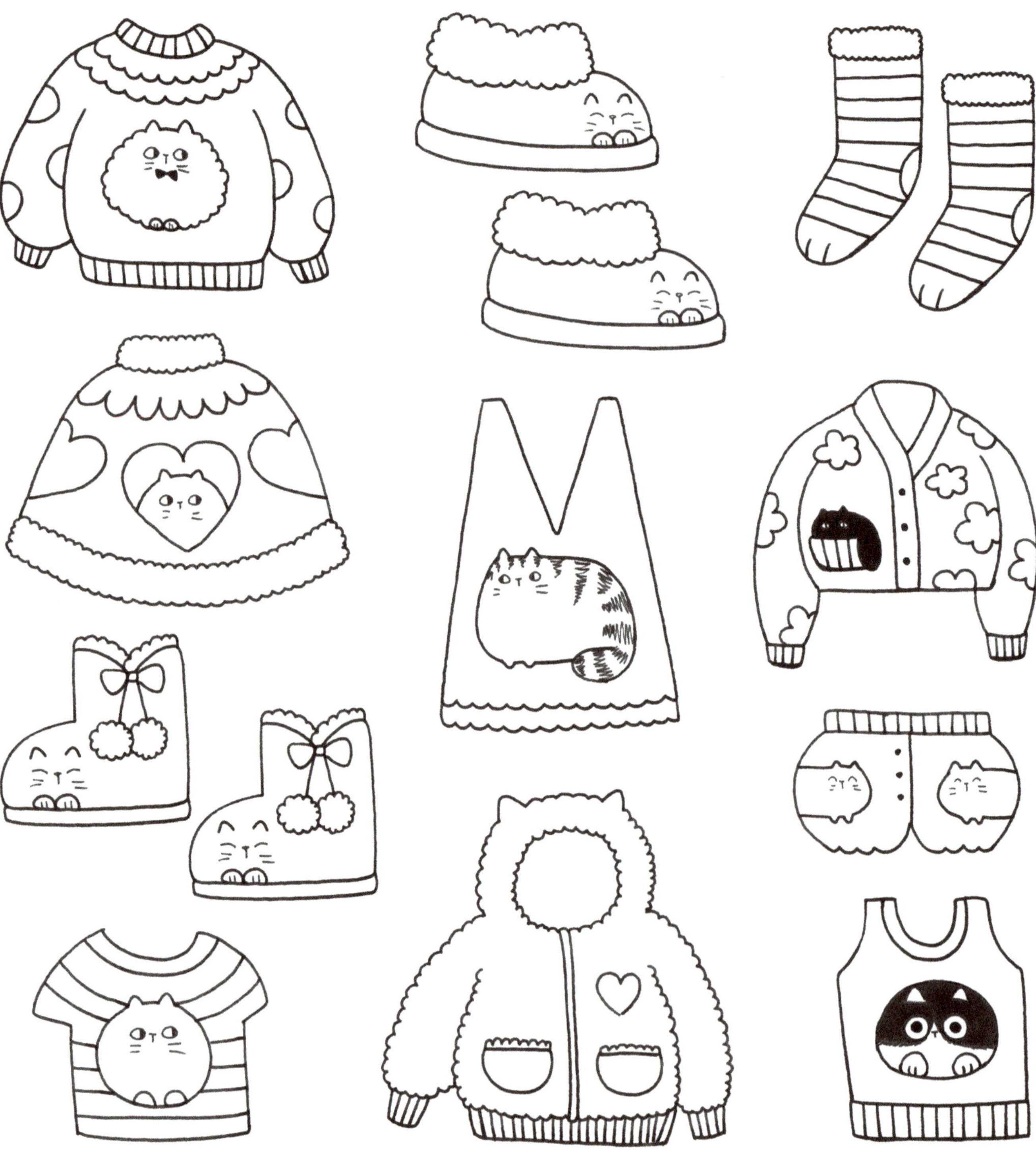

Doodle some cat designs on the clothes below. Don't forget to add color!

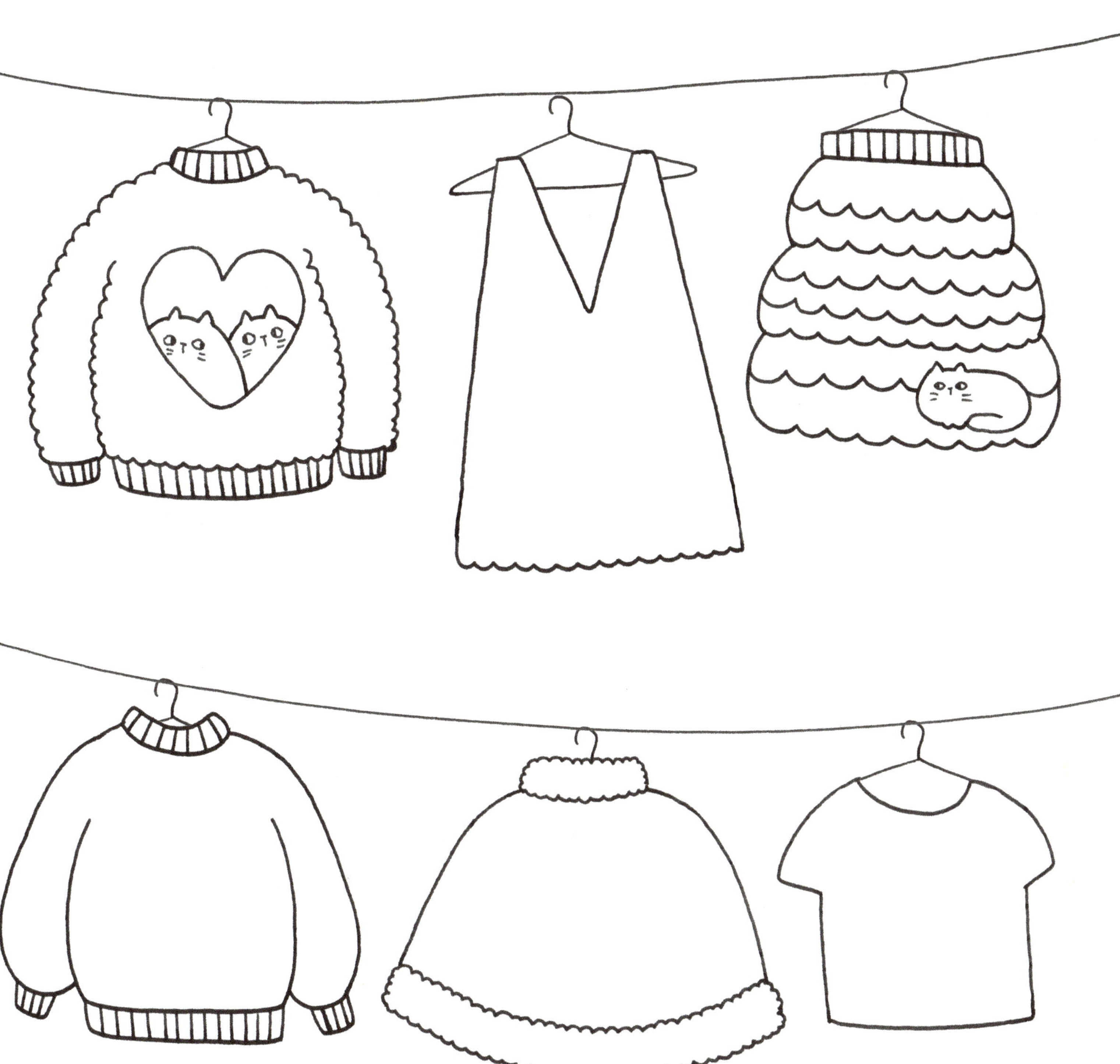

RAINY DAY GEAR

Do you like a rainy day? I love it! On rainy days, I get to stay home drawing and coloring while listening to the rhythm of the falling rain. Grab your colored pencils and lose yourself in coloring these pages—perhaps on a rainy day?

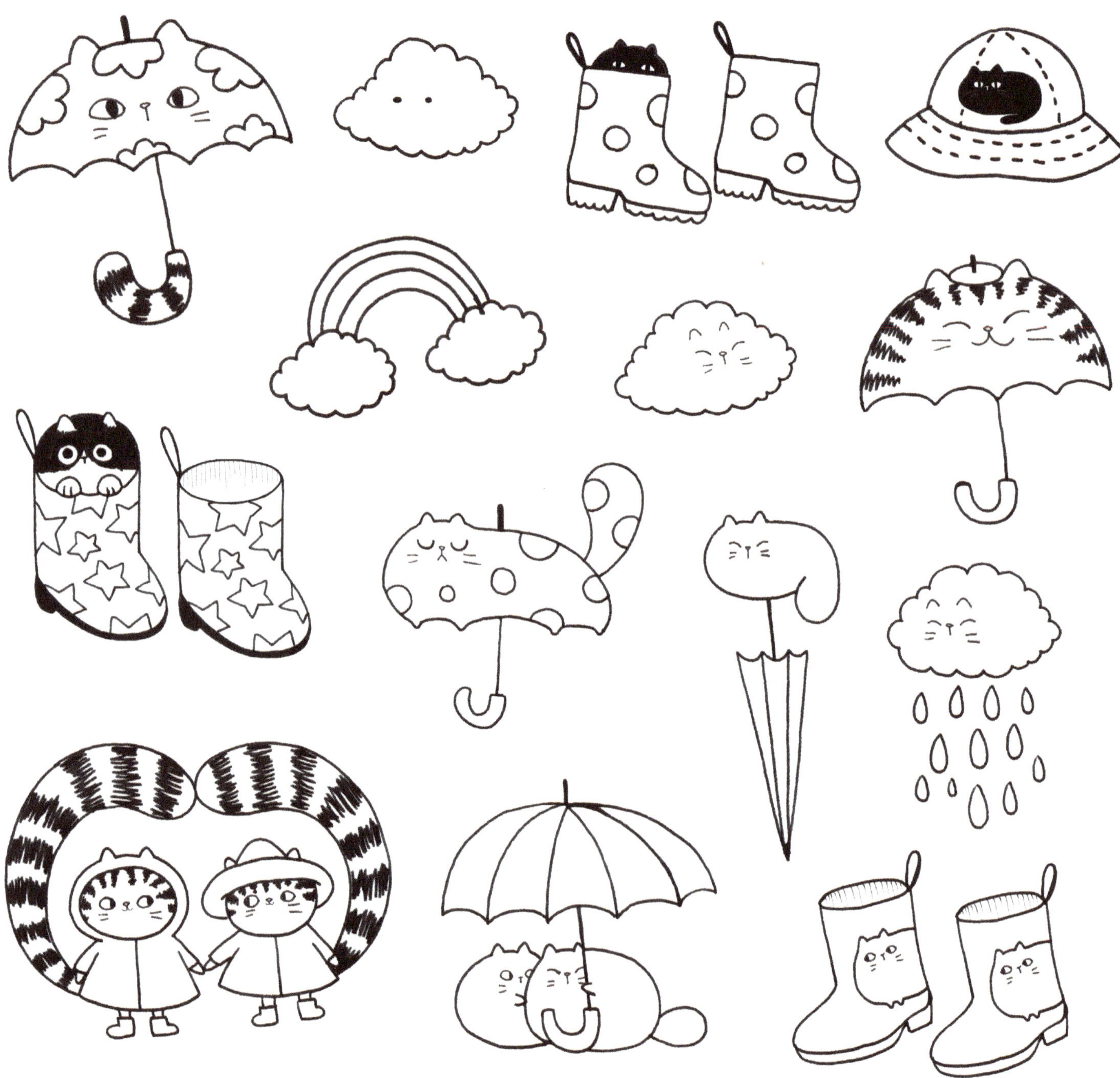

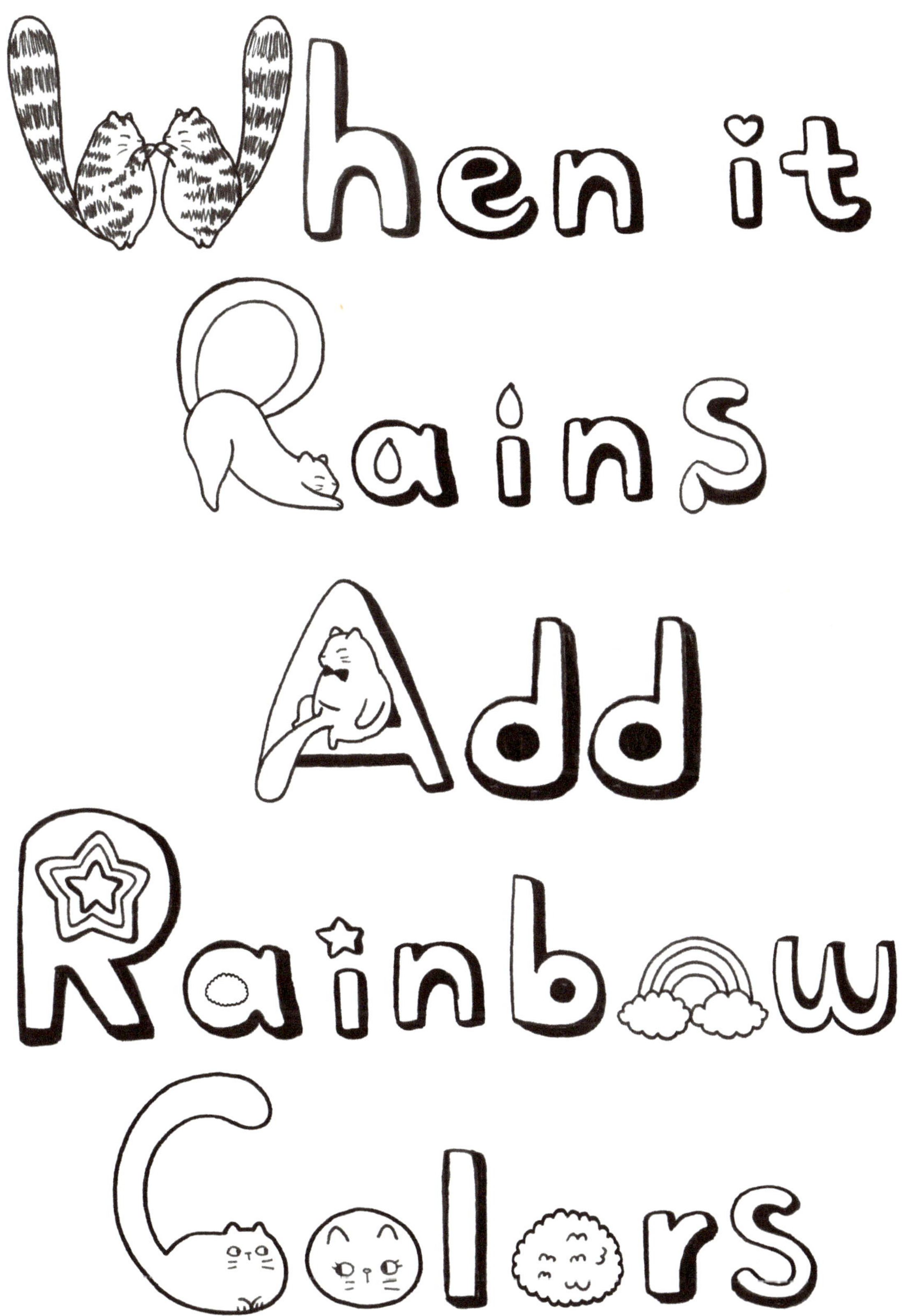
When it
Rains
Add
Rainbow
Colors

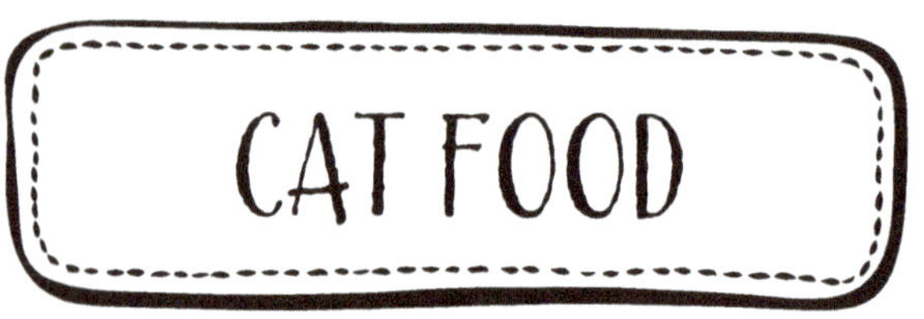
CAT FOOD

A balanced meal consists of a healthy serving of veggies and fruit. Would you add any of these to your next meal?

FIVE A DAY: FELINE FRUITS & VEGGIES

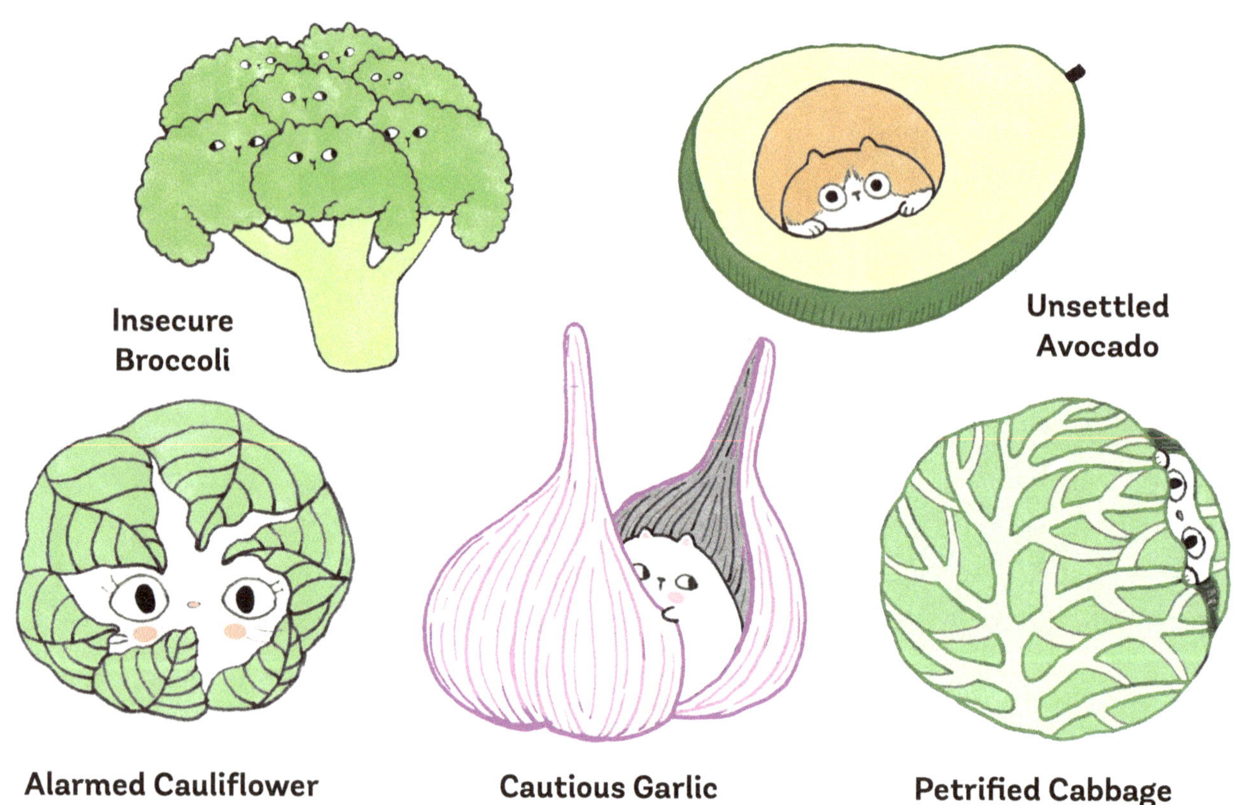

Insecure Broccoli

Unsettled Avocado

Alarmed Cauliflower

Cautious Garlic

Petrified Cabbage

SCARED MUSHROOM

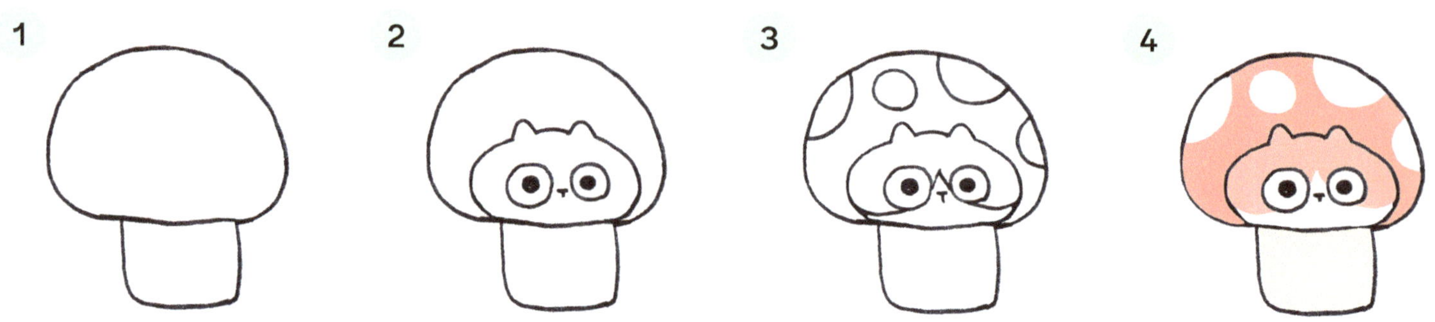

Draw your emotional veggies here.

Worried Broccoli

COOL COCONUT

Add a straw for an instant thirst quencher.

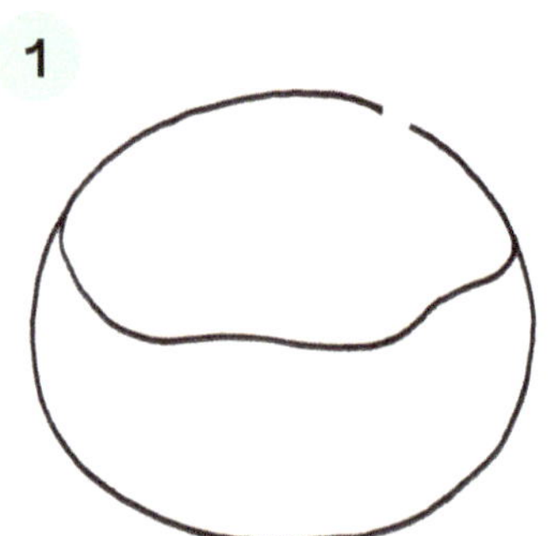

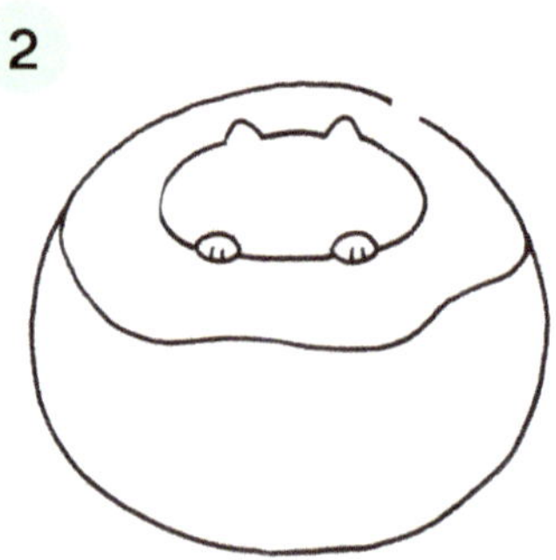

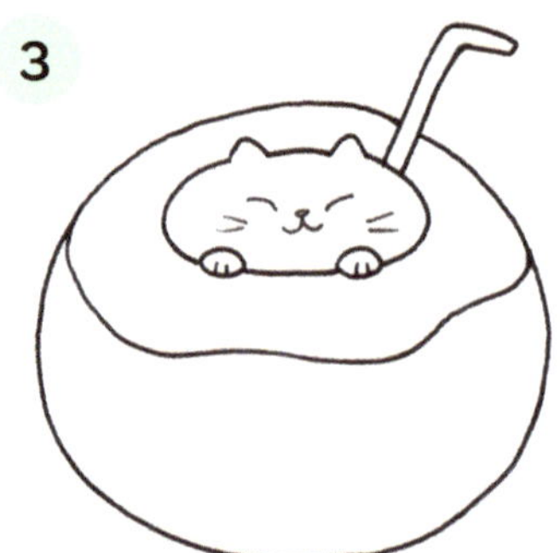

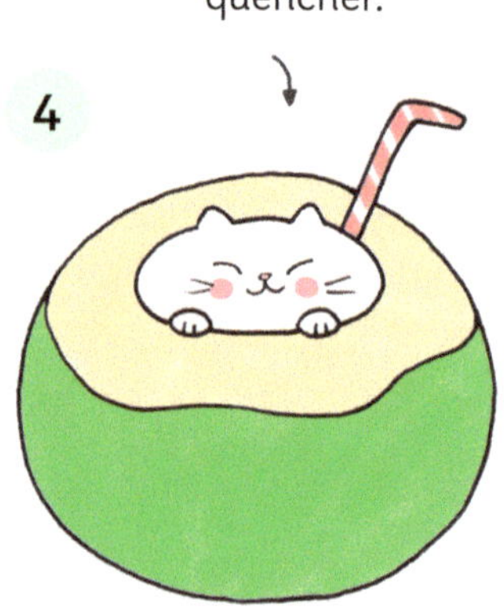

PURRFECT PEACH

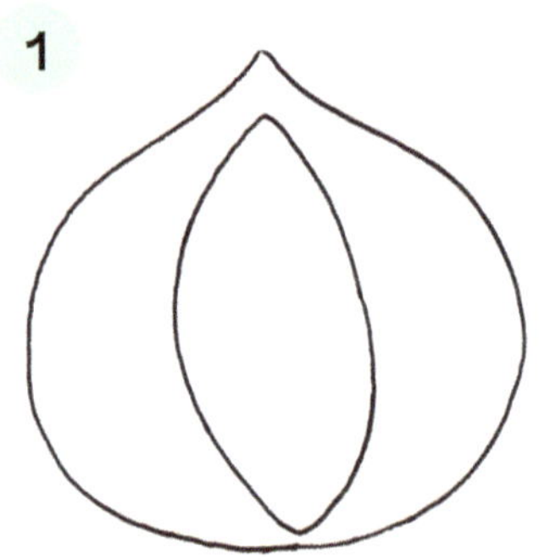

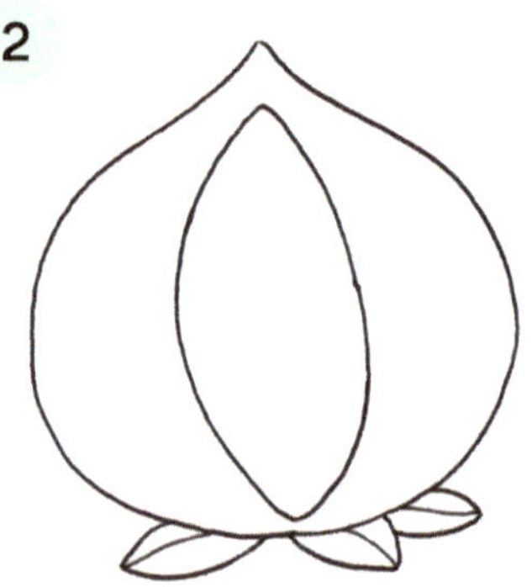

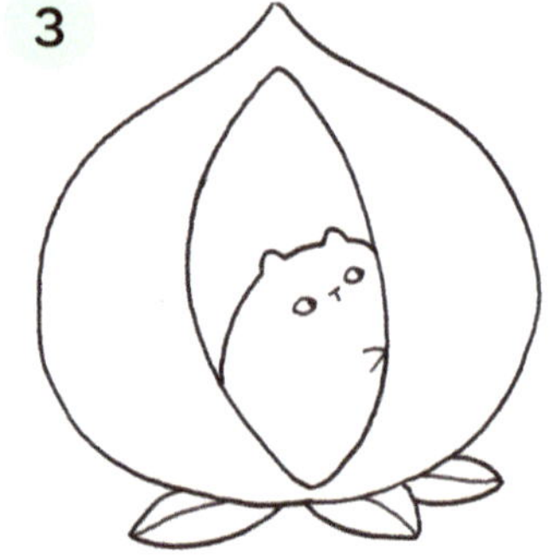

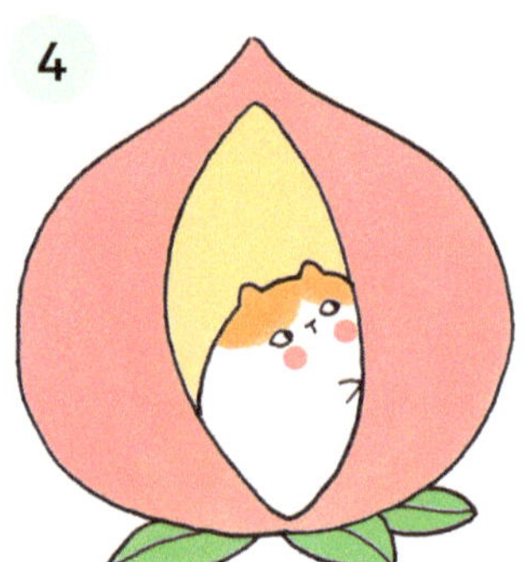

MATURE BANANA

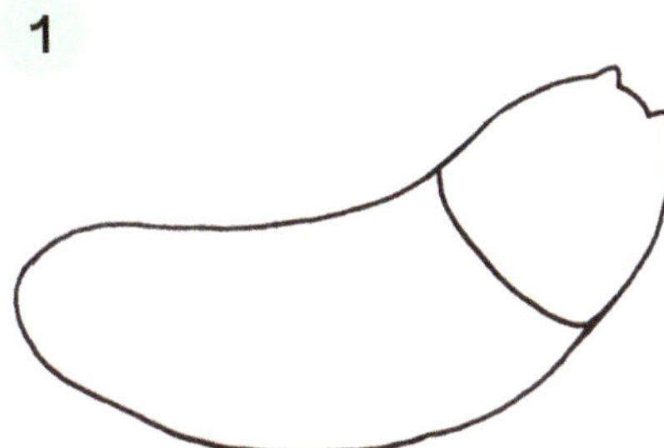

1

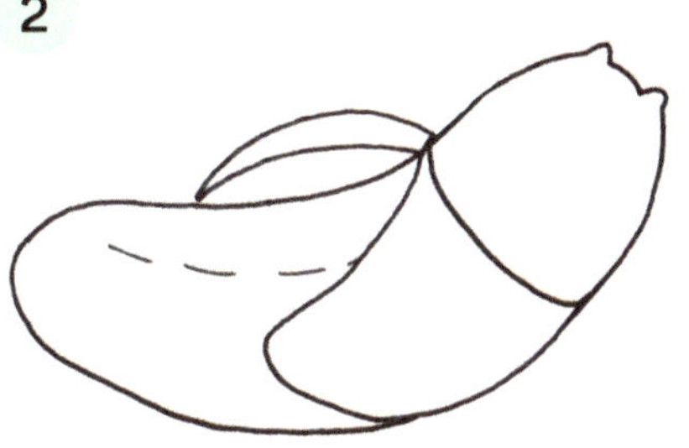

2

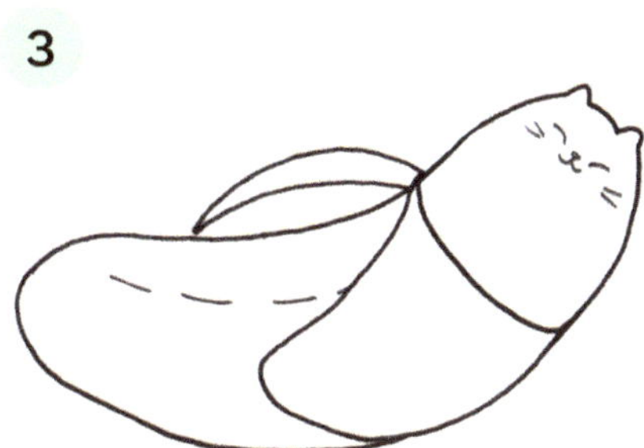

3

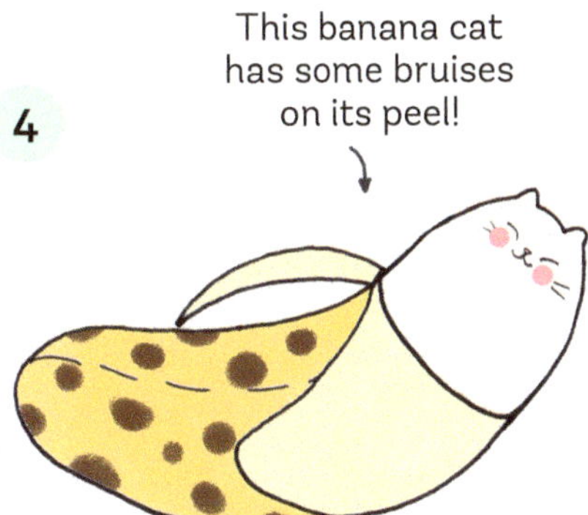

4

This banana cat has some bruises on its peel!

TANGERINE TABBY

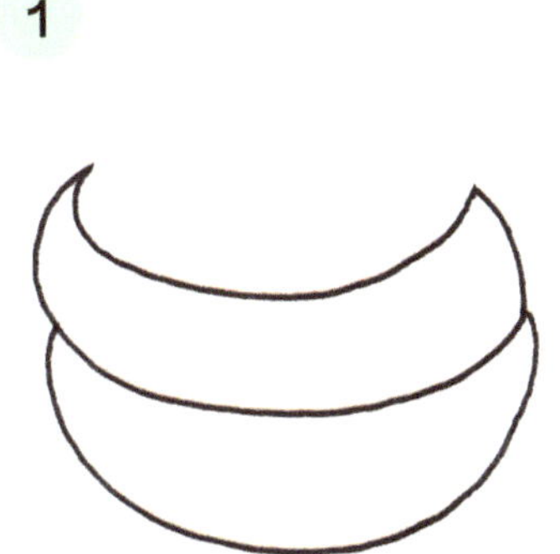

1

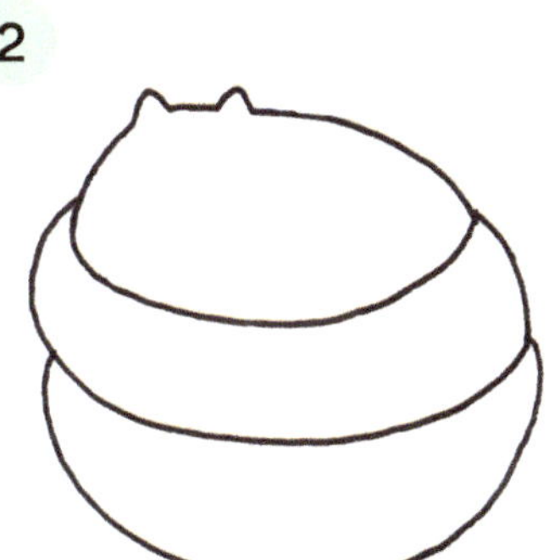

2

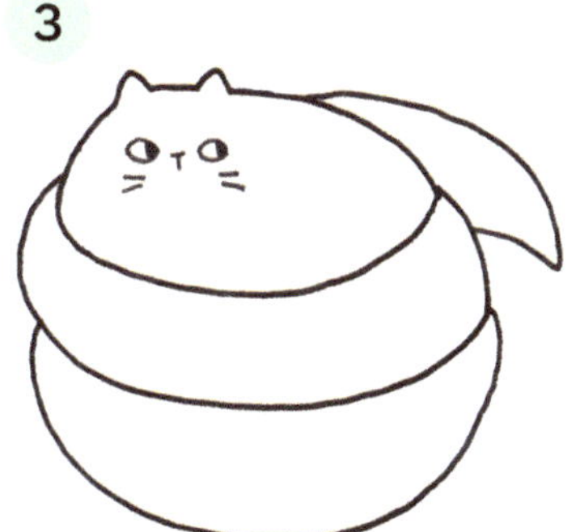

3

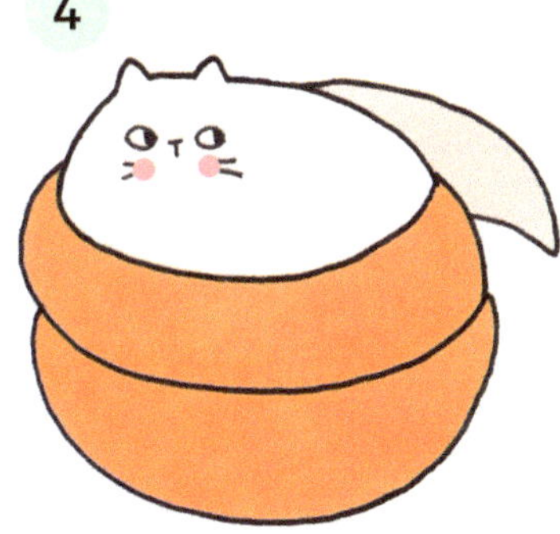

4

KIWI KITTY

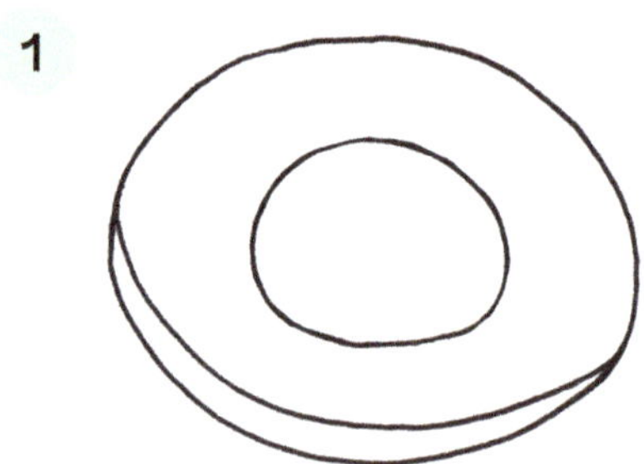

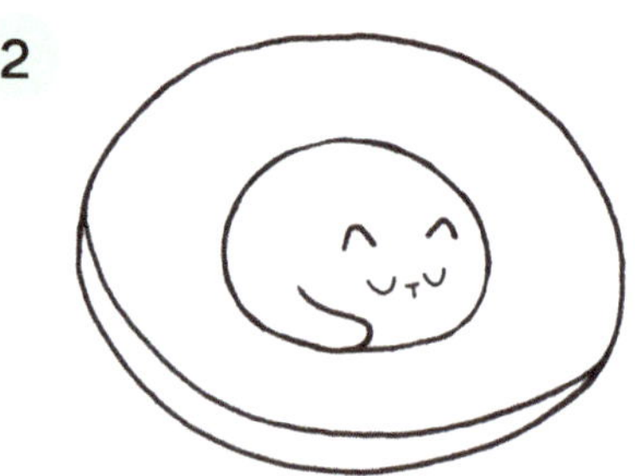

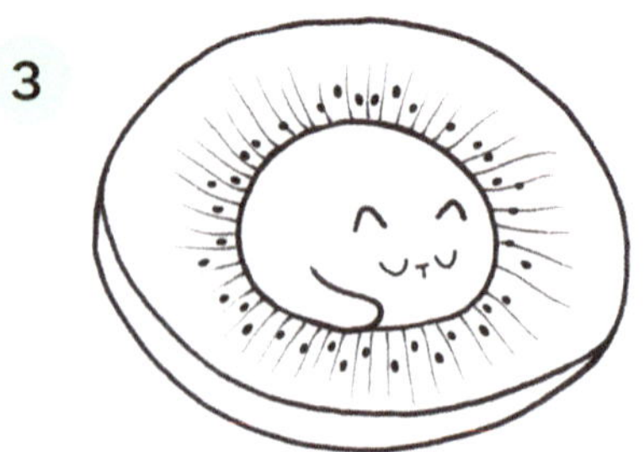

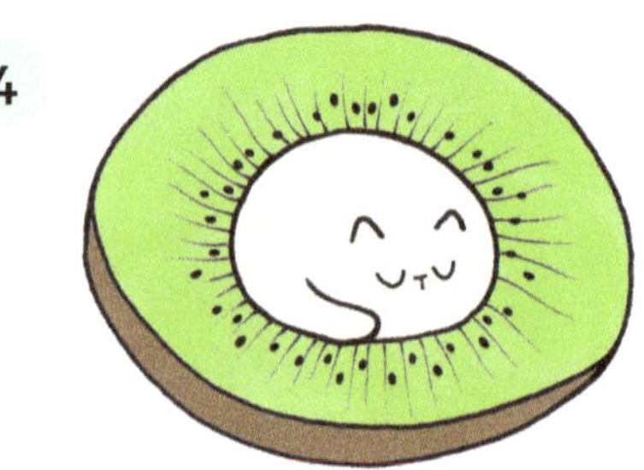

KING DURIAN KITTY CATS

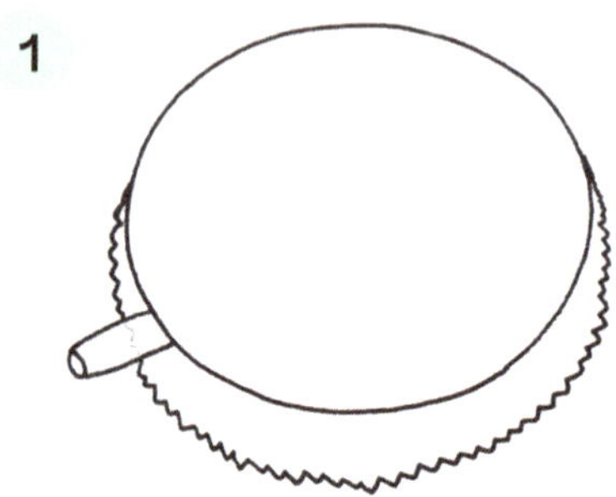

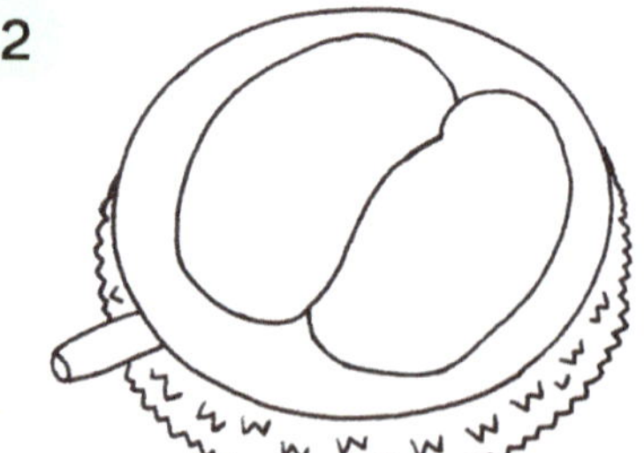

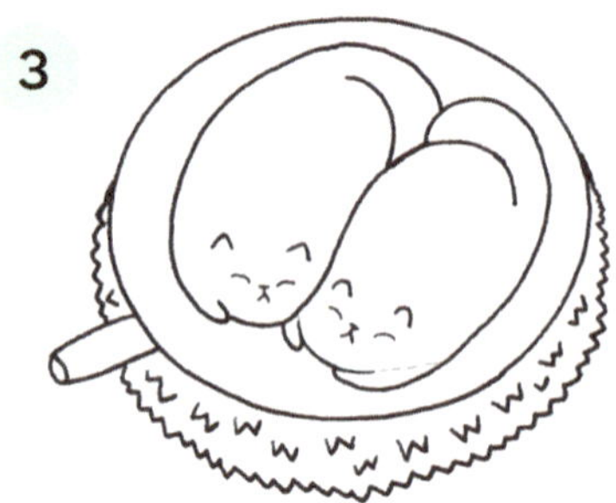

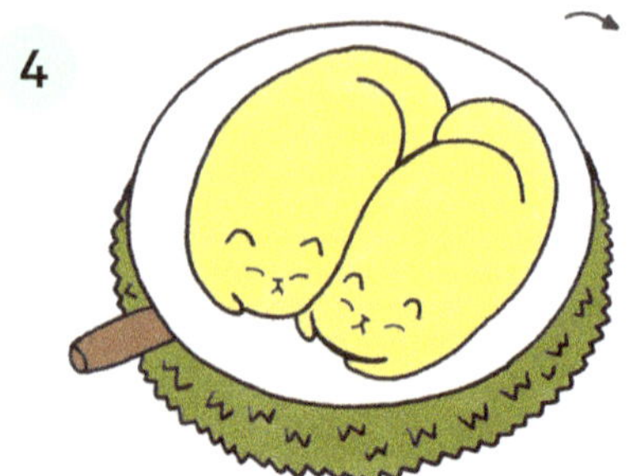

The durian is a large fruit from Southeast Asia that has a strong smell and rich taste.

Now doodle your own feline fruits!

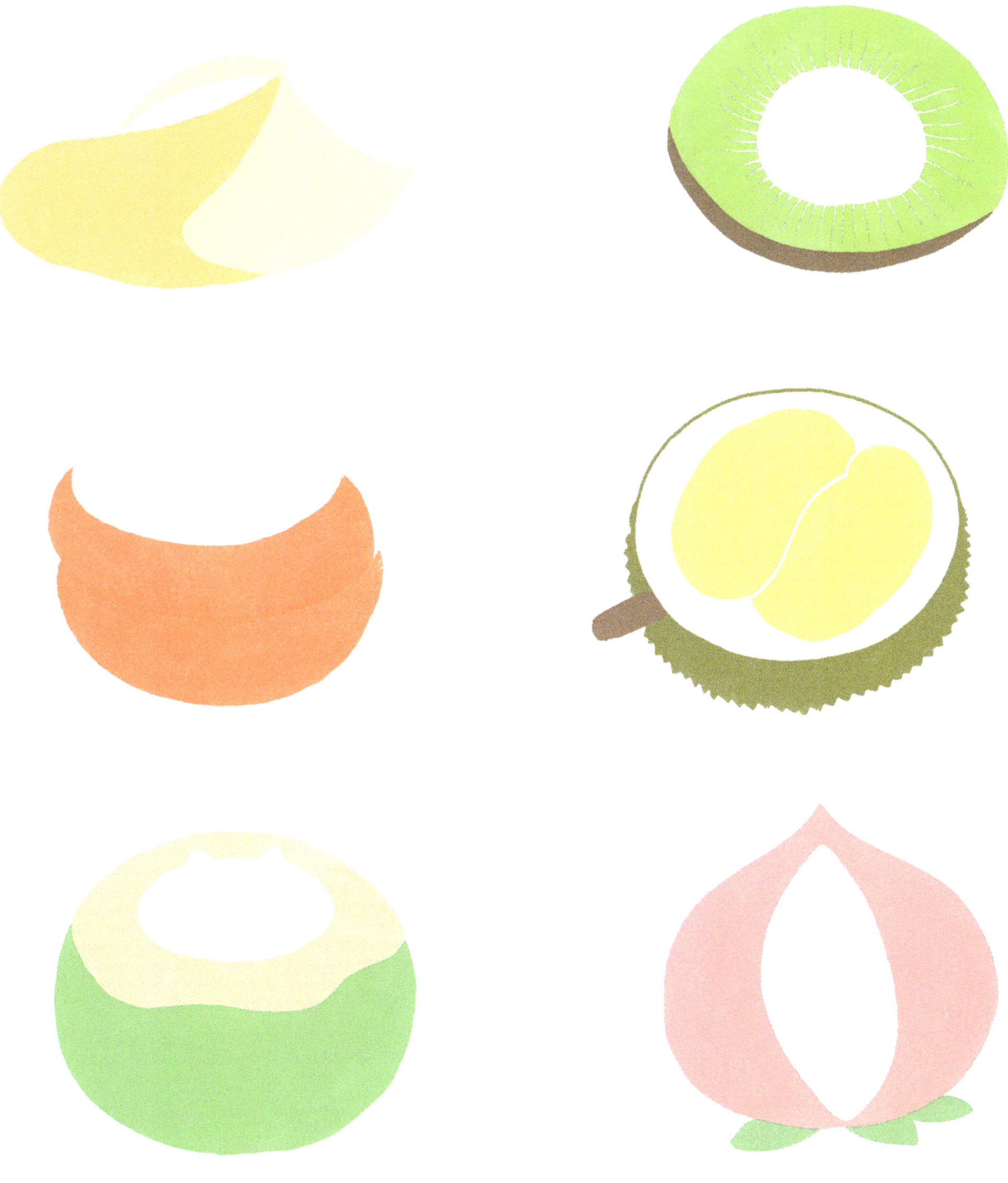

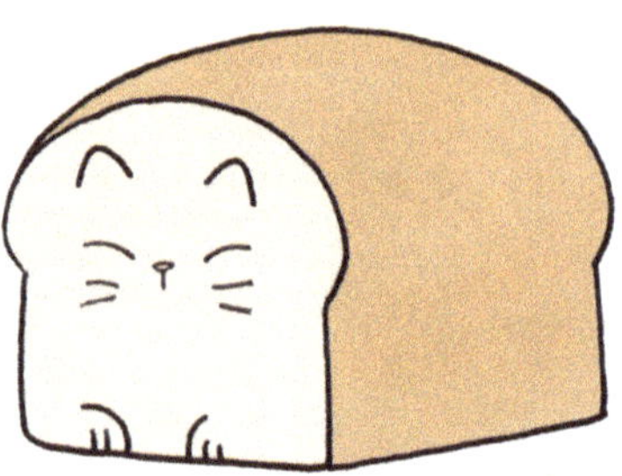

White loaf
Fine and simple

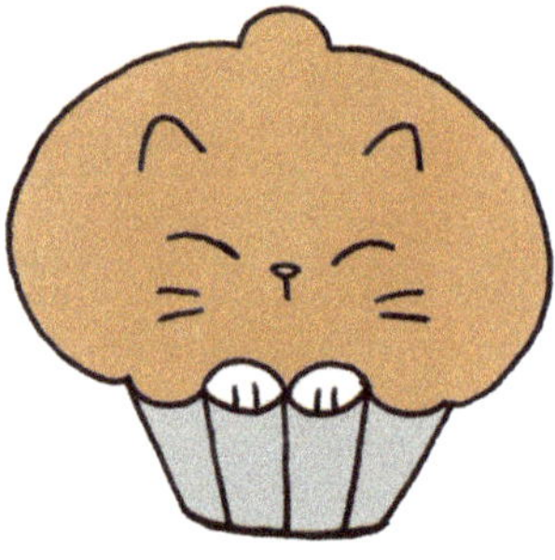

Muffin
Soft and buttery

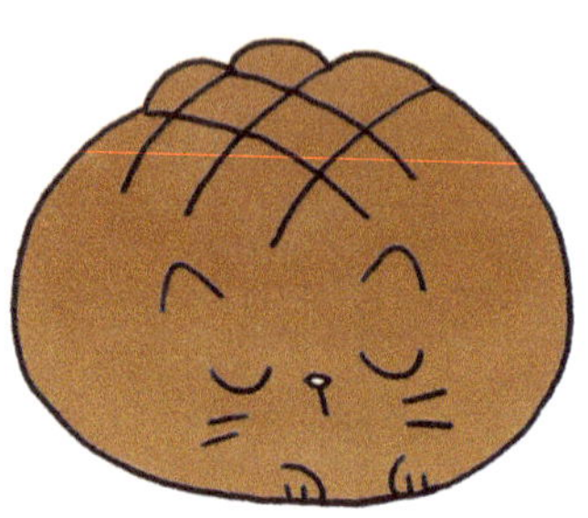

Sourdough
Sour and airy

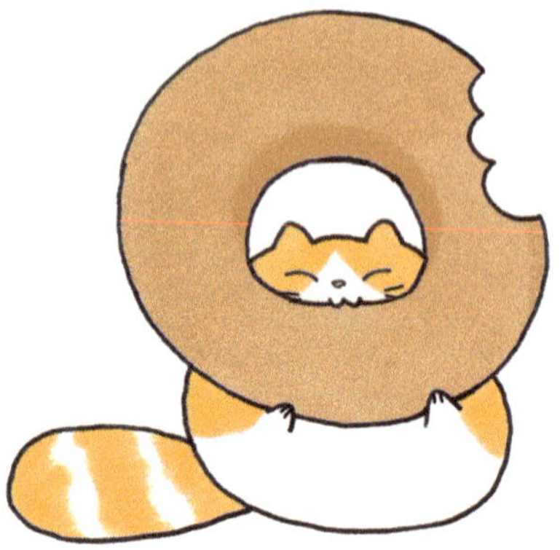

Bagel
Dense and chewy

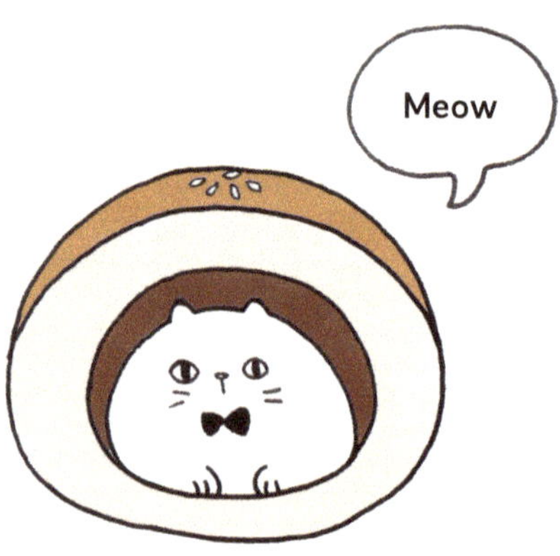

Mochi bun
Elastic with a great
depth of flavor.

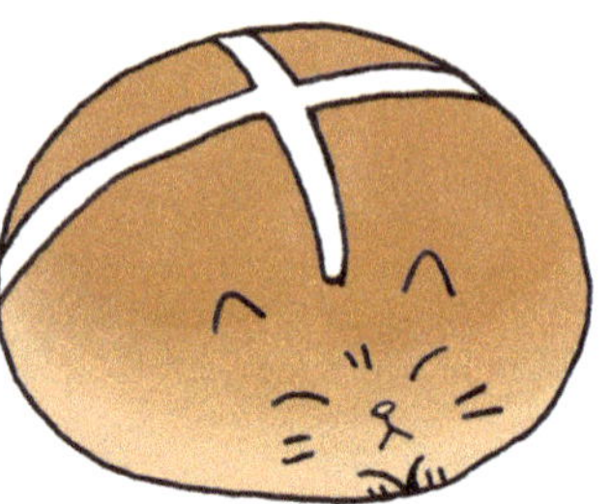

Cross bun
Cross and spicy with a
hint of cinnamon

BIG LOAF

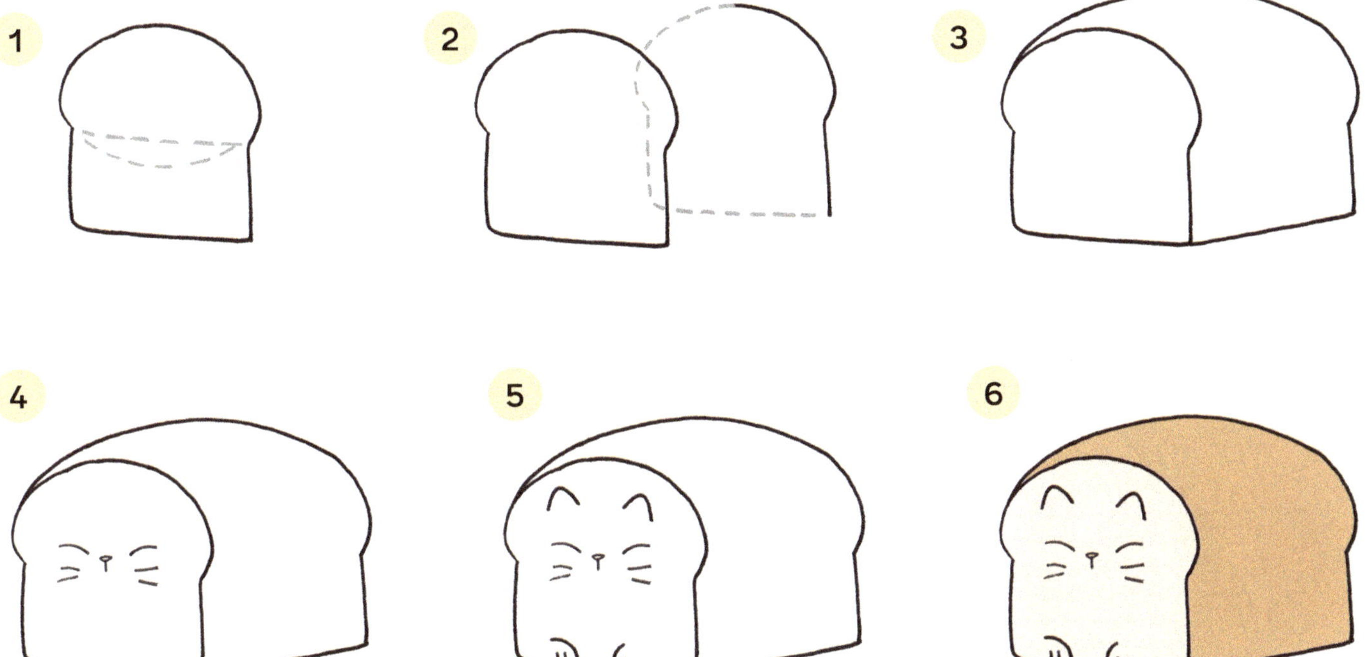

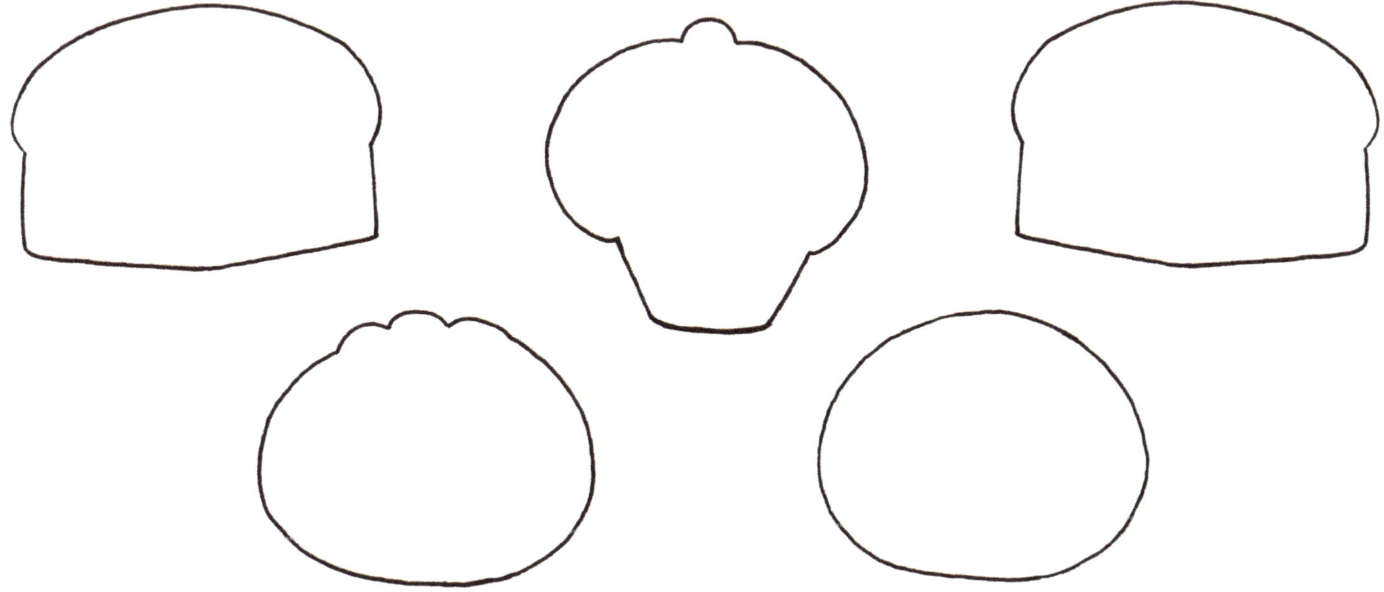

Doodle your own cat bread below.

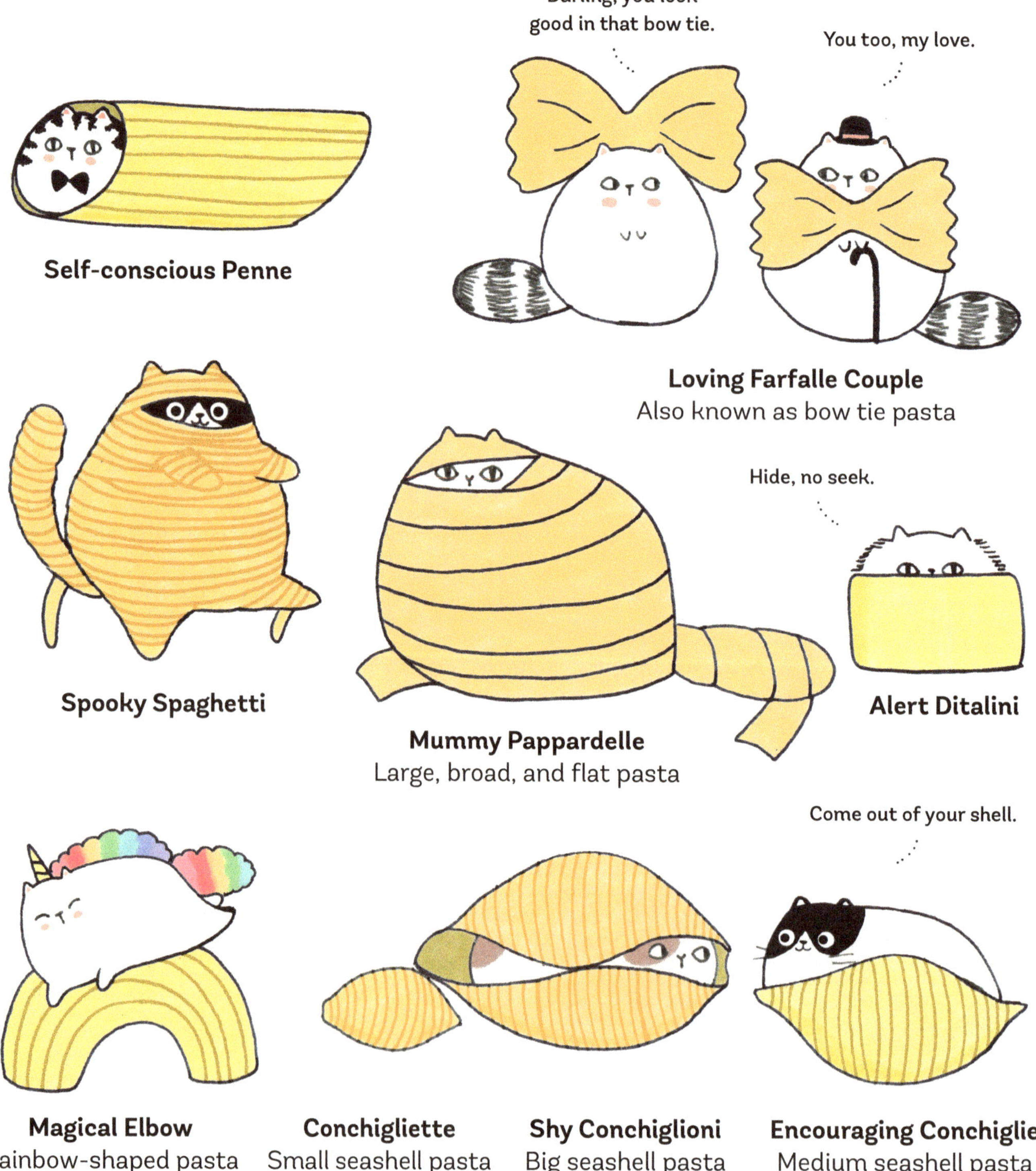

Self-conscious Penne

Loving Farfalle Couple
Also known as bow tie pasta

Spooky Spaghetti

Mummy Pappardelle
Large, broad, and flat pasta

Alert Ditalini

Magical Elbow
Rainbow-shaped pasta

Conchigliette
Small seashell pasta

Shy Conchiglioni
Big seashell pasta

Encouraging Conchiglie
Medium seashell pasta

Turn the pasta into cats-a!

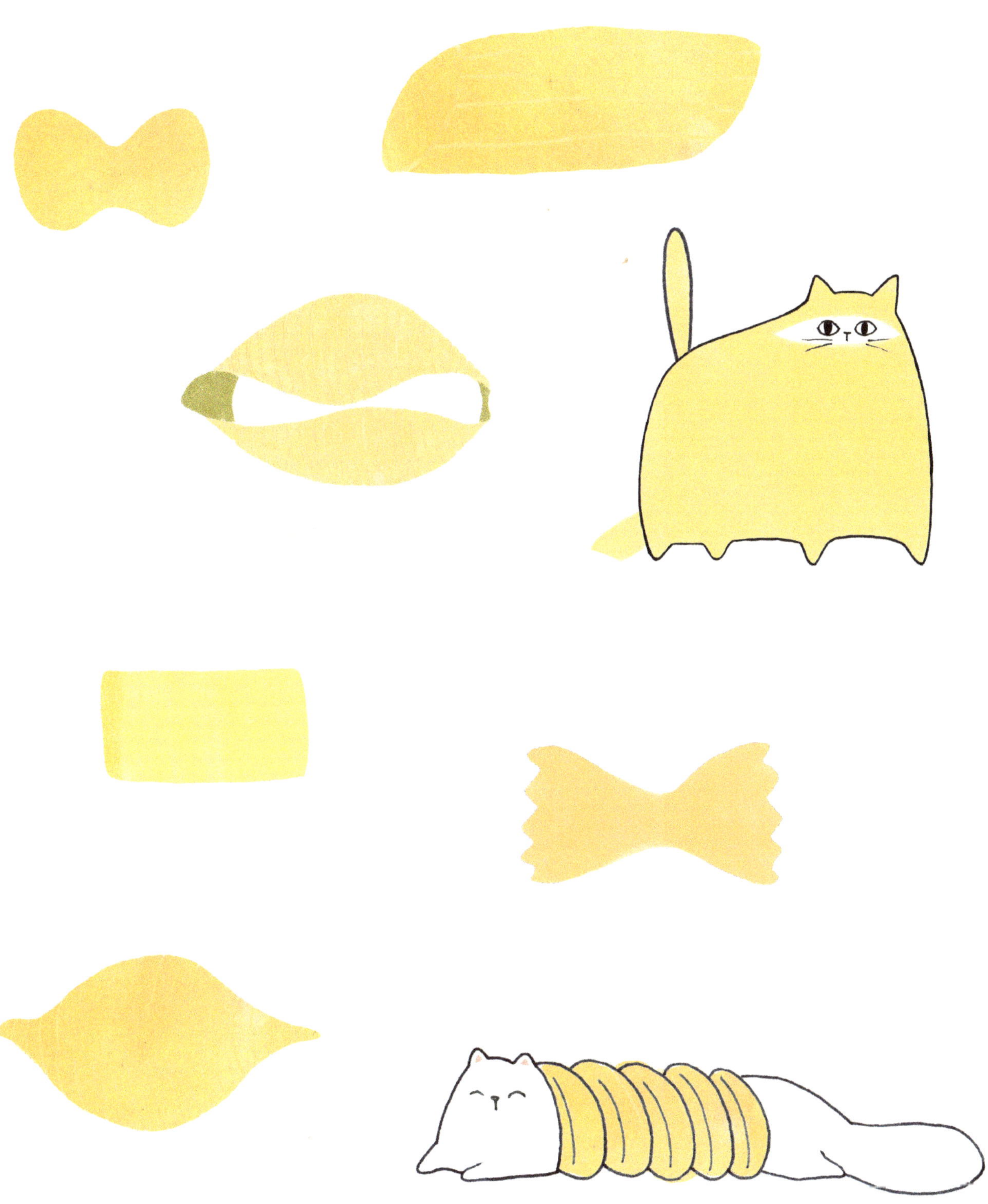

OVERJOYED POPCORN

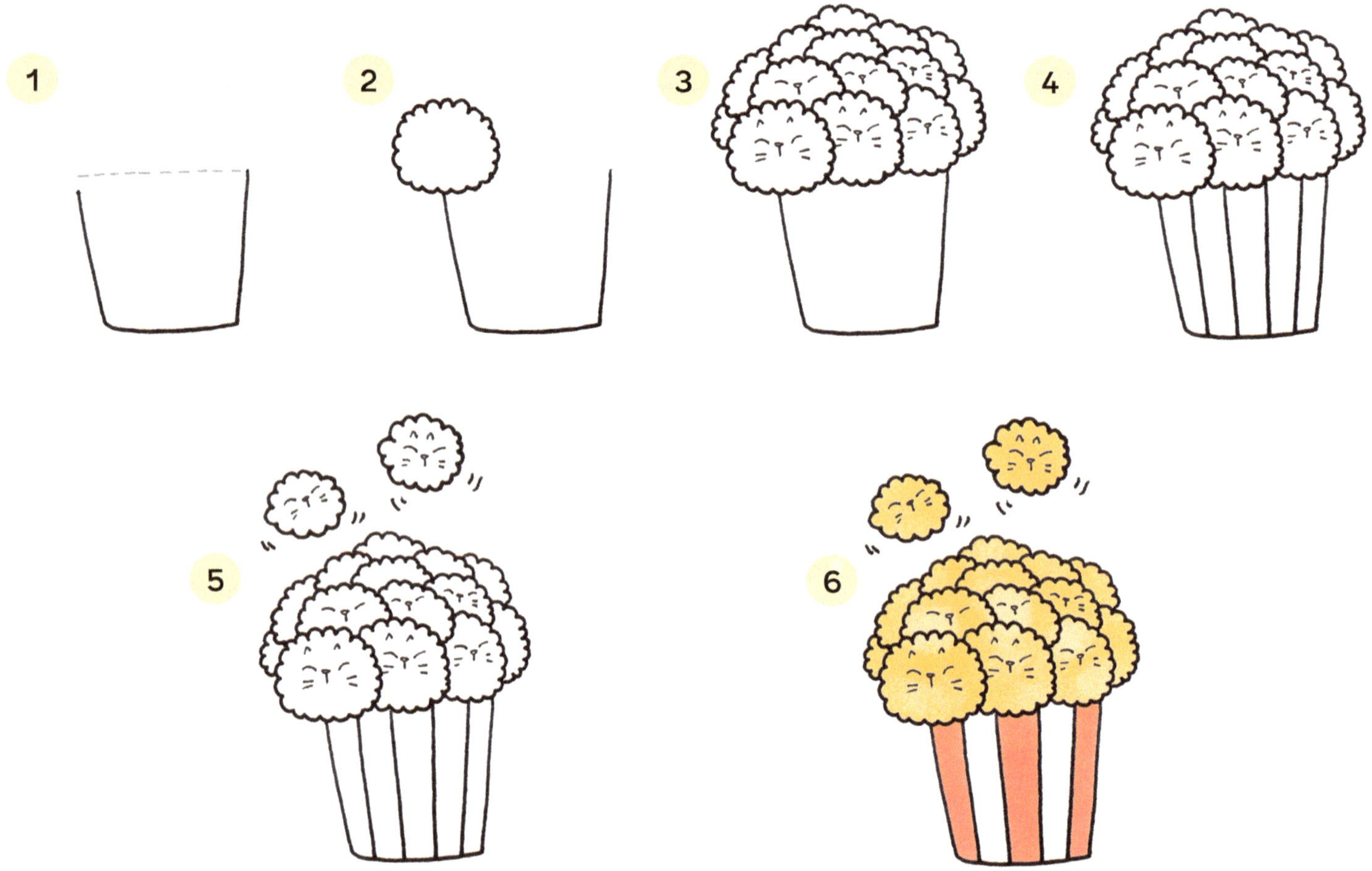

1

2

3

4

5

6

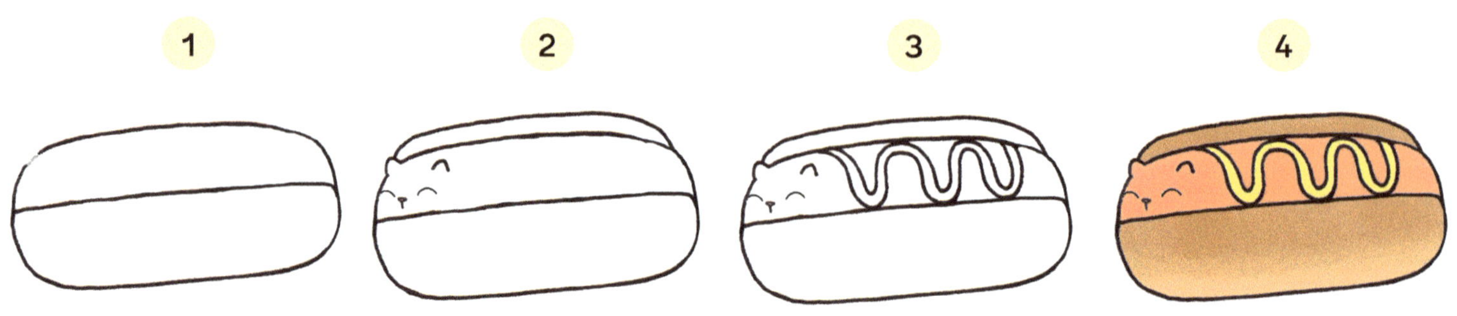

SMILEY HOT DOG-CAT

1

2

3

4

COMFY BURGER

 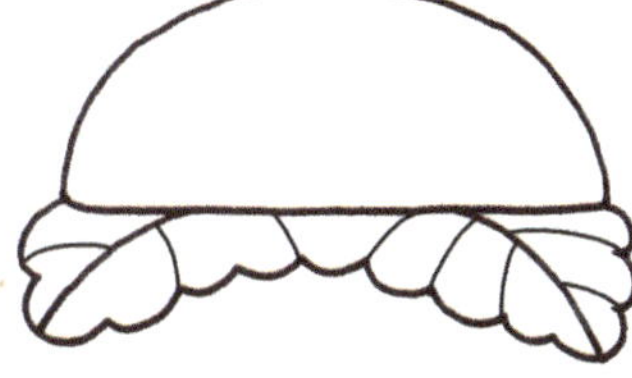

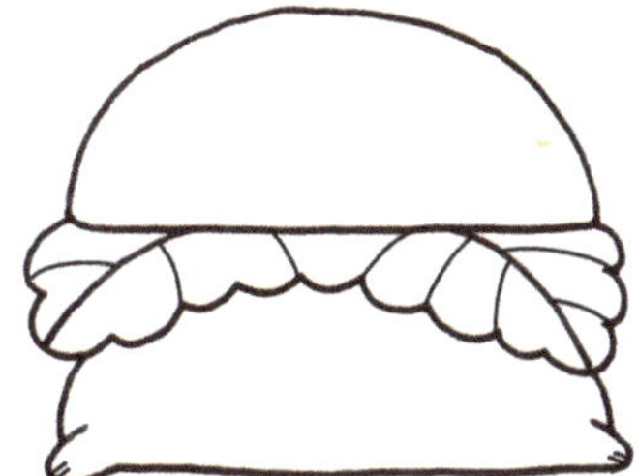

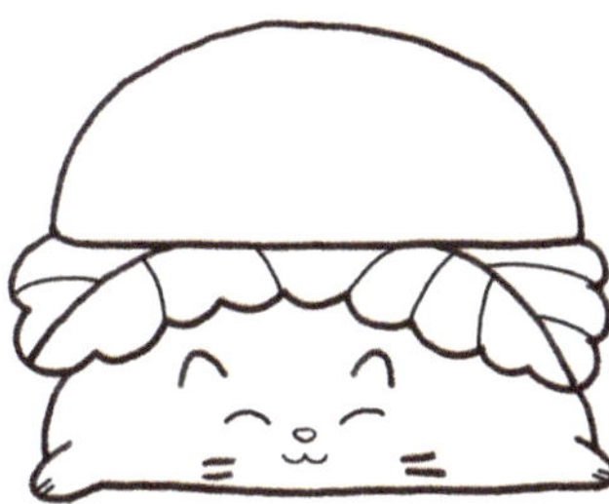

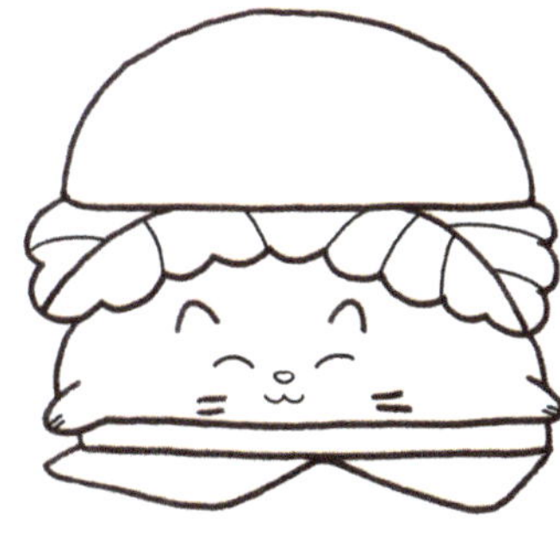

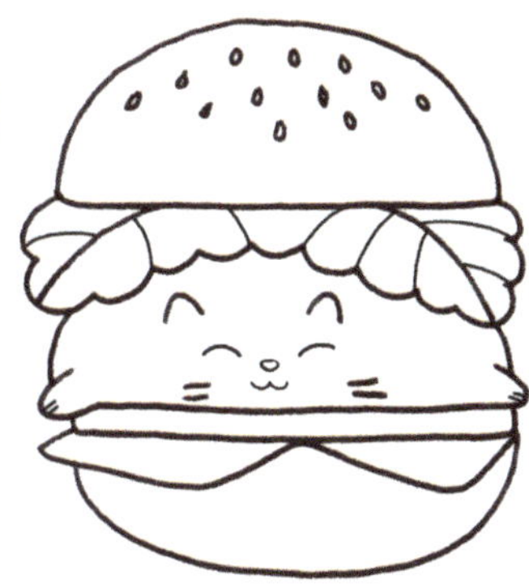

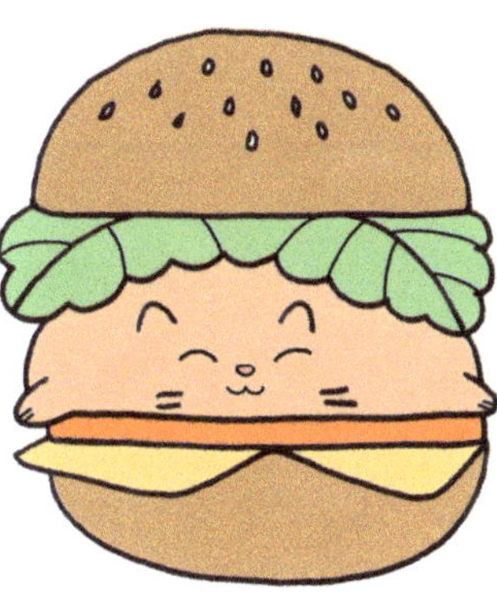

CLAUSTROPHOBIC TACO

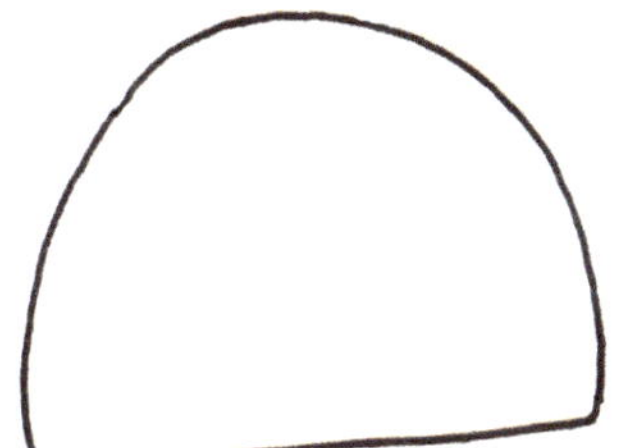

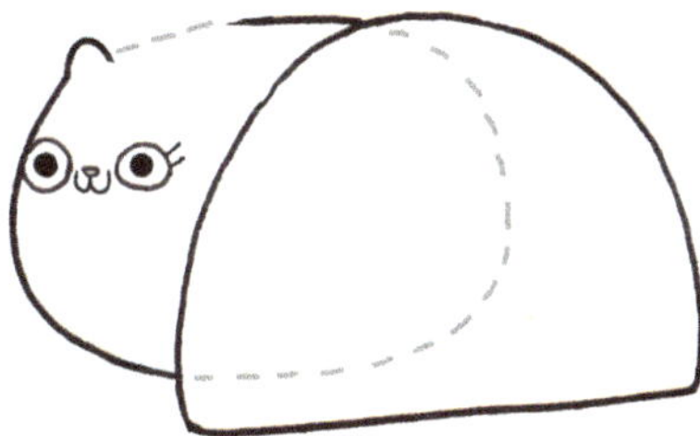

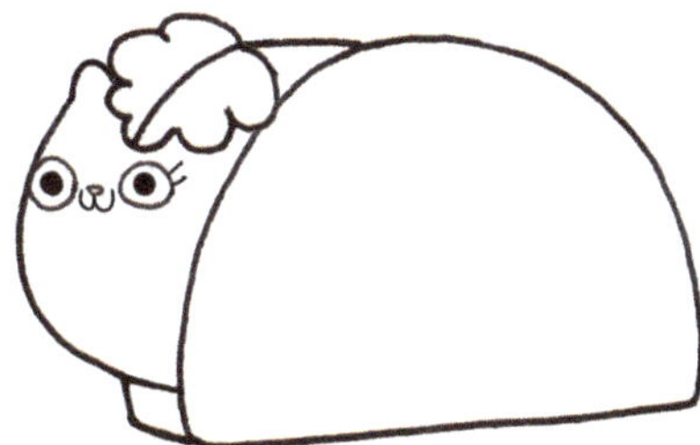

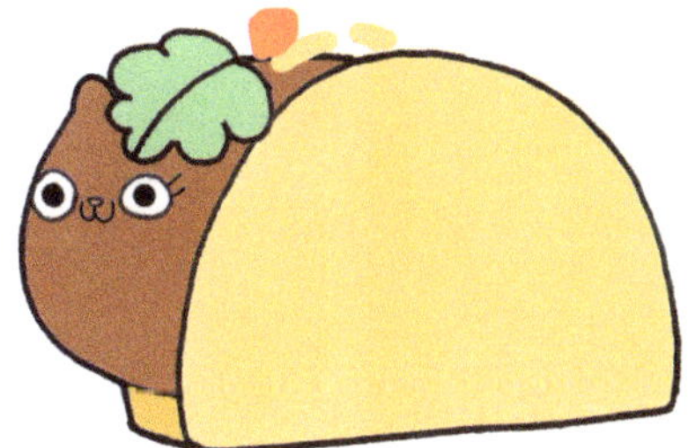

RESTED PANCAKE

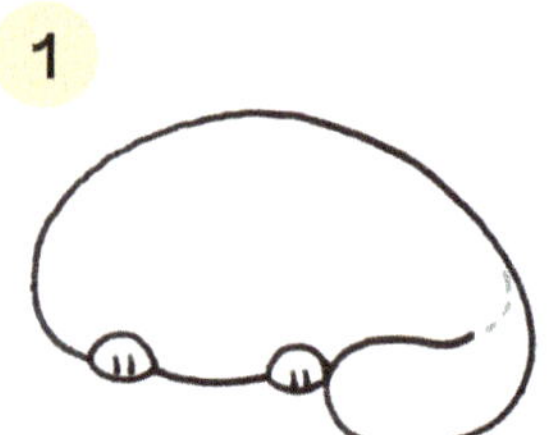

1

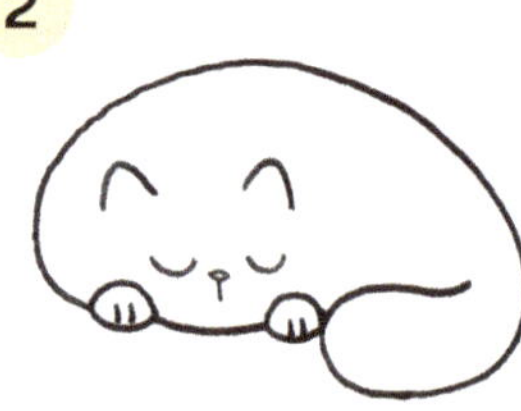

2

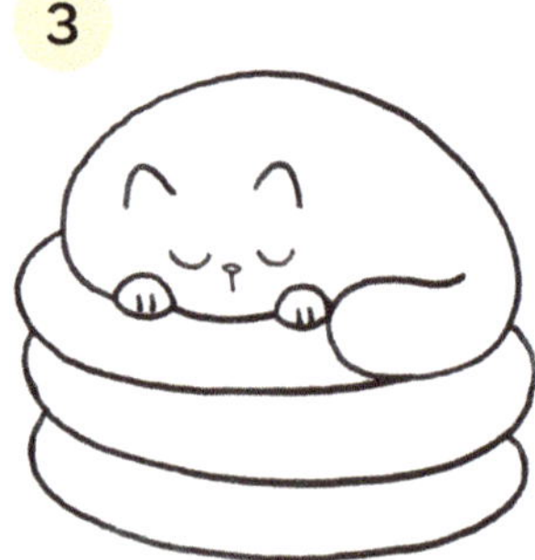

3

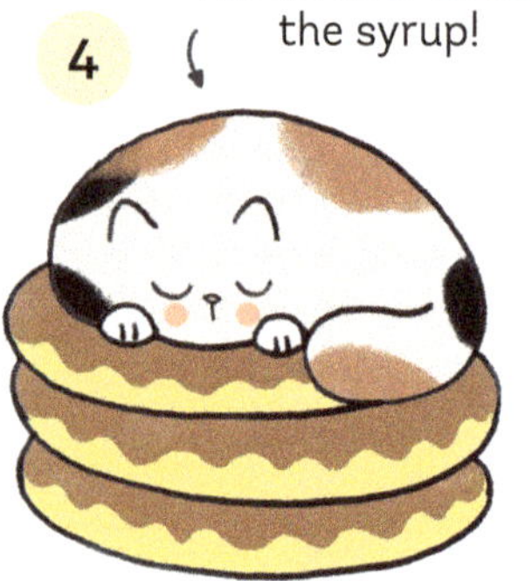

4

Remember to add the syrup!

- -

CHEERFUL INSTANT NOODLES

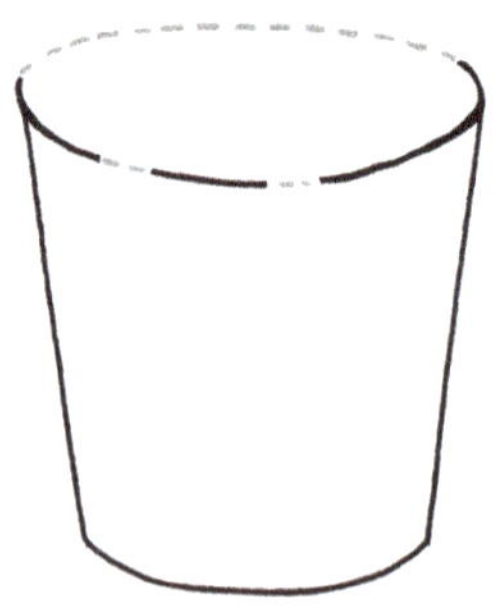

1

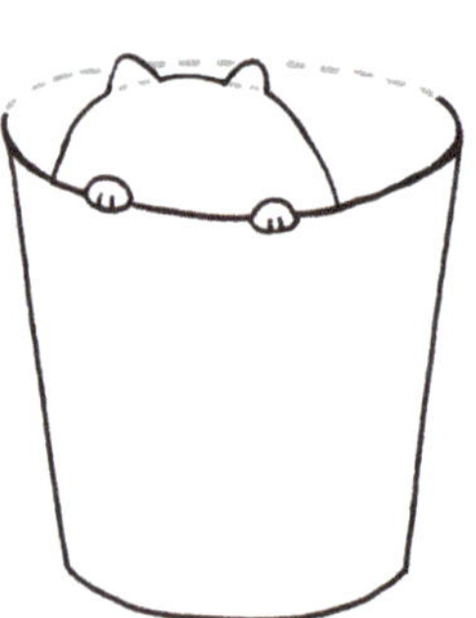

2

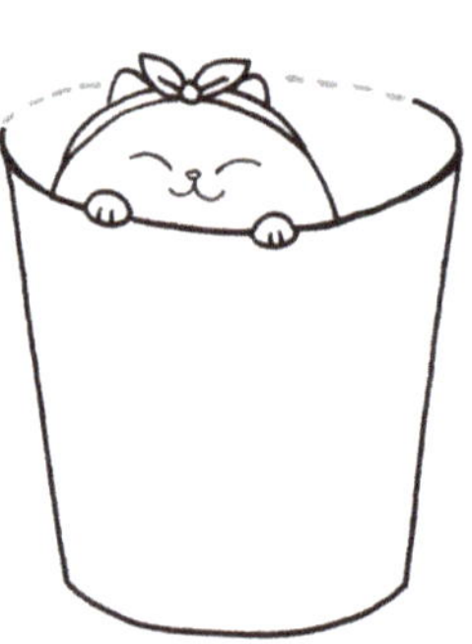

3

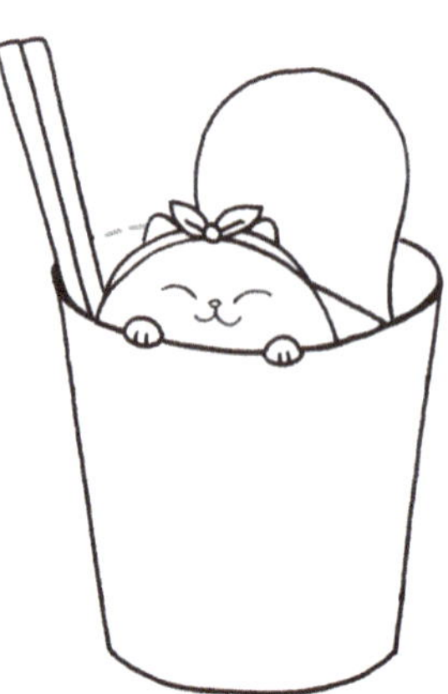

4

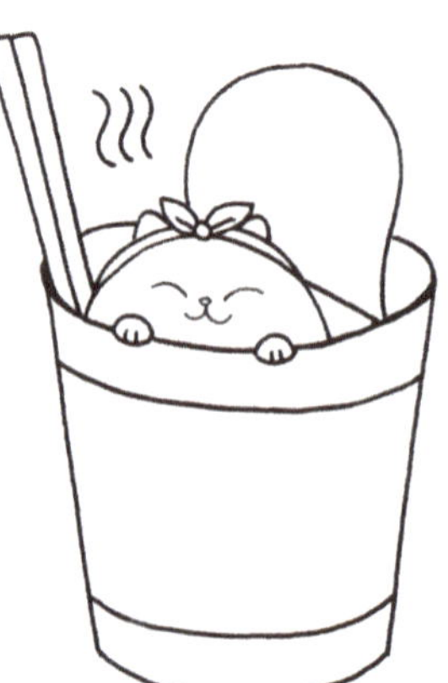

5

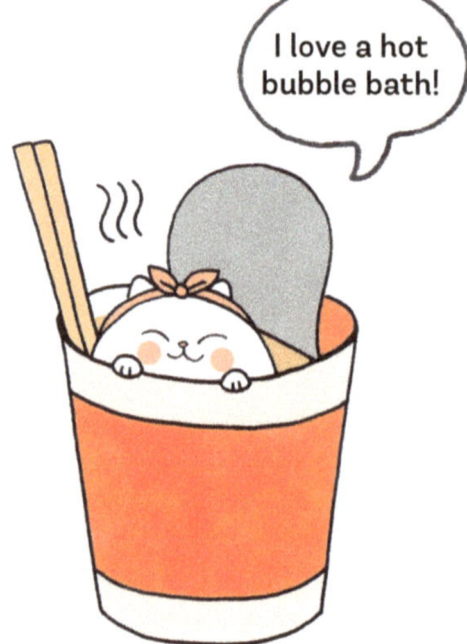

6

Cook up your comfort food from these yummy shapes!

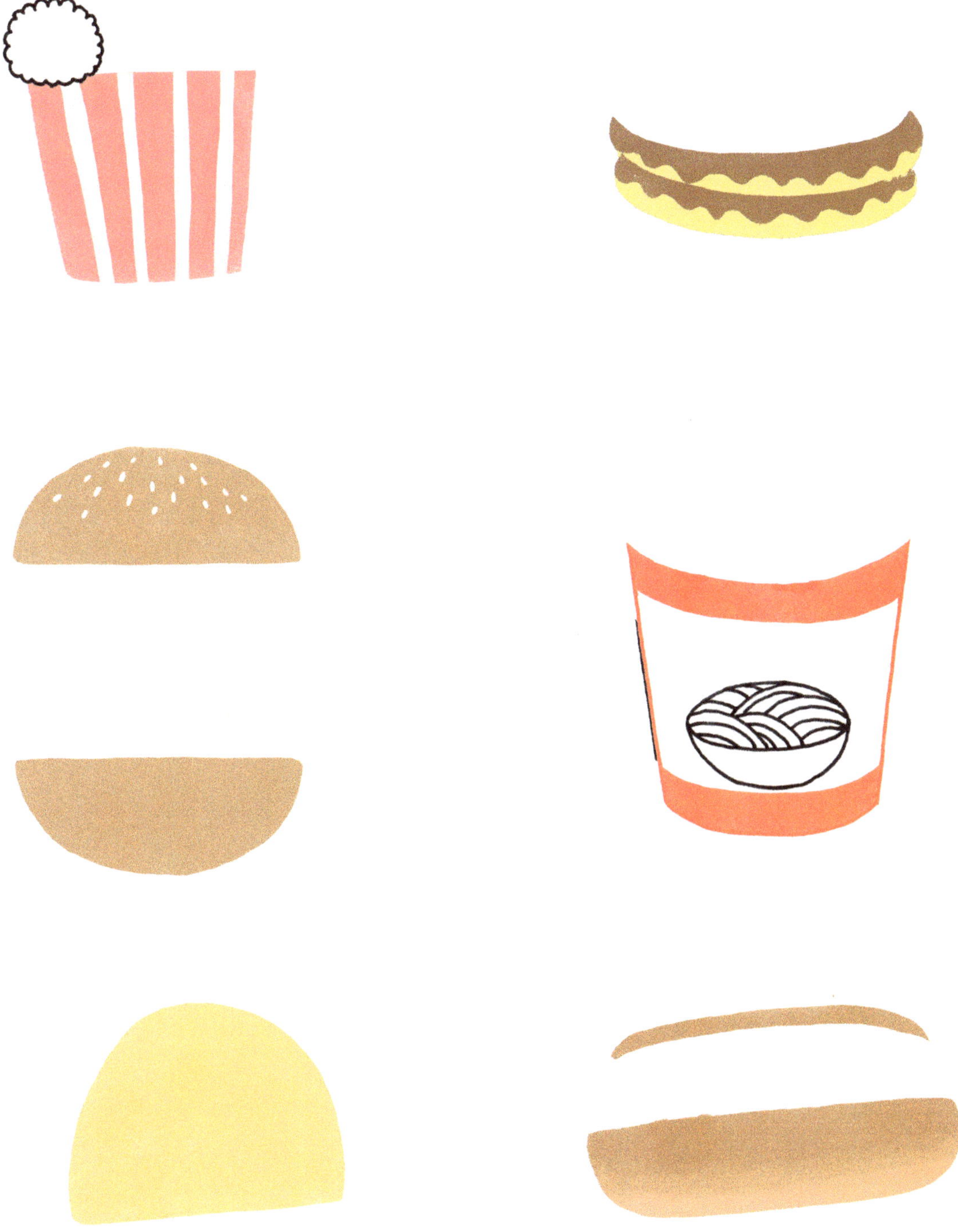

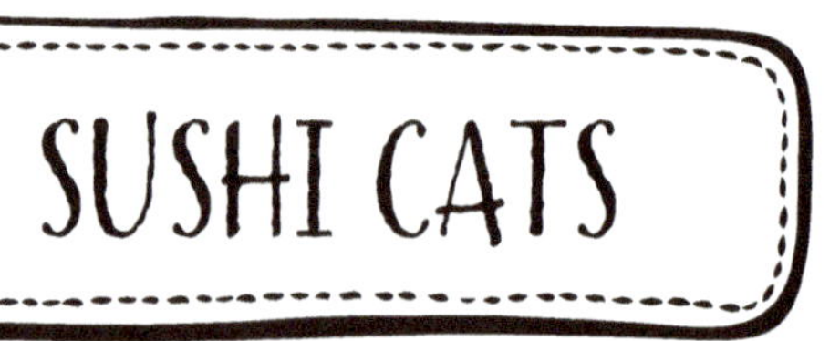

Here we are serving up some yummy sushi cats.

SLEEPY NIGIRI

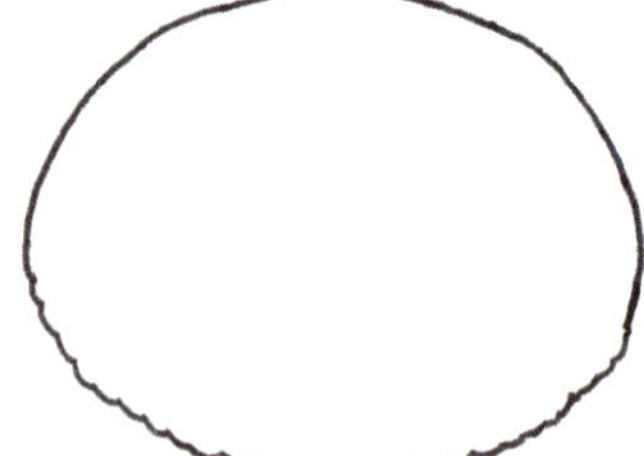

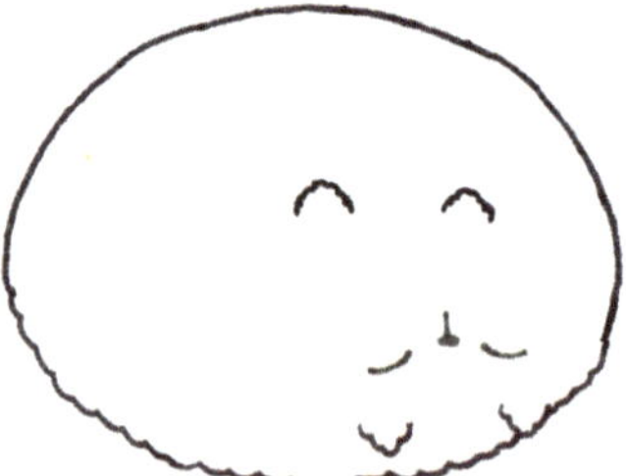

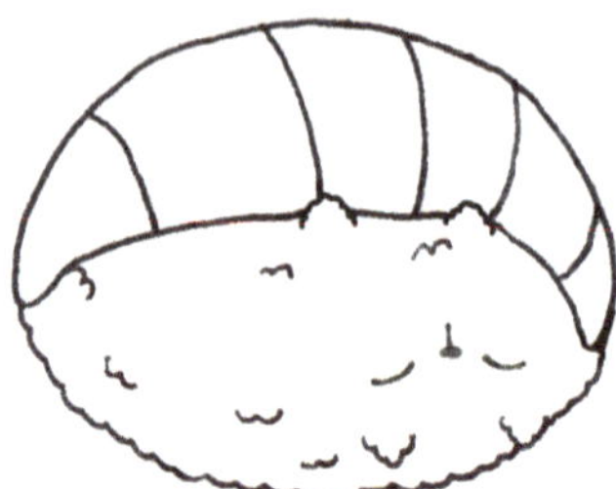

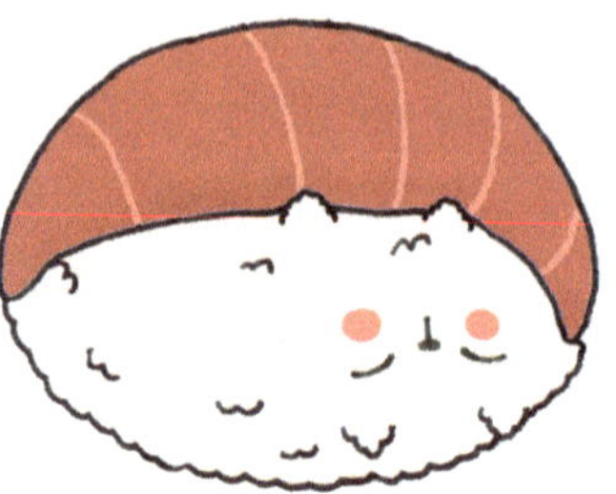

FLOPPY SASHIMI

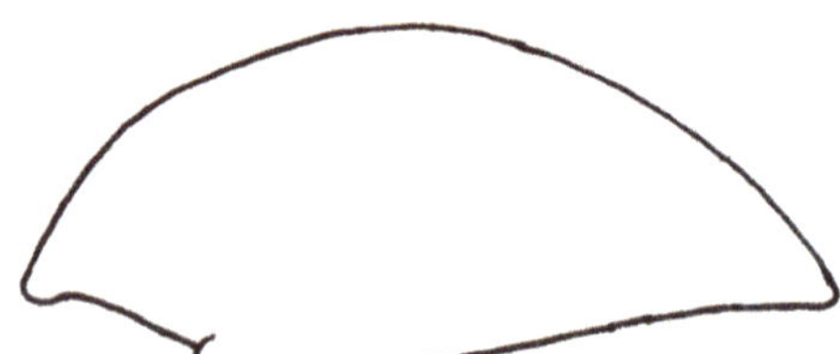

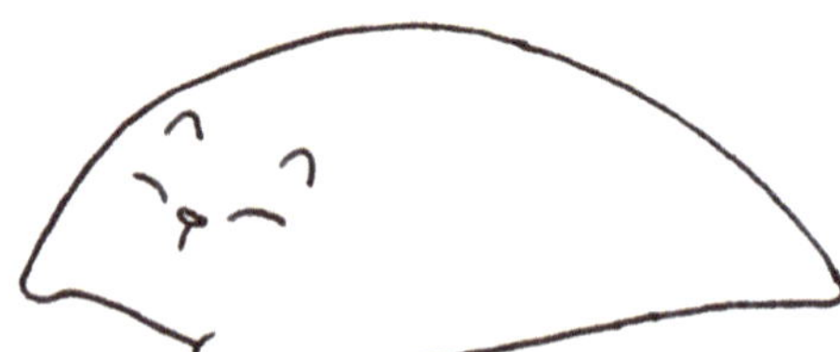

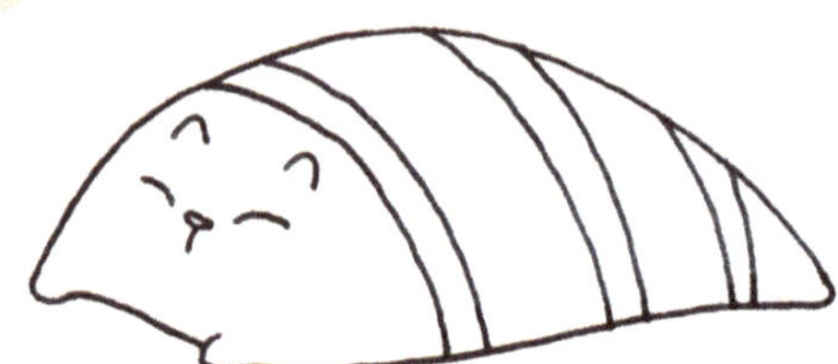

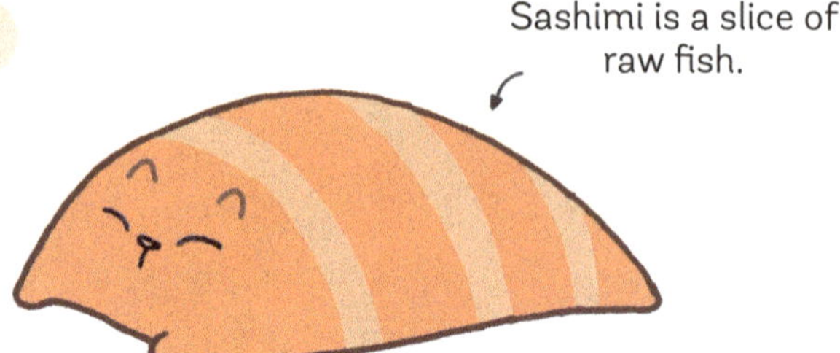

Sashimi is a slice of raw fish.

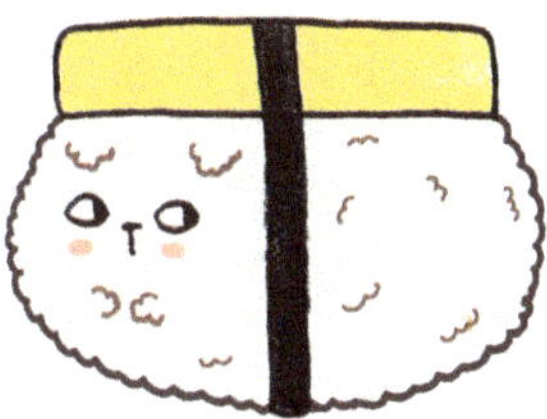

Tamago Sushi
A sushi made with omelet.

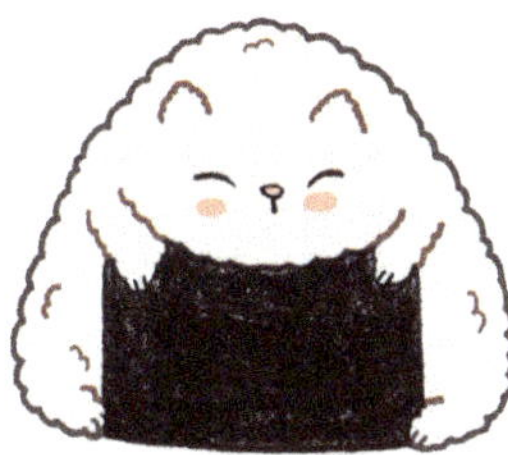

Triangle Onigiri
A rice ball.

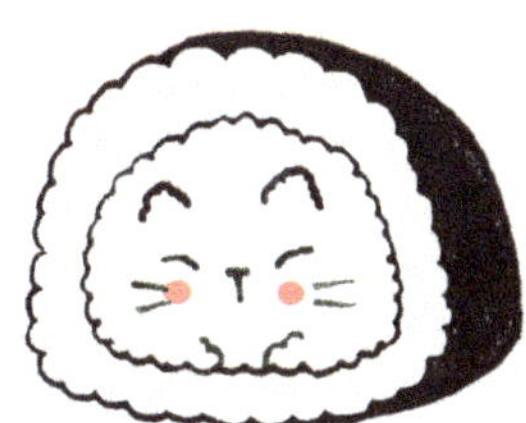

Rolled-up Maki
Maki is a rice cylinder with seaweed.

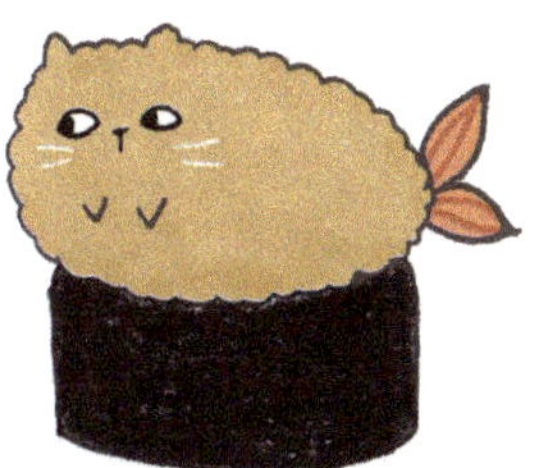

Prawn Tempura Maki
A battered and deep-fried maki.

Complete these sushi!

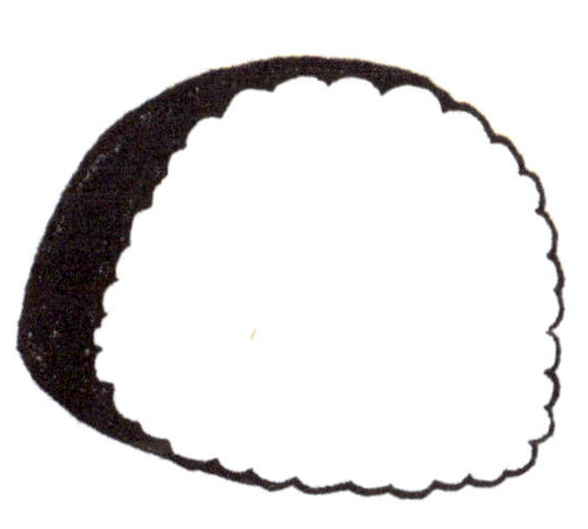

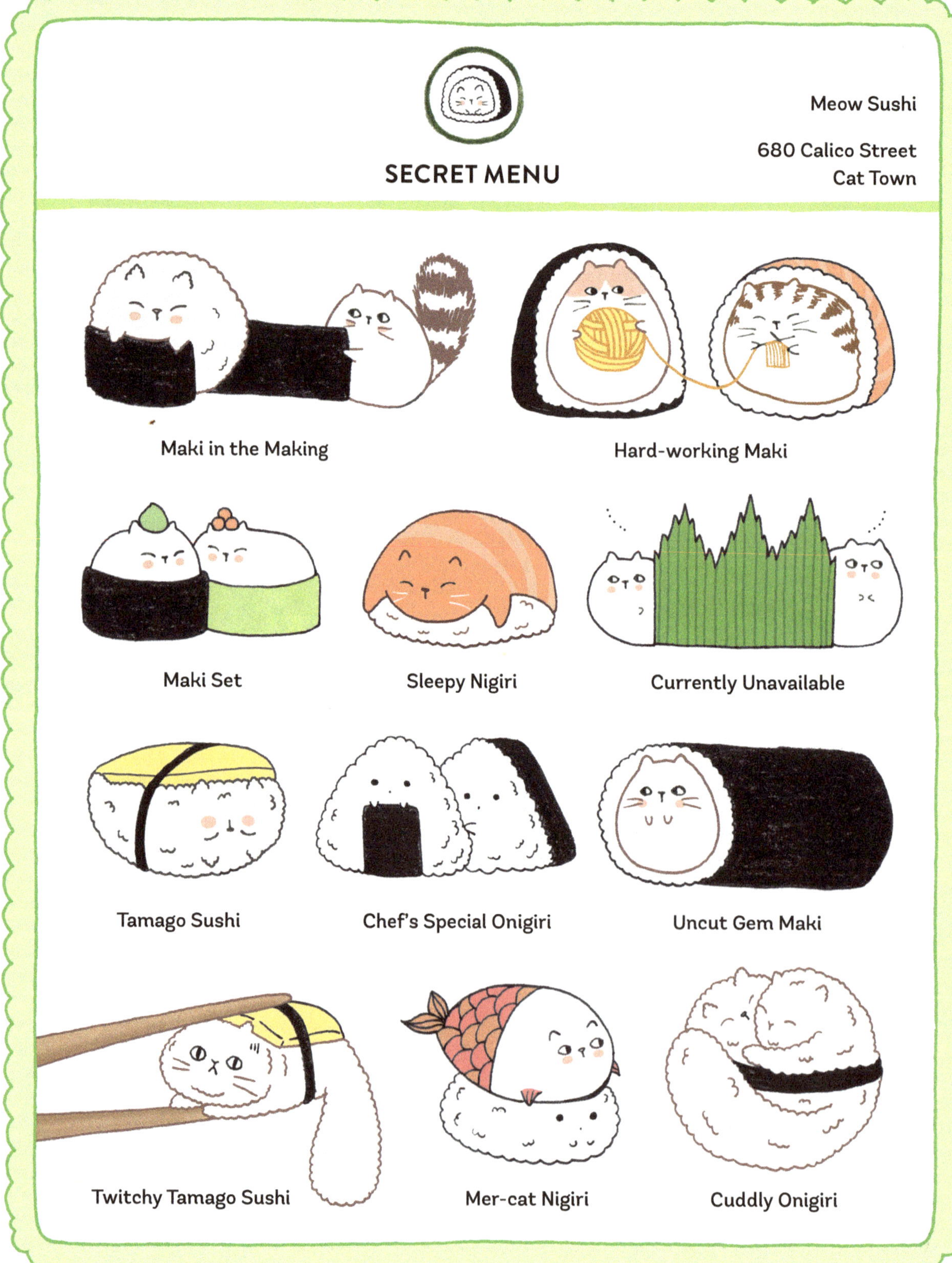

Meow Sushi
680 Calico Street
Cat Town
SECRET MENU
Maki in the Making
Hard-working Maki
Maki Set
Sleepy Nigiri
Currently Unavailable
Tamago Sushi
Chef's Special Onigiri
Uncut Gem Maki
Twitchy Tamago Sushi
Mer-cat Nigiri
Cuddly Onigiri

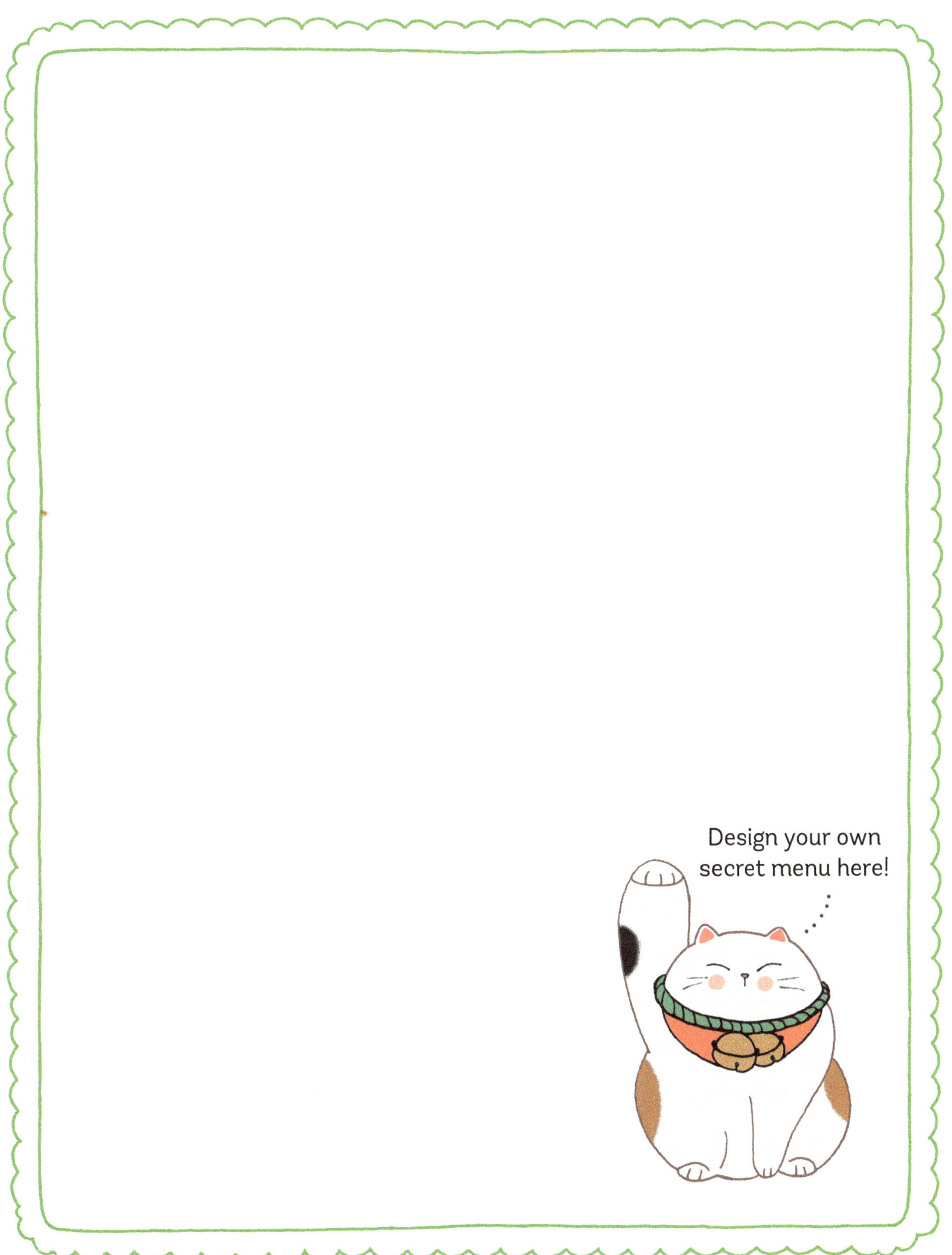

Design your own
secret menu here!

Cats and food have always been my biggest inspirations. Here are some of my favorite foods. Why not color them in? Don't forget to add color to the words on the opposite page.

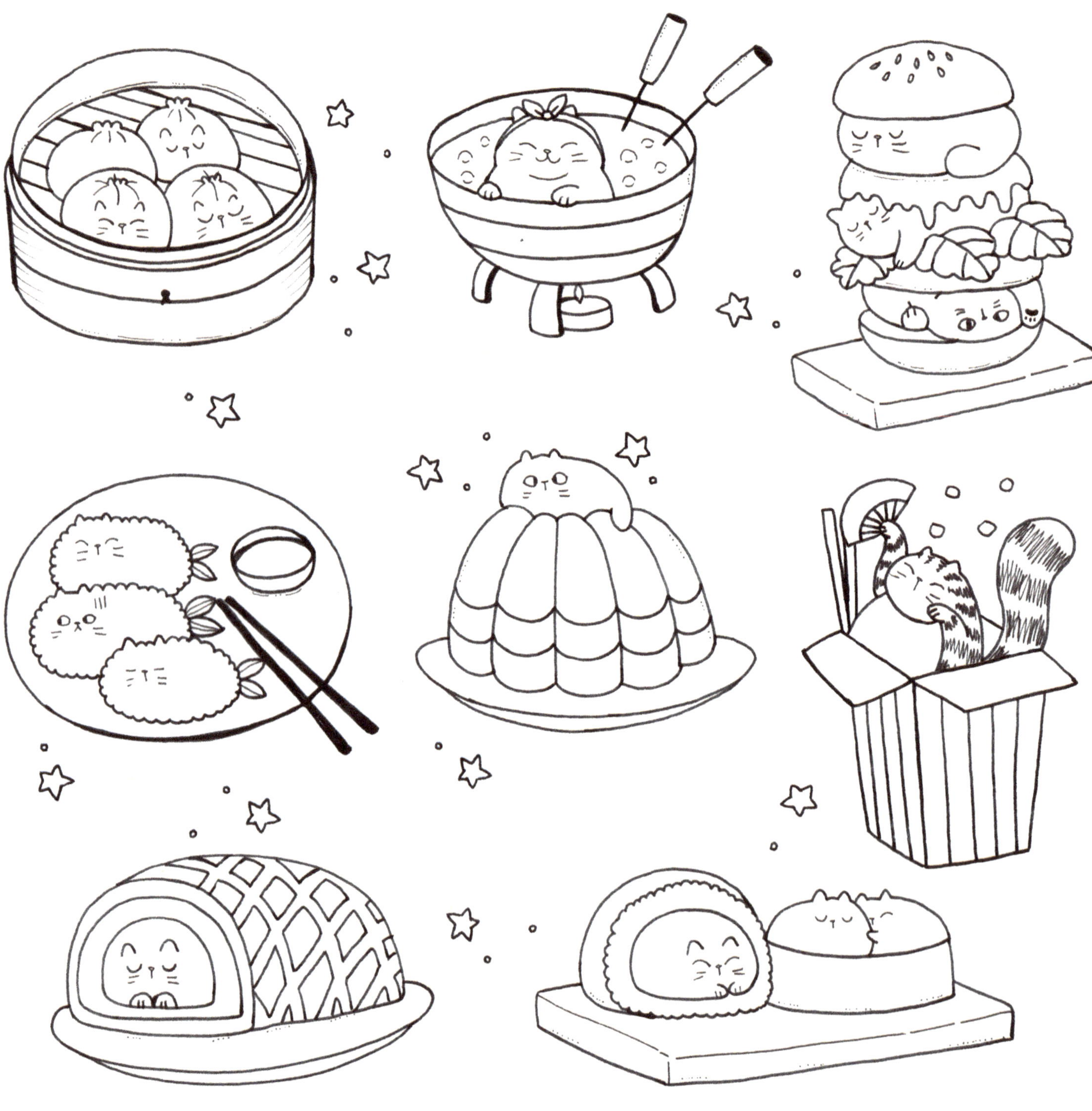

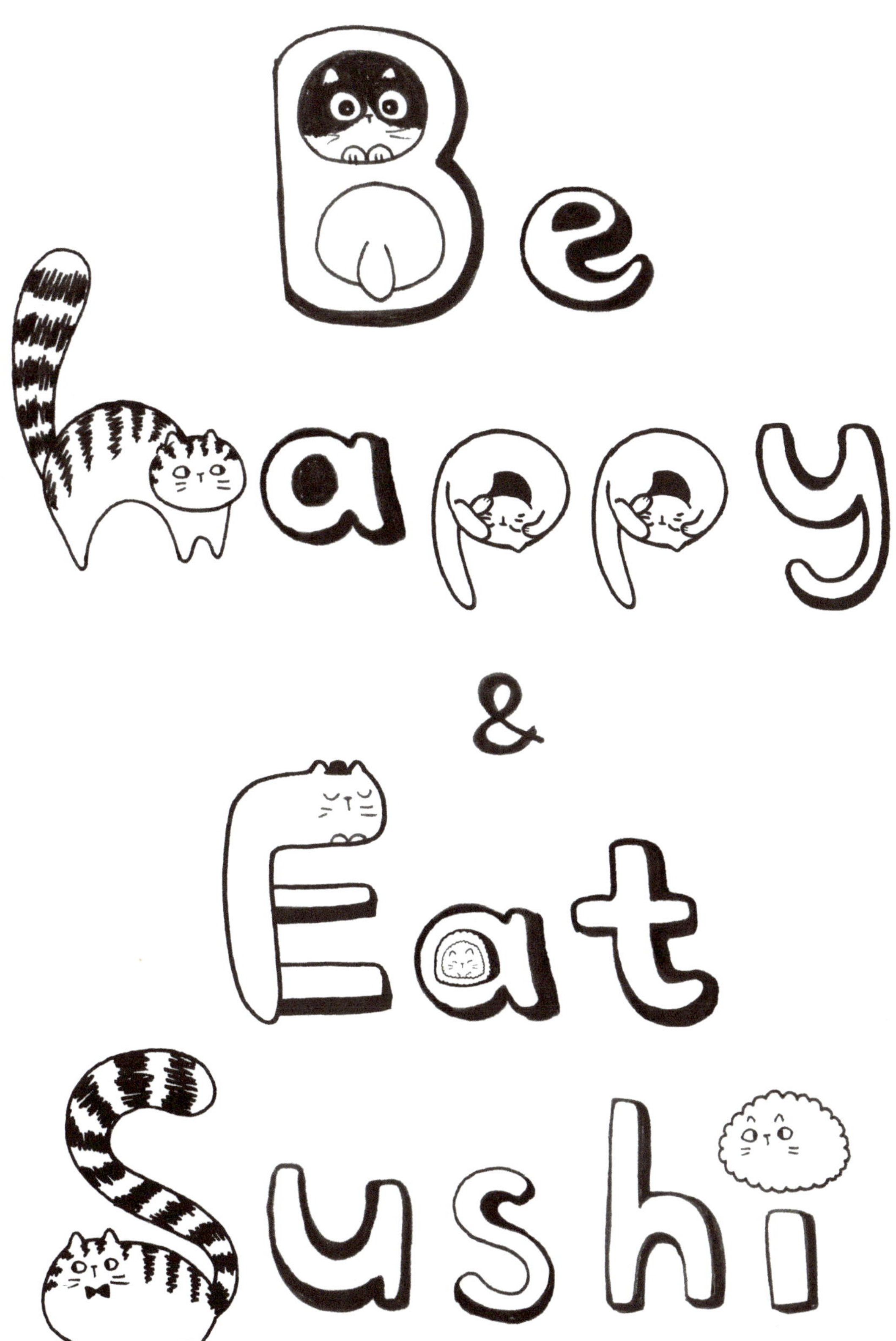
Be happy
&
Eat Sushi

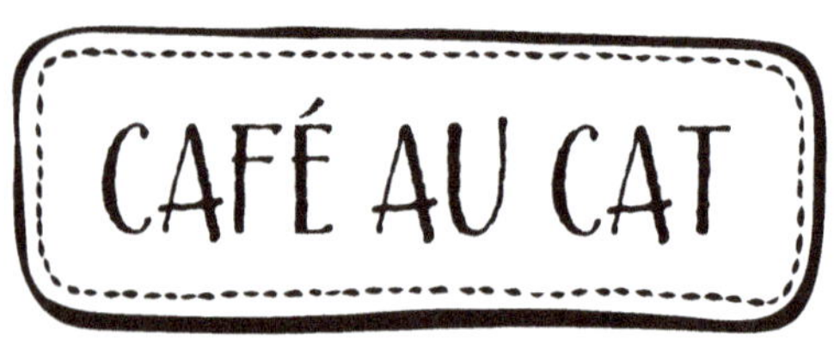

Now let's turn our attention to caffeinated cat drinks, shall we?

GINGER TABBY LATTE

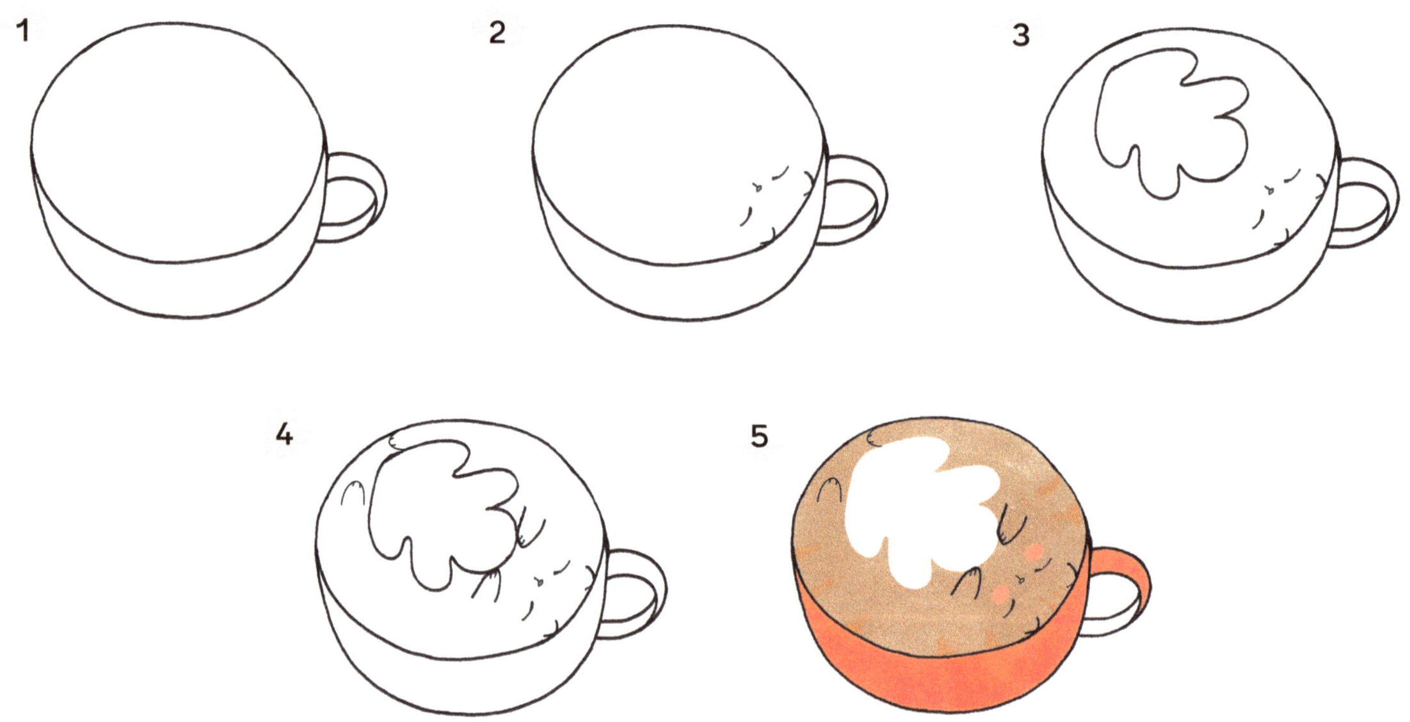

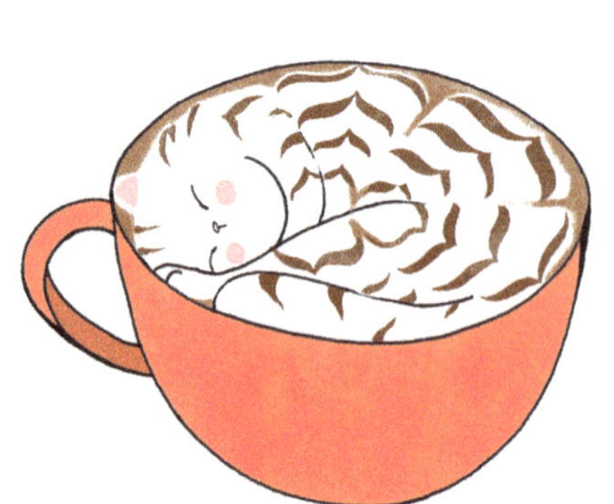

Tabby Mocha

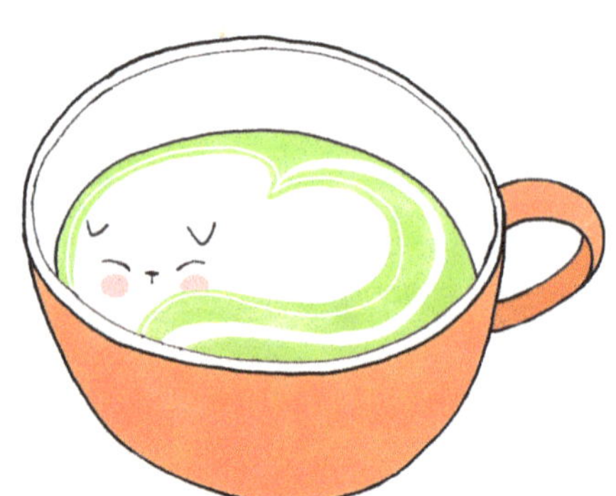

Moggy Matcha Latte

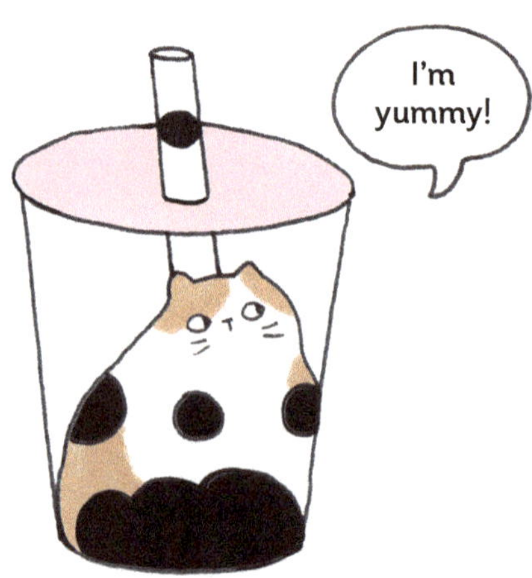

Calico Bubble Tea

Color these café cats in!

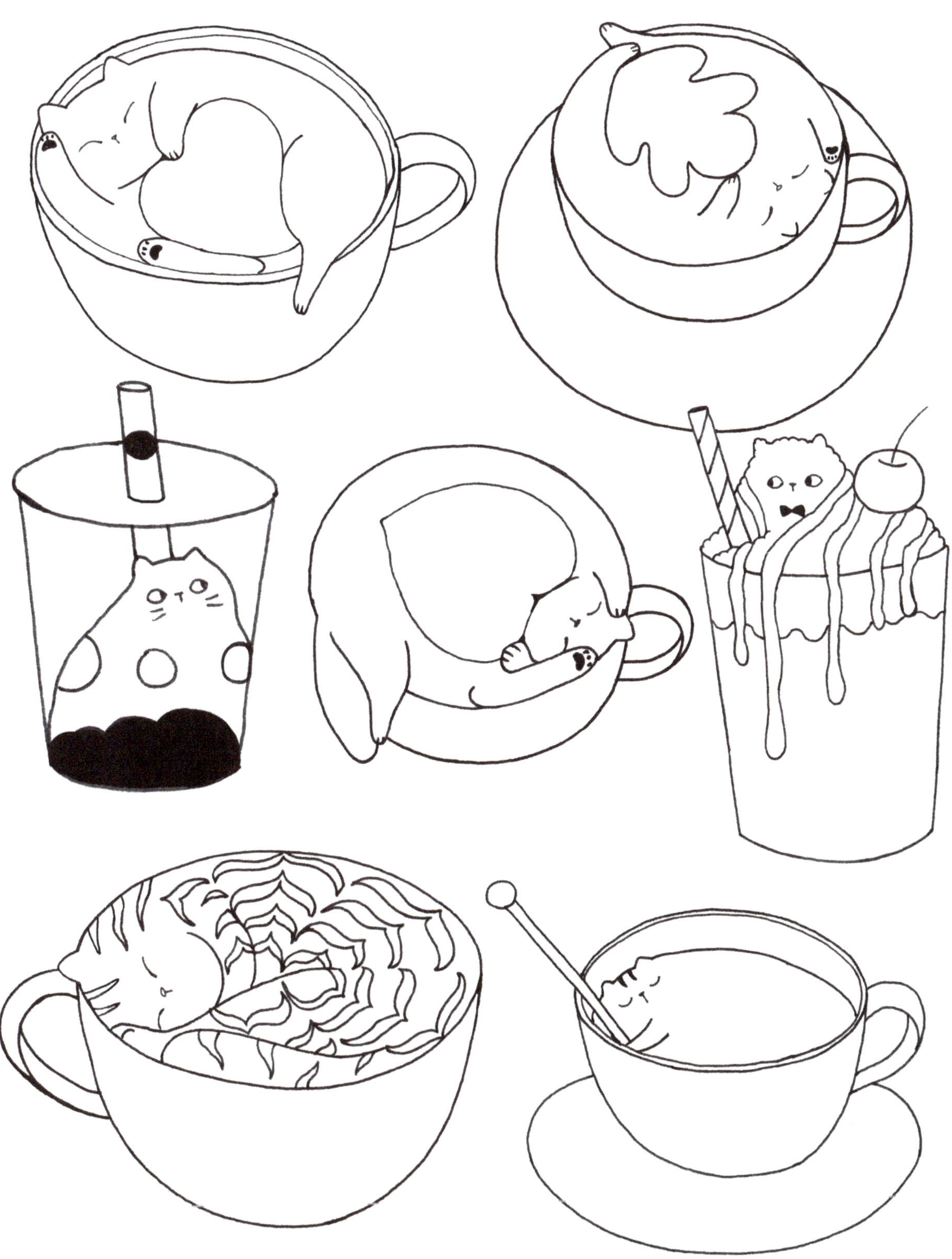

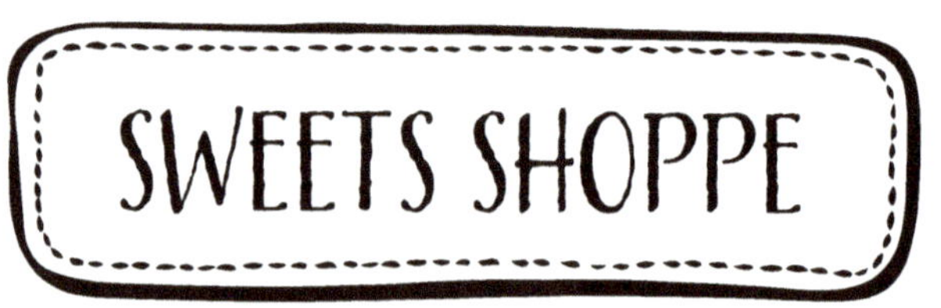

SWEETS SHOPPE

Which flavor would you like?

MACARONS

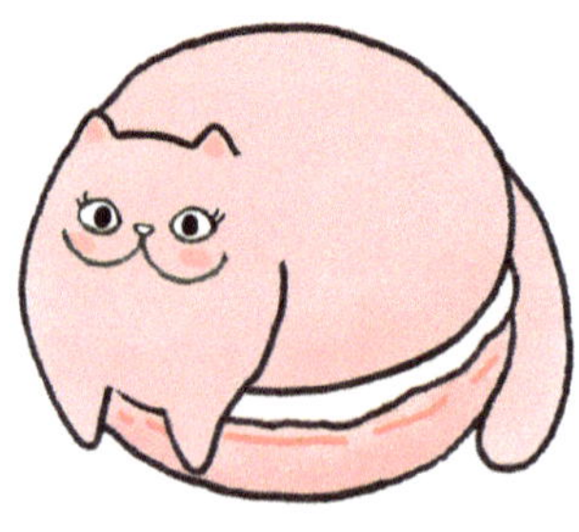

Rose

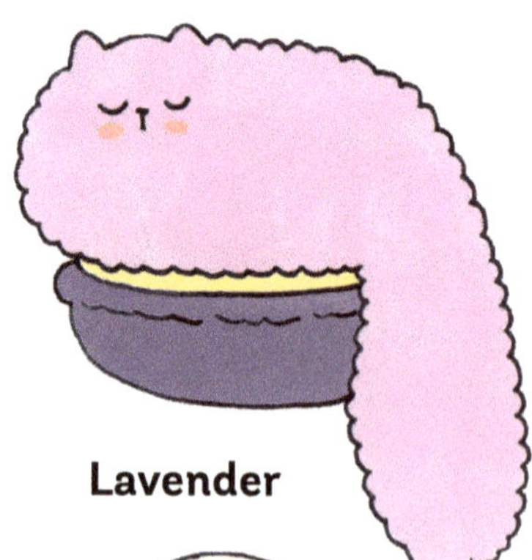

Lavender

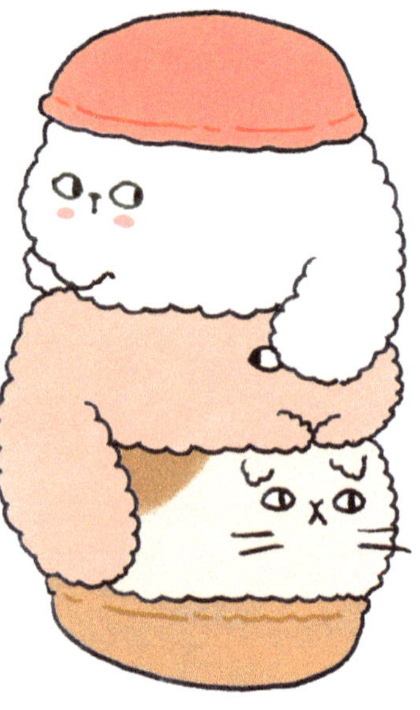

Trio
Lemon, peach, and coffee

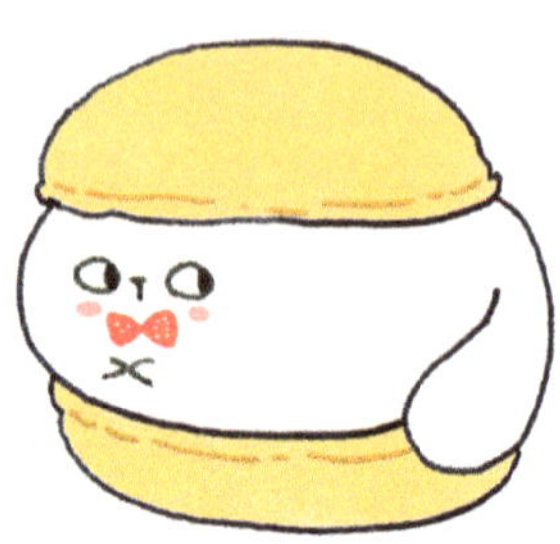

Lemon

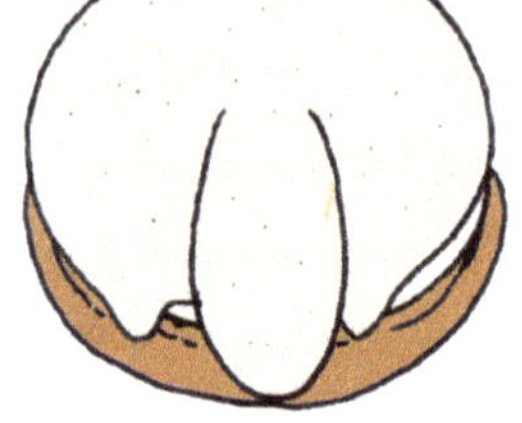

Vanilla and Caramel

LICORICE & STRAWBERRY MACARON

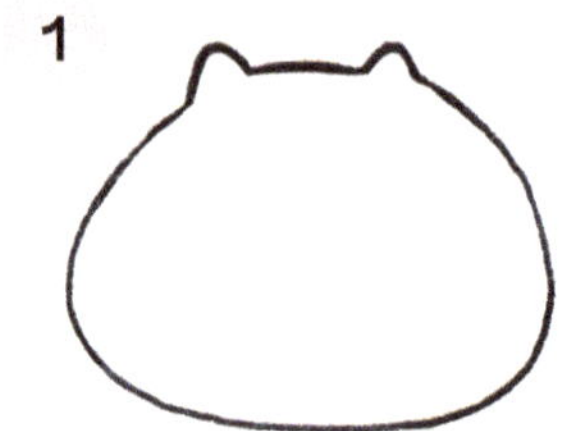

1

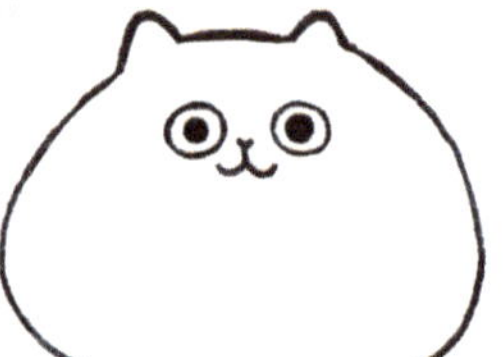

2

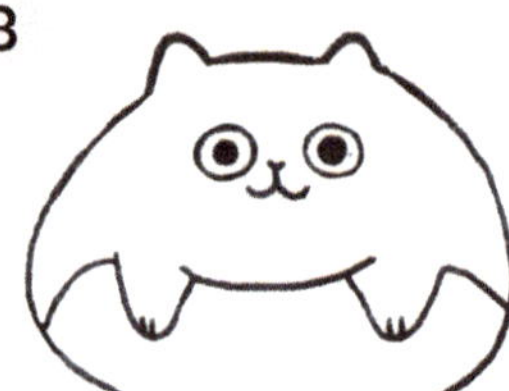

3

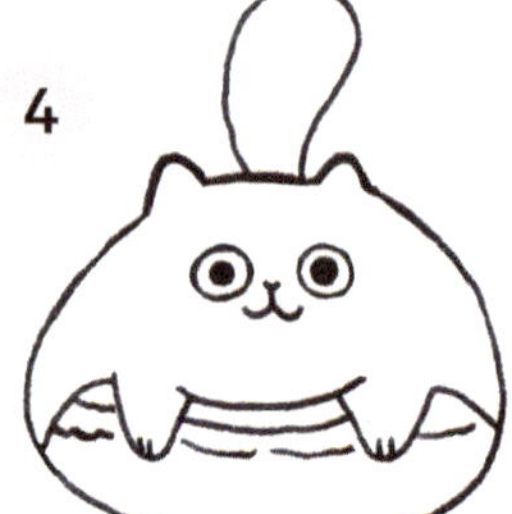

4

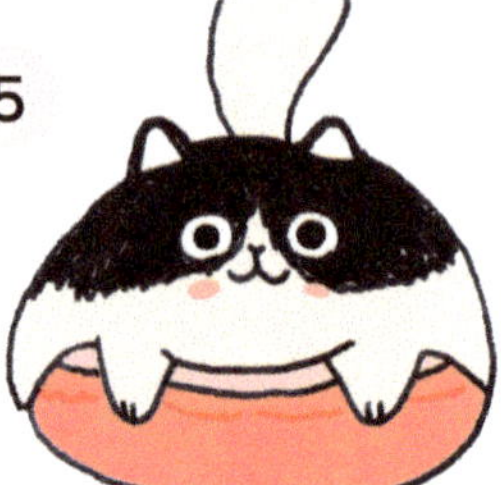

5

Use the shapes below as a guide to create your own macaron cats. Don't worry about going over the shapes, let your pen roam free!

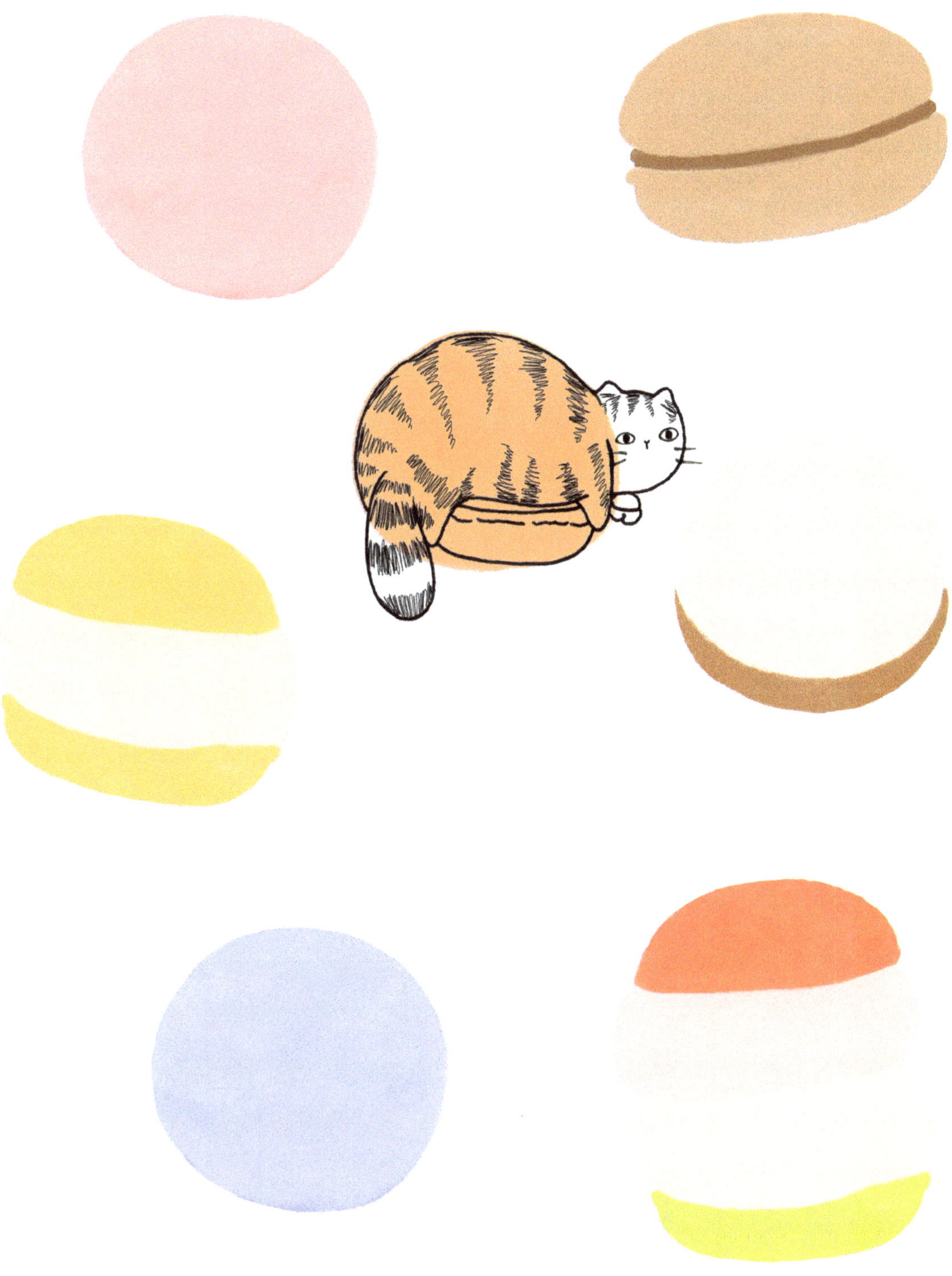

SOPHISTICATED GATO GELATO

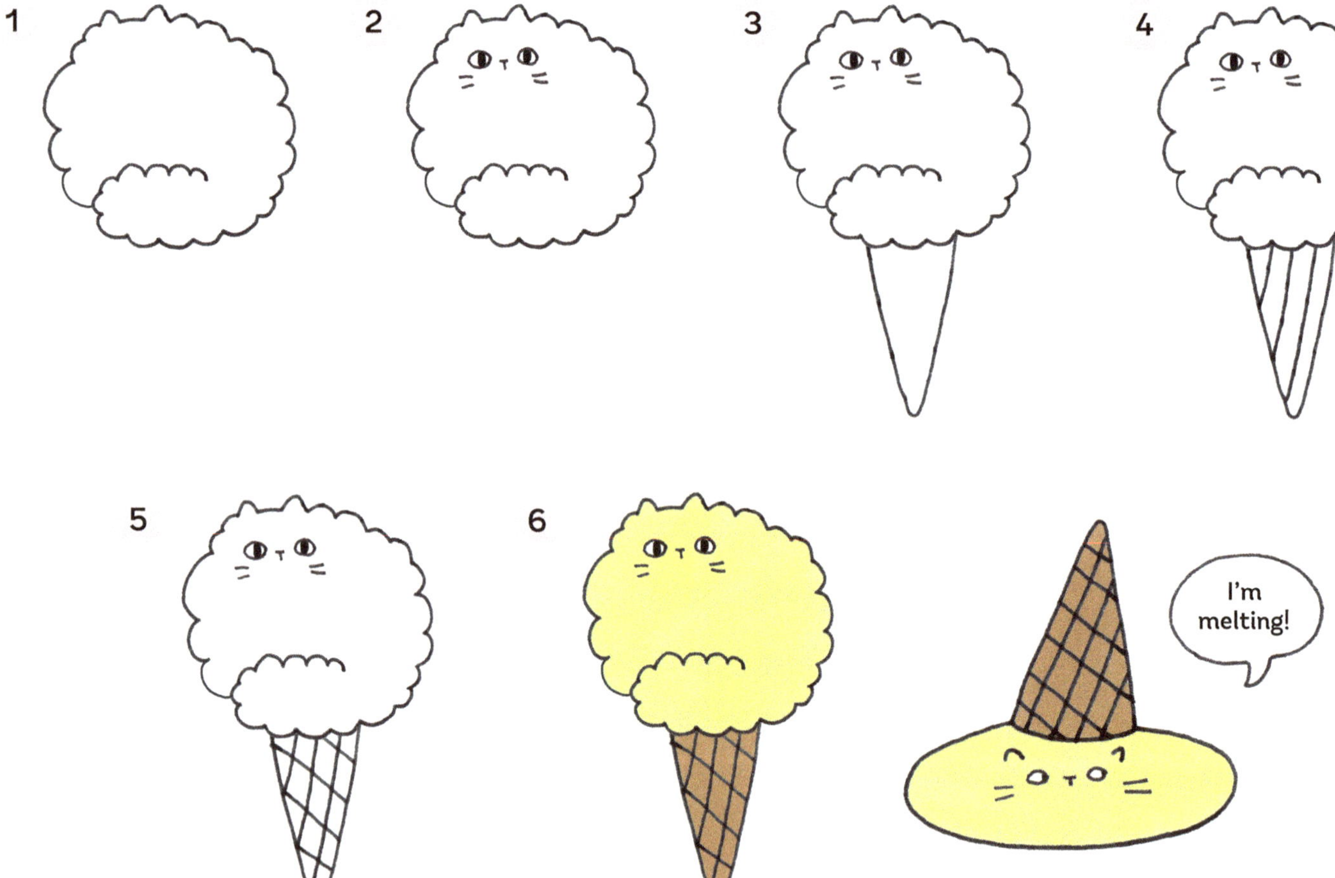

1

2

3

4

5

6

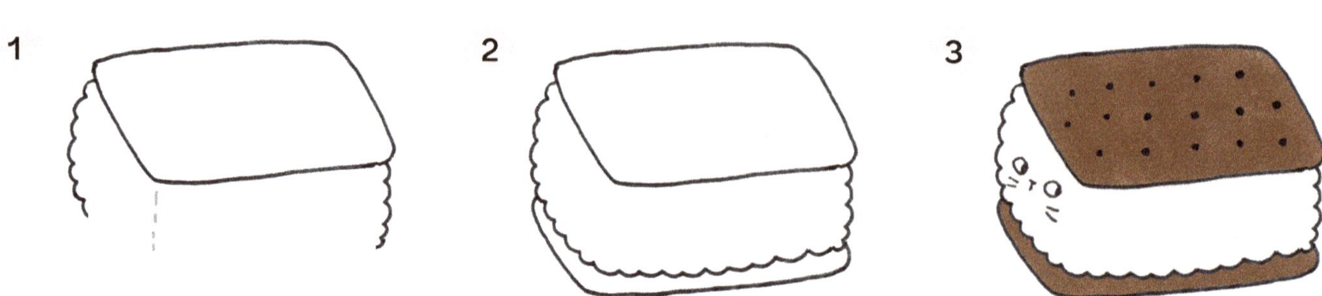

Soupy ice cream

VANILLA ICE CREAM CATWICH

1

2

3

TANGLED ICE LOLLY

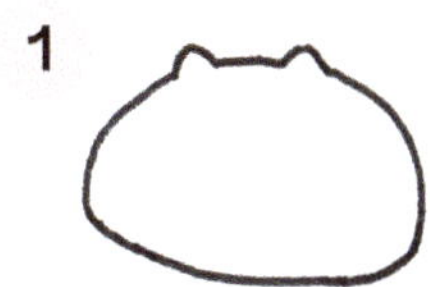

1

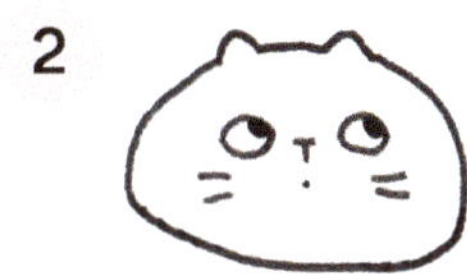

2

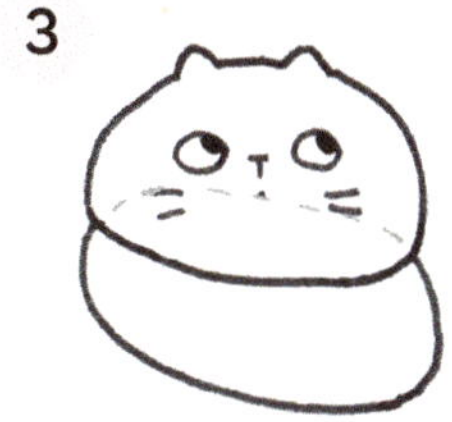

3

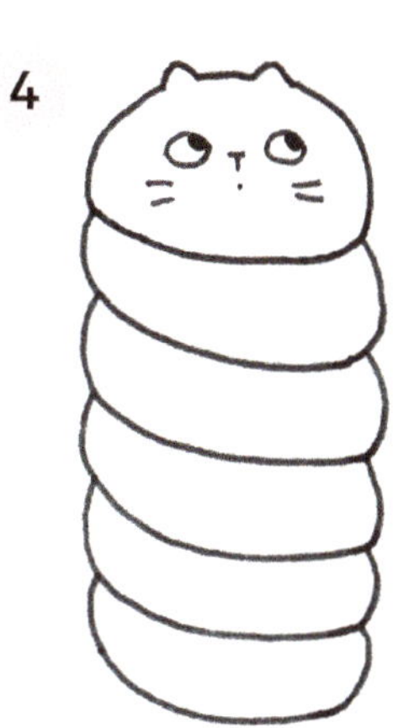

4

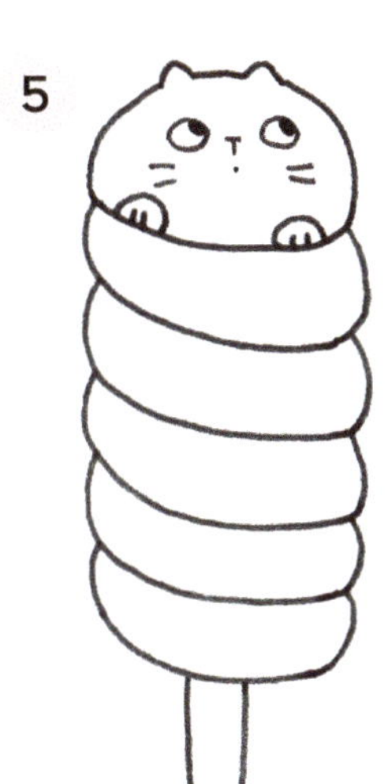

5

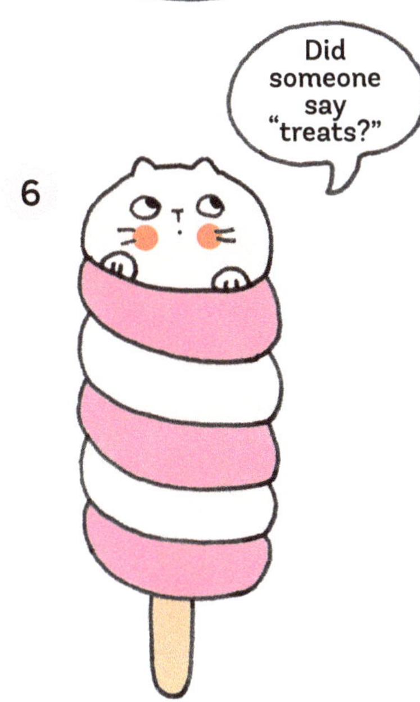

6

MELTING DOUBLE STICK

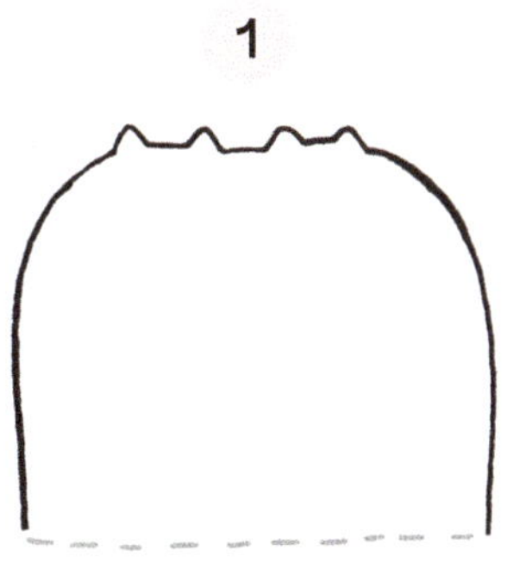

1

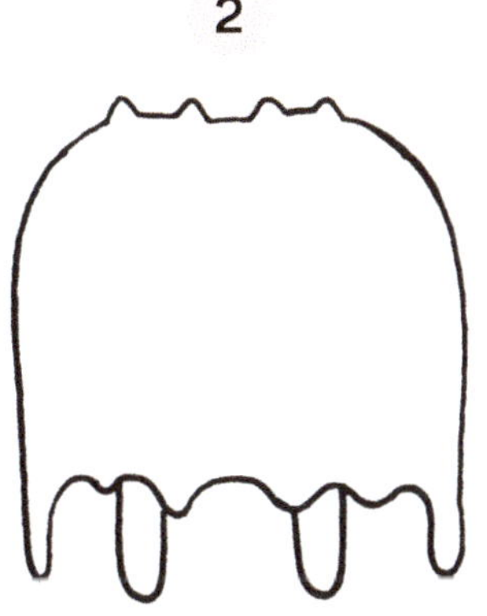

2

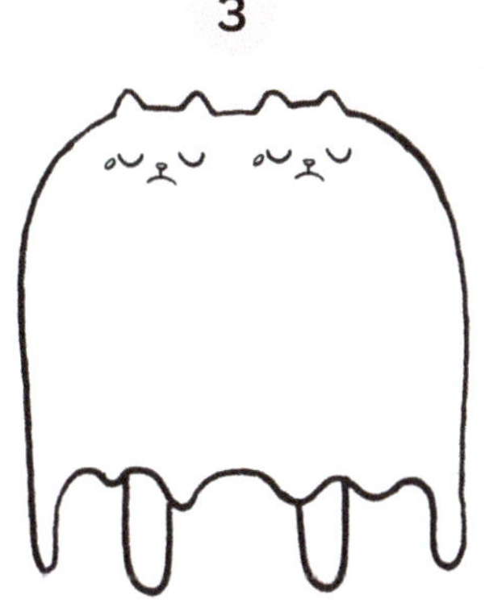

3

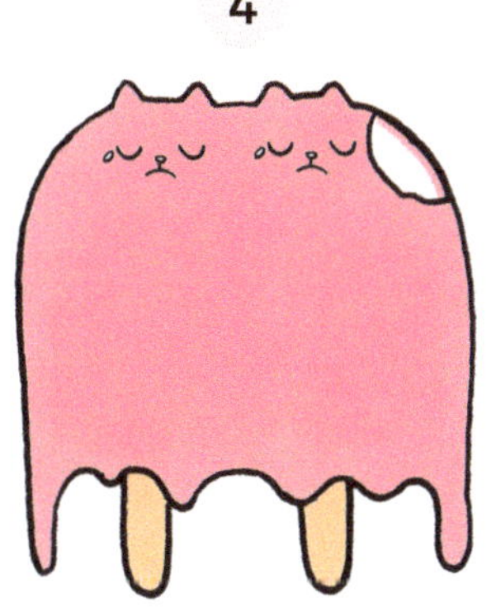

4

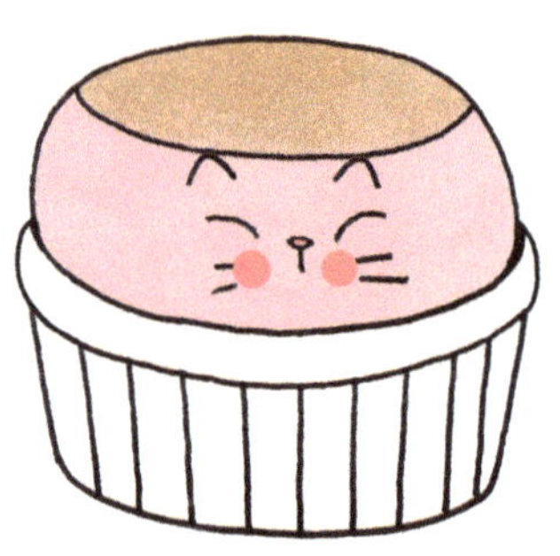

Soufflé
Delicate and light

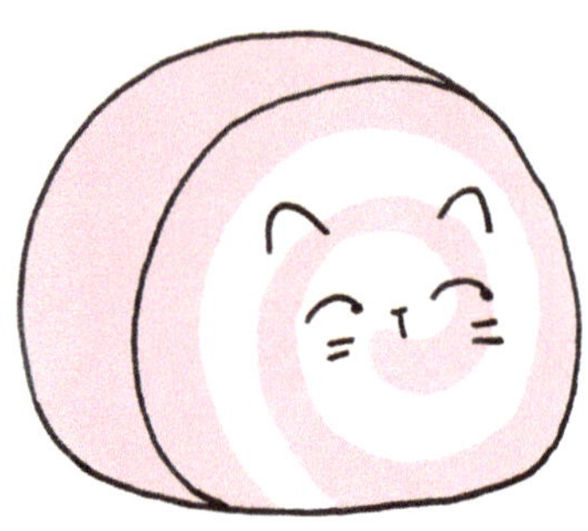

Swiss roll
Dizzy and delicious
rolled sponge cake
with jam

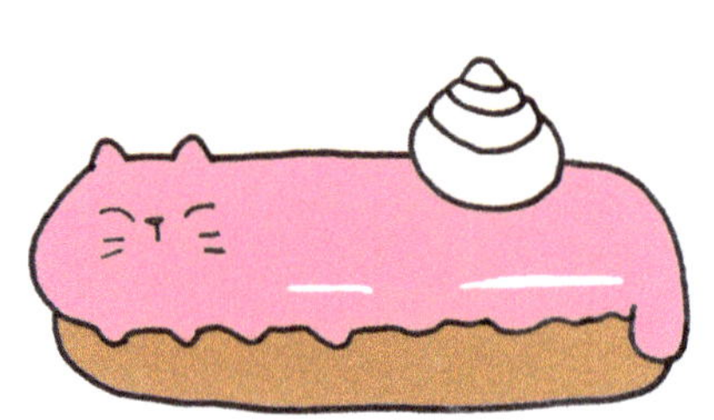

Éclair
Glossy and silky

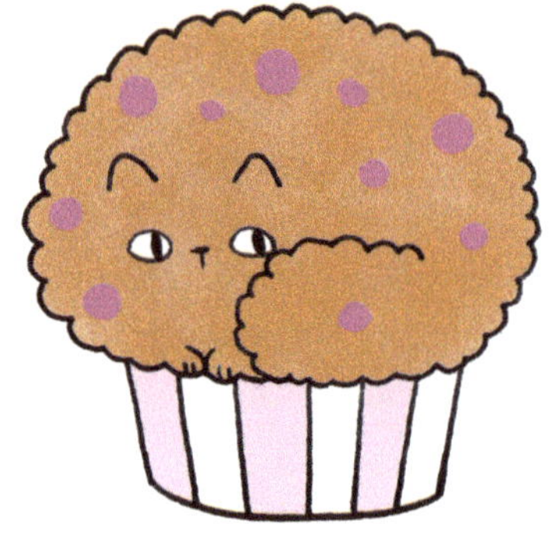

Muffin
Filling and portable

CAT CAKE DONUTS

1

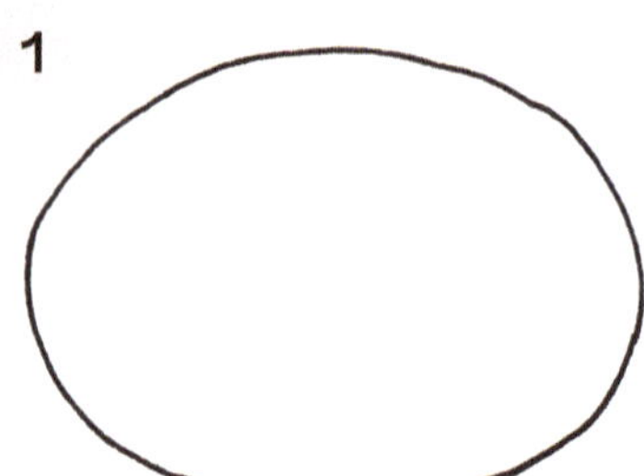

2

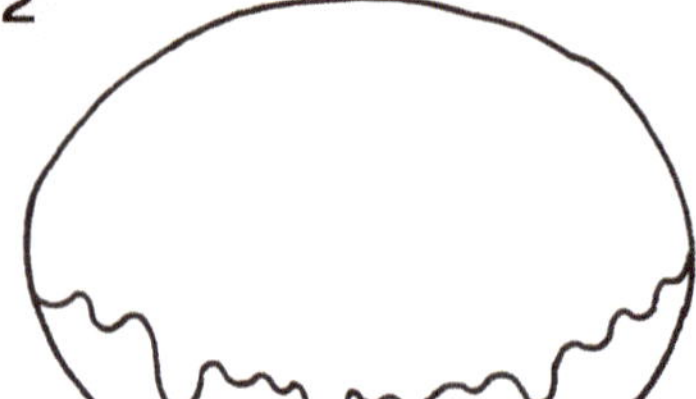

3

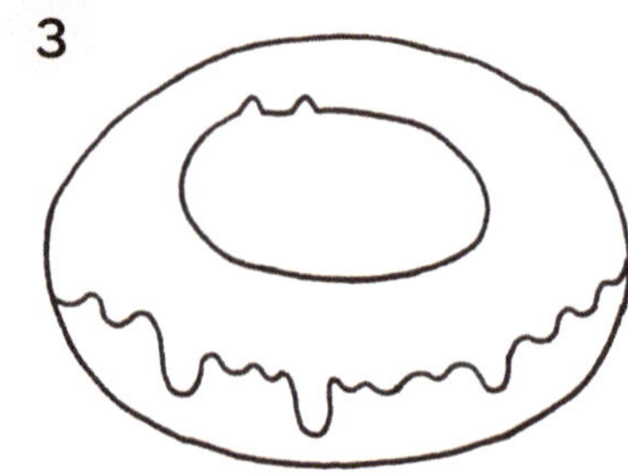

4

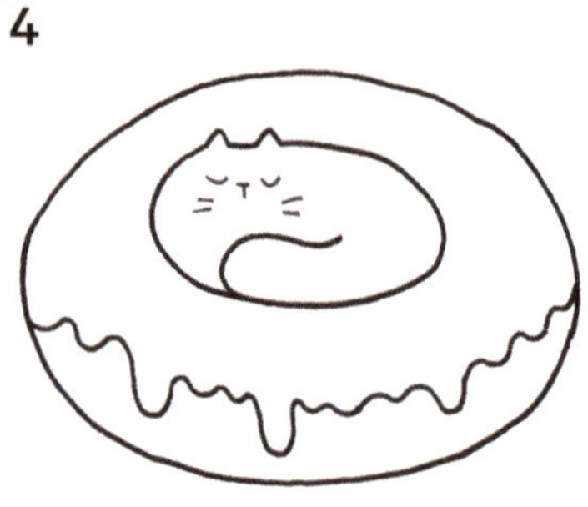

5

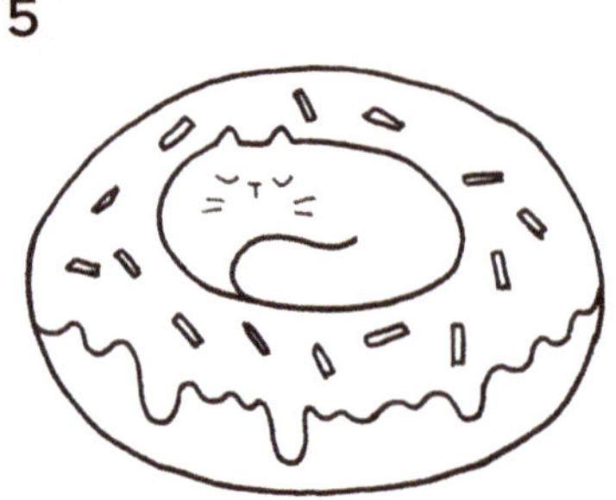

6

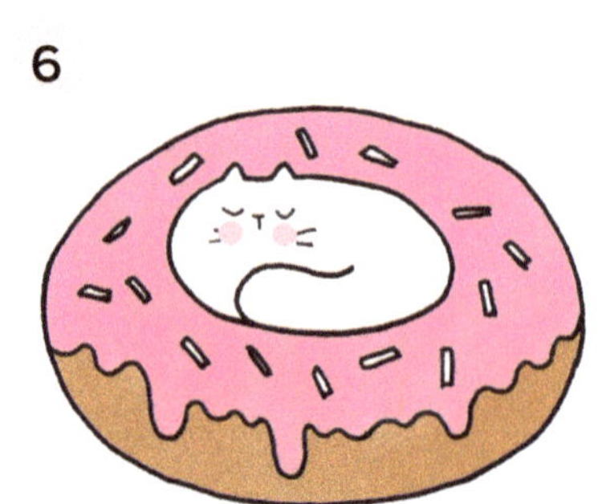

Turn these simple shapes into super cute cat desserts.

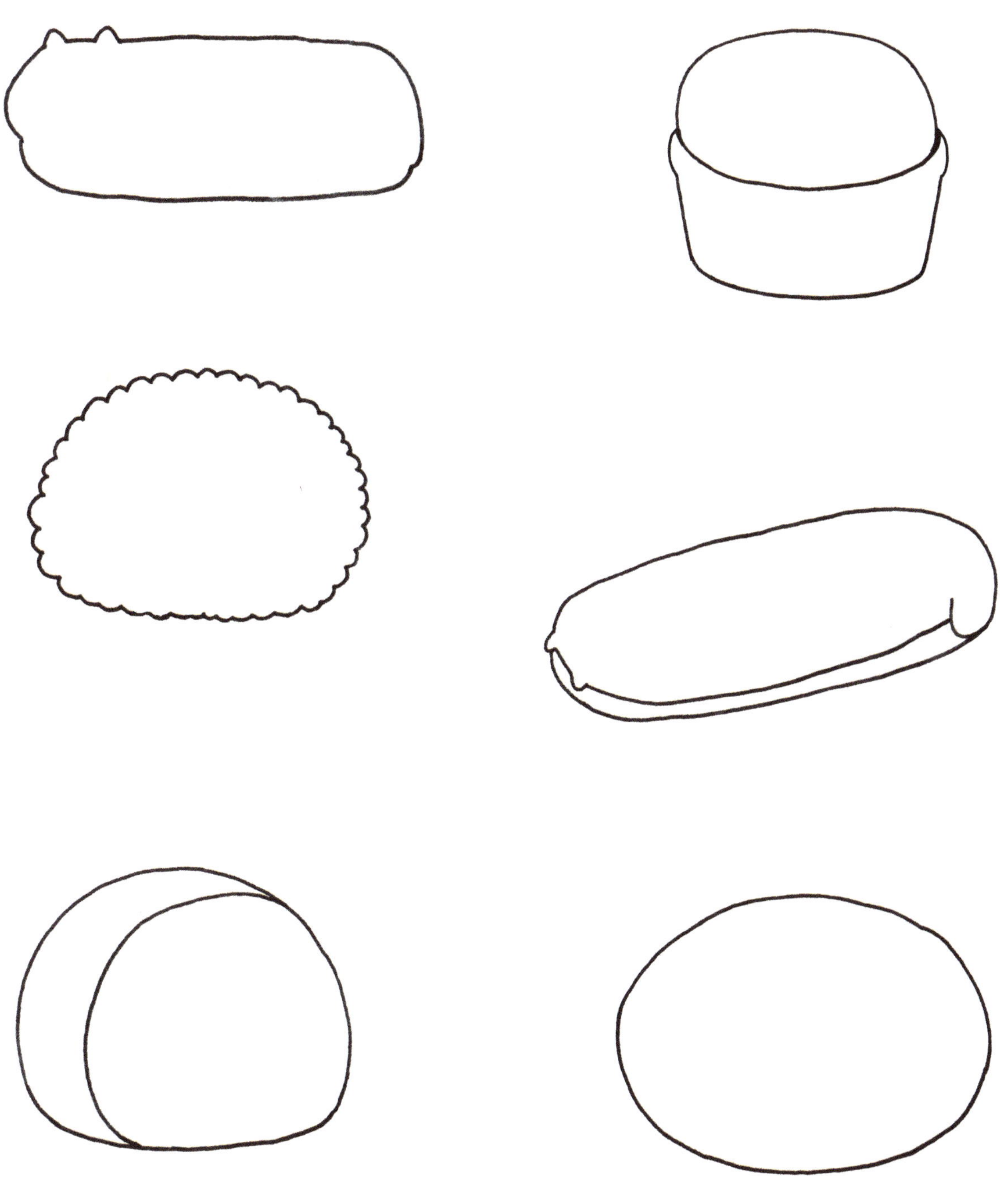

When I think about donuts and desserts, I think about trips to the bakery with my mom when I was a kid. It always makes me smile. Do desserts give you any happy memories? Now channel those happy thoughts into your coloring! Fill the cake stands on the opposite page delicious desserts. How about a cat cake or a delicious macaron?

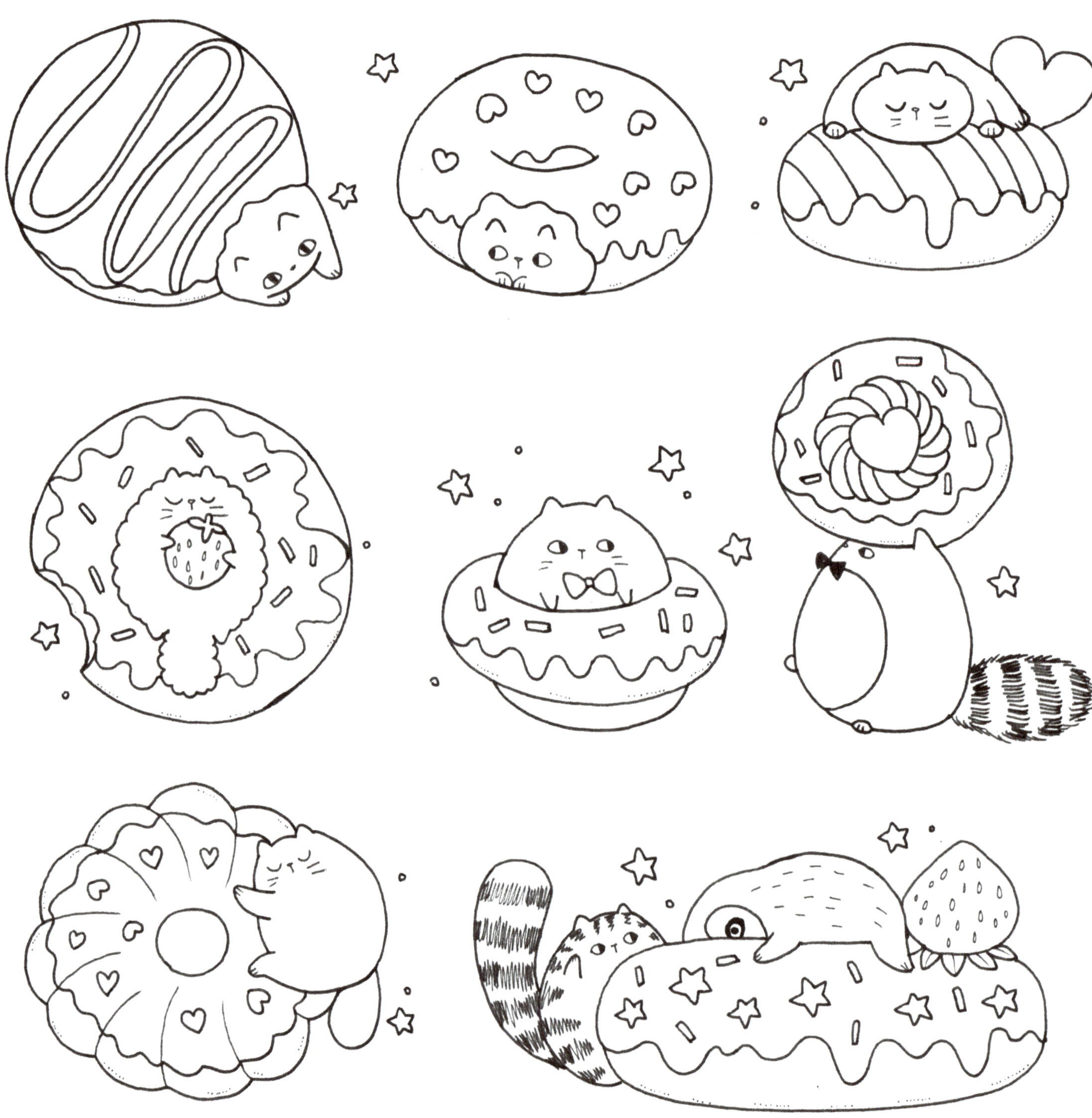

CAT LADY'S CROCKERY

Follow the steps below to draw a cat-themed tea service.

TEAPOT

1
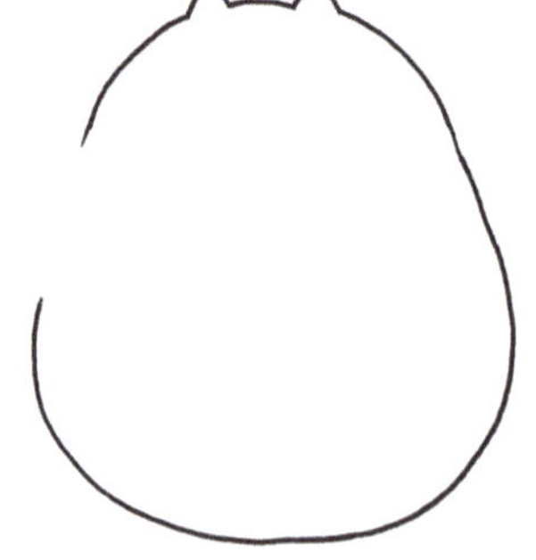

2
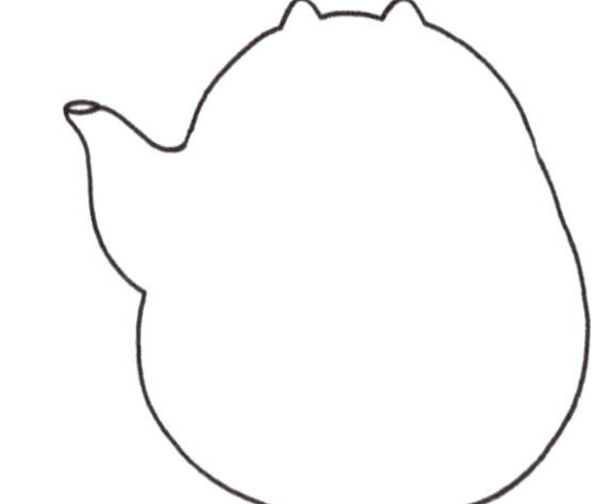

3
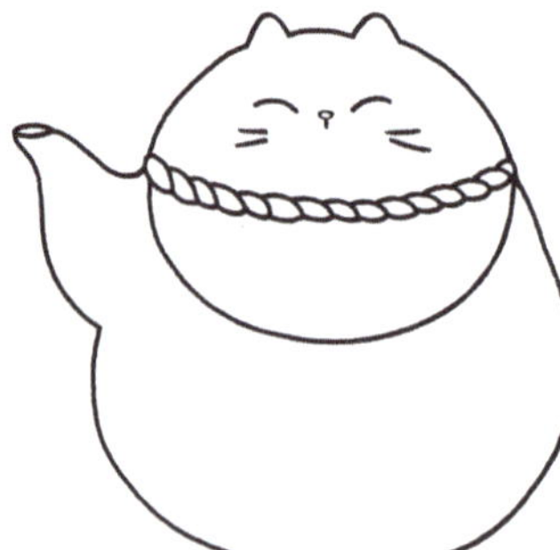

4
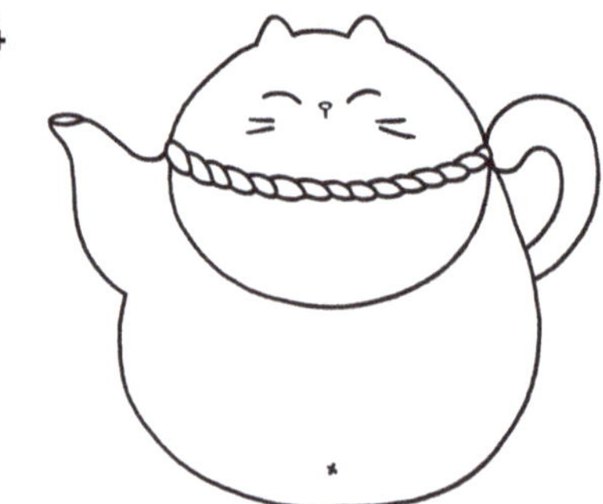

5
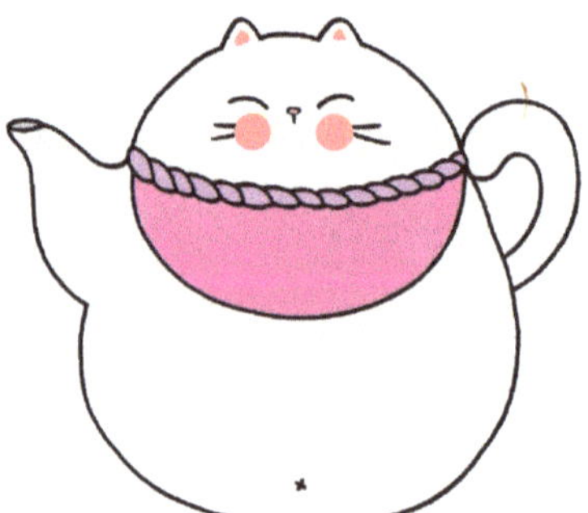

MUG

1
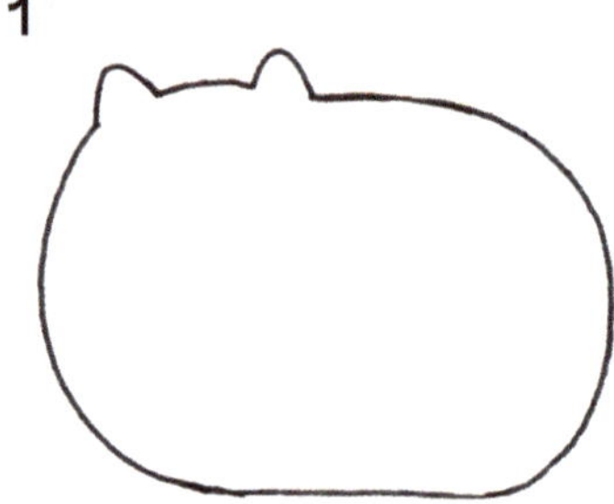

2
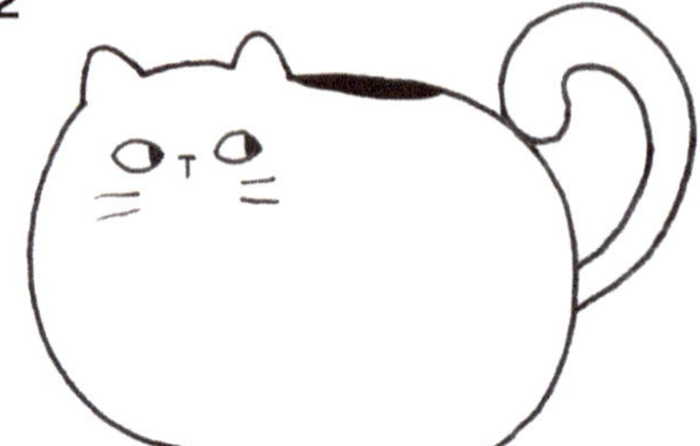

3
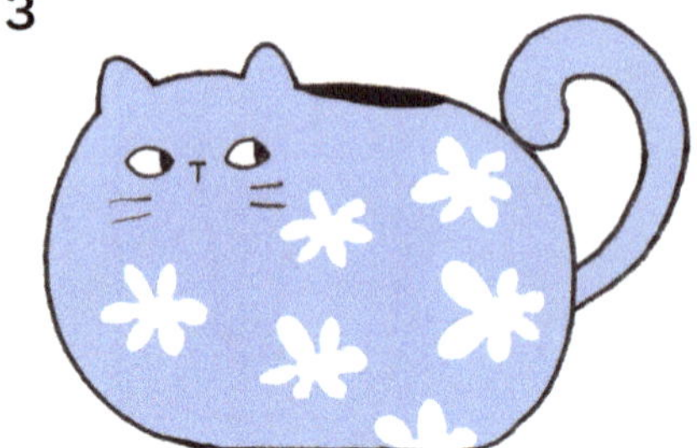

Fill in the shelves with your own cat crockery.

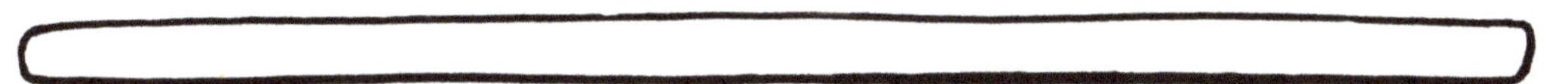

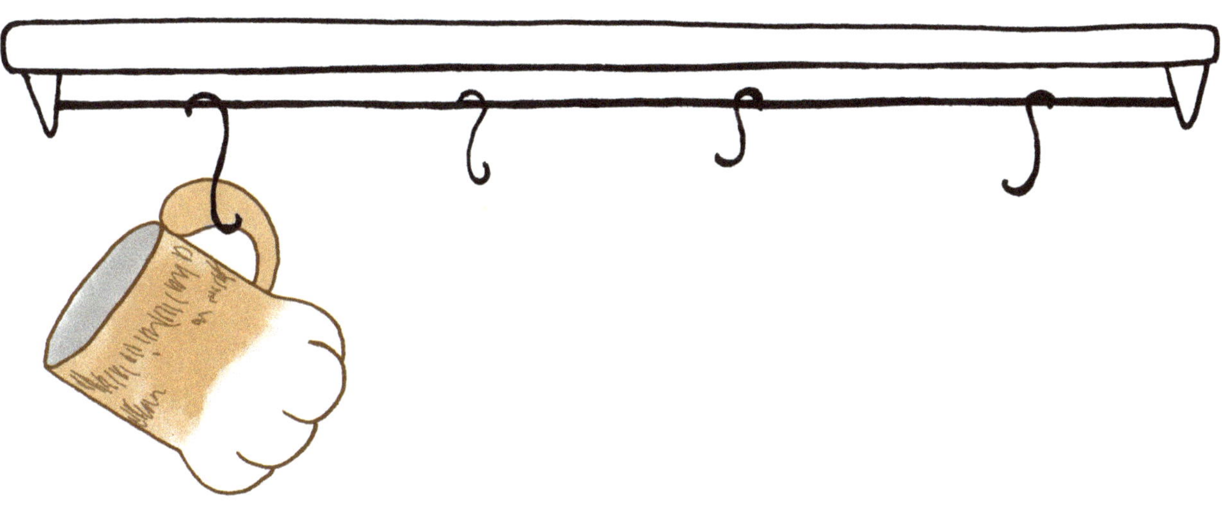

Doodle some wonderful flowers or patterns on the crockery, and then color in all of the designs.

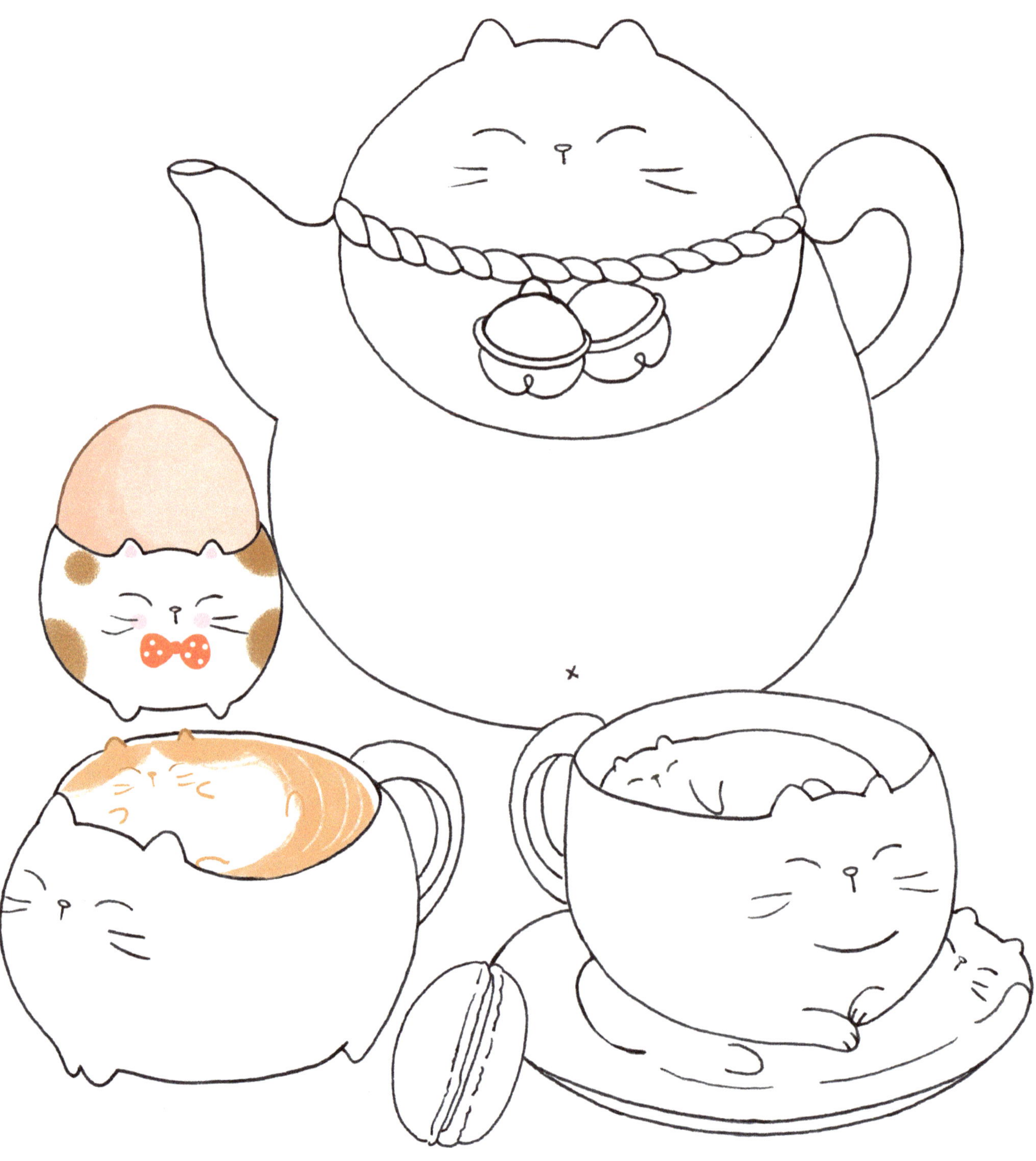

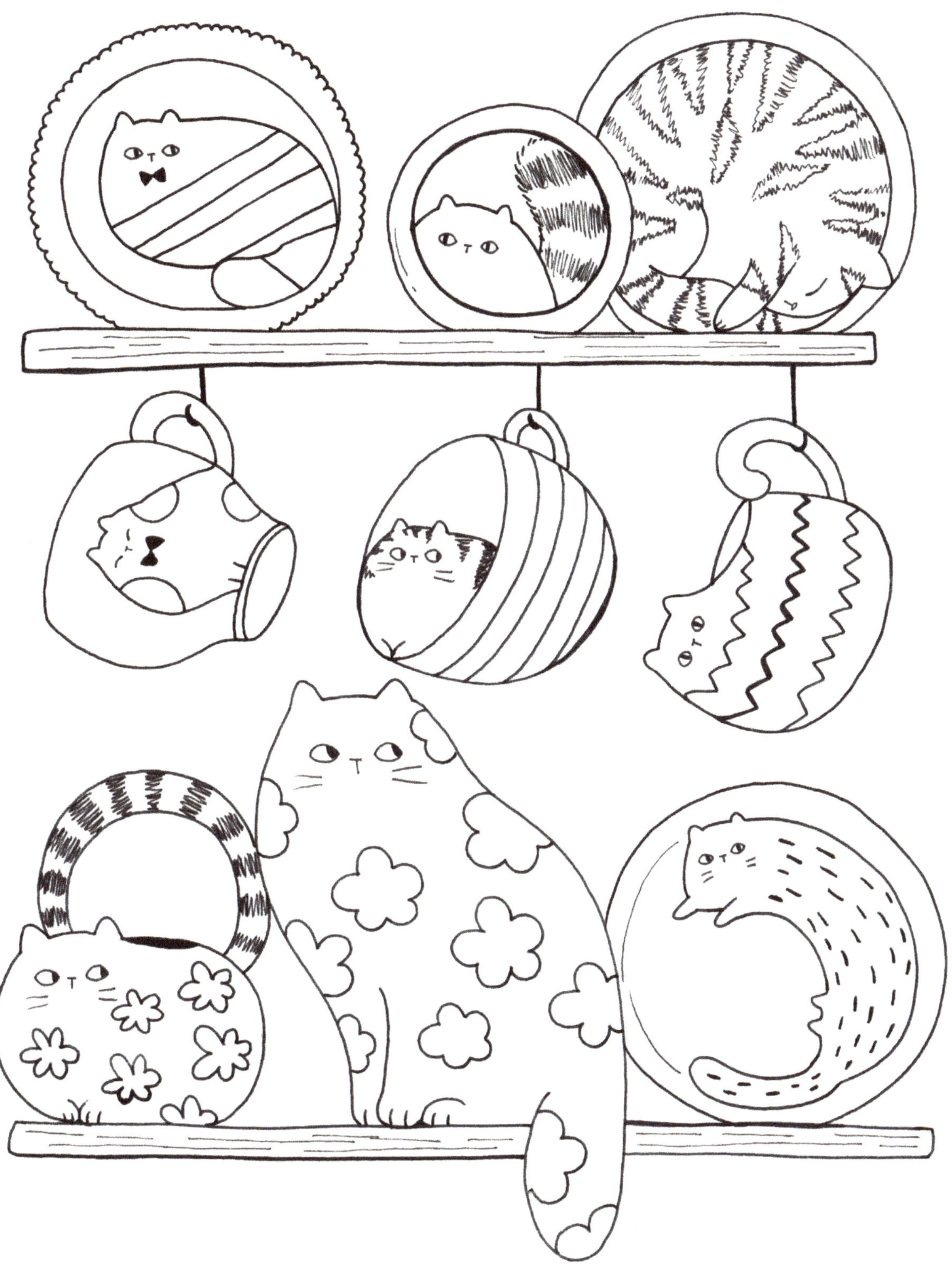

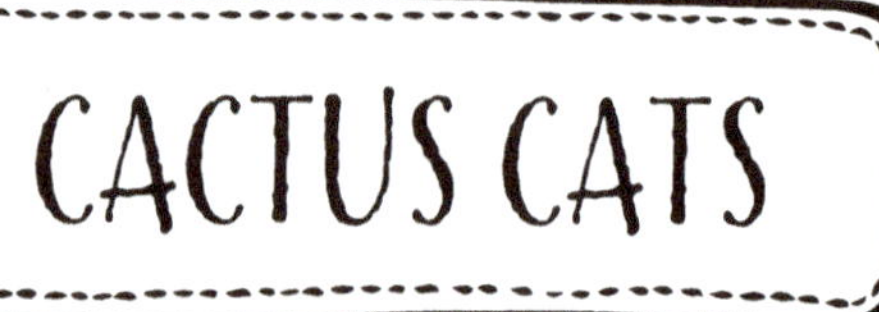

Can you identify these cat cacti? They are all a bit prickly!

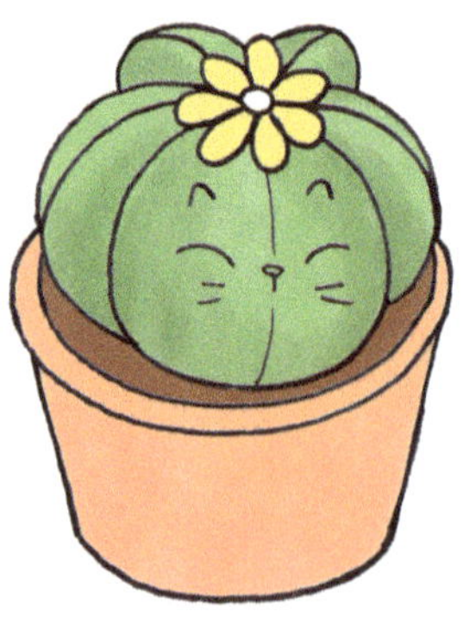

Bishop's cat
Reflect on the things you are grateful for.

Prickly pear
Do yoga.

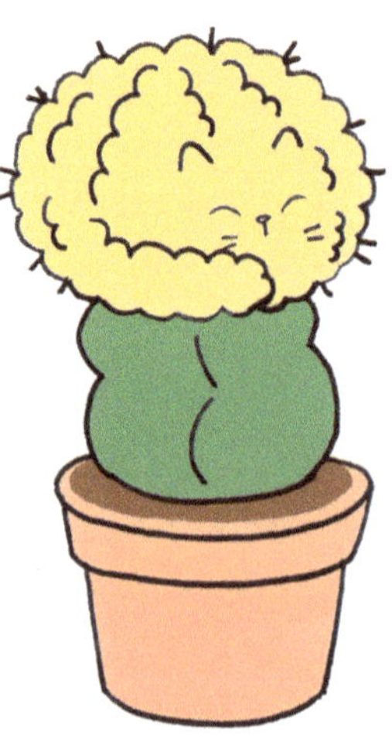

Moon cactus
Sit in the sunlight.

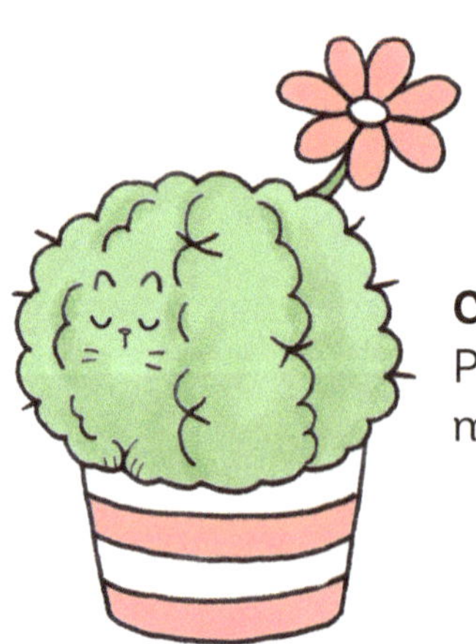

Chin cactus
Practice mindfulness.

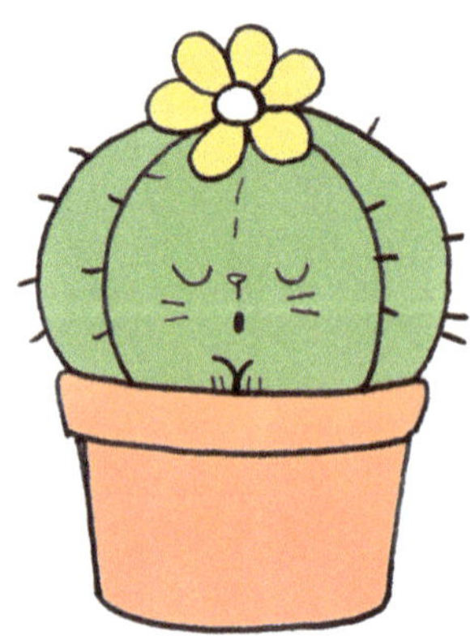

Barrel cactus
Breathe in, breathe out. Meditate.

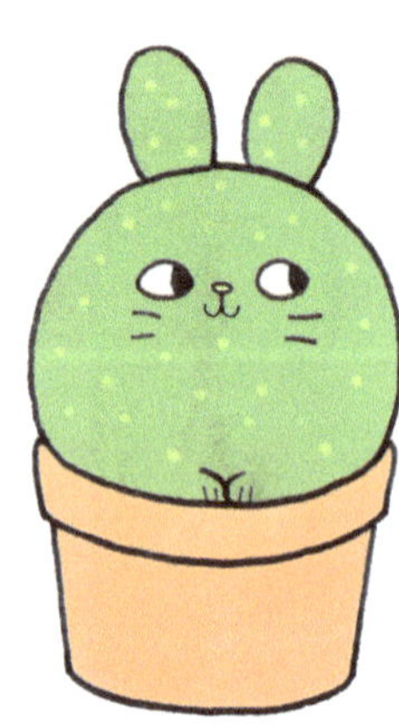

Bunny ear cactus
Eat nutritious food.

BUNNY EAR

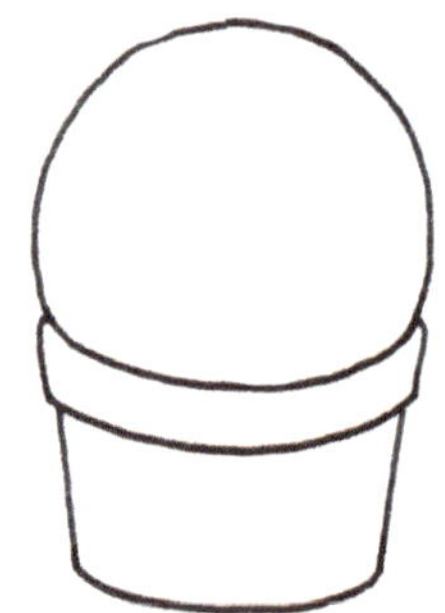

1

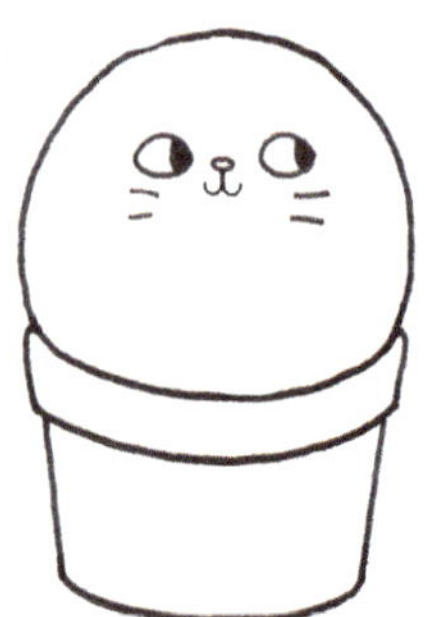

2

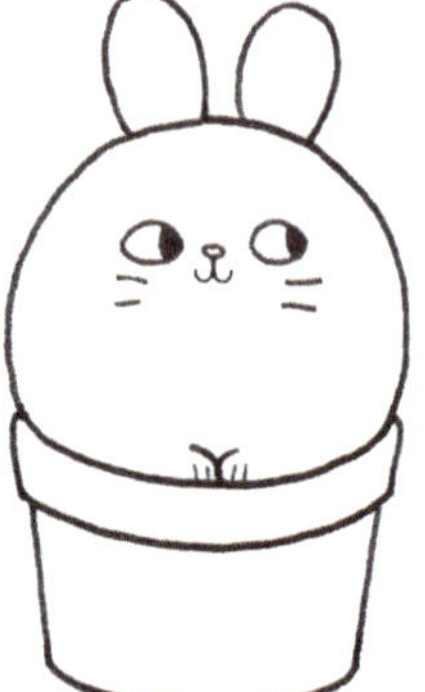

3

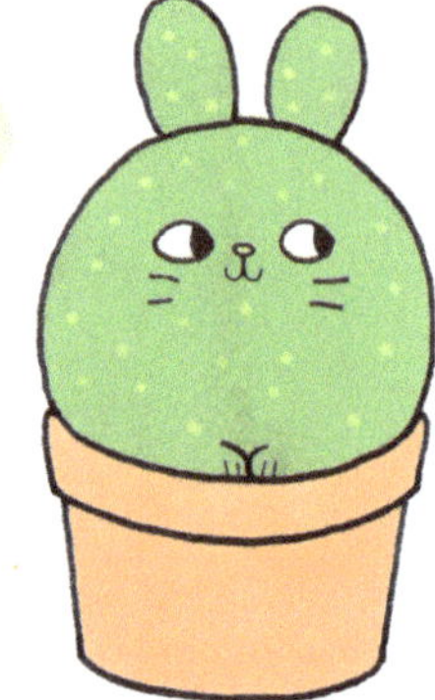

4

Add details to these cacti.

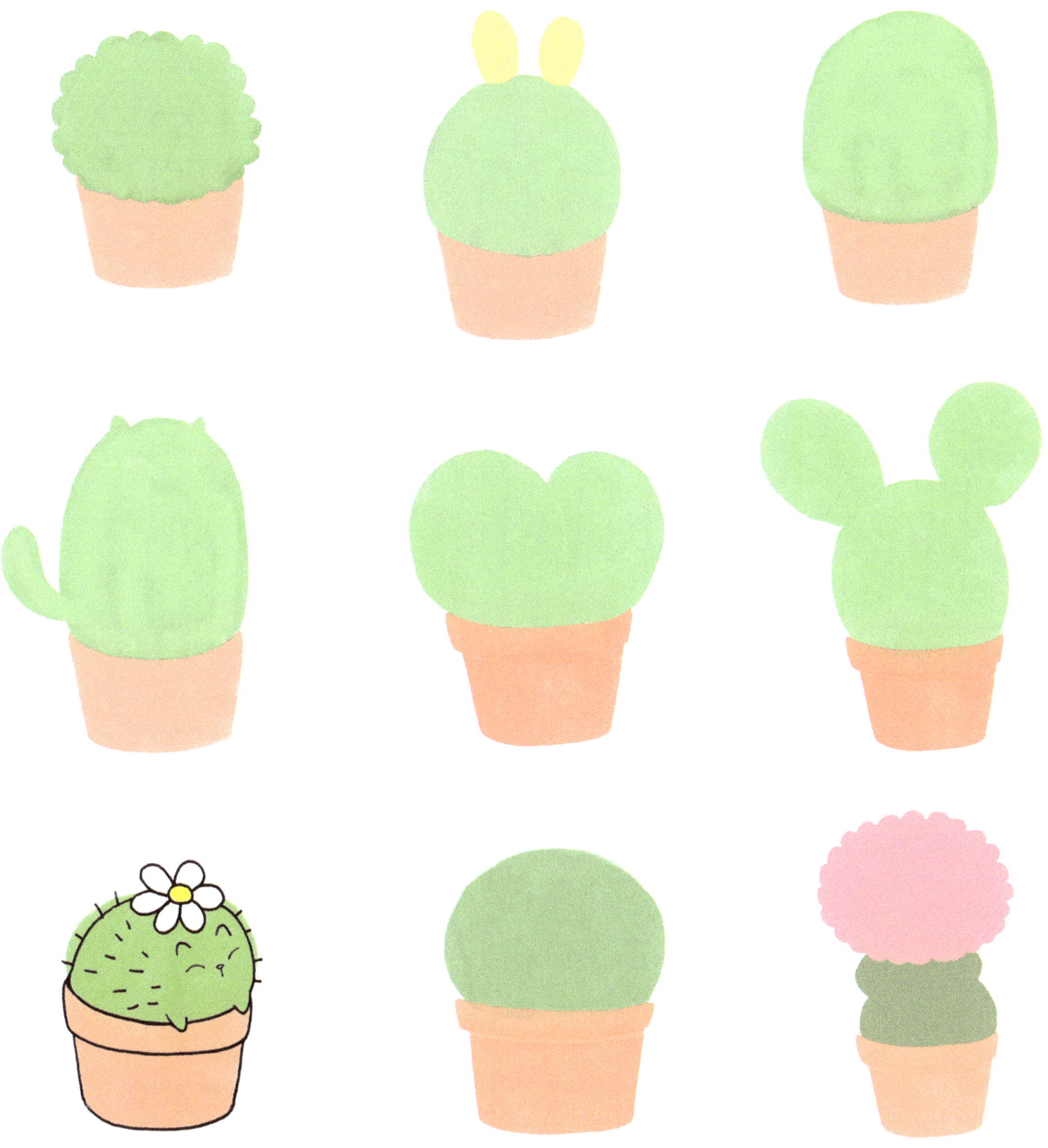

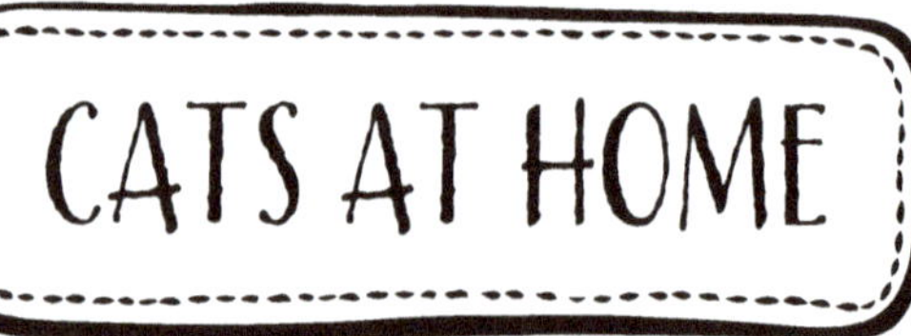

Follow the steps below to draw some fun cat things you might have at home.

BOOKSHELF

1
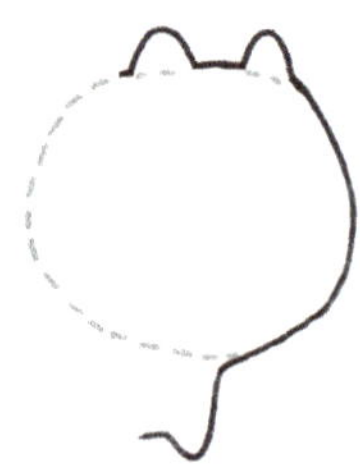

2
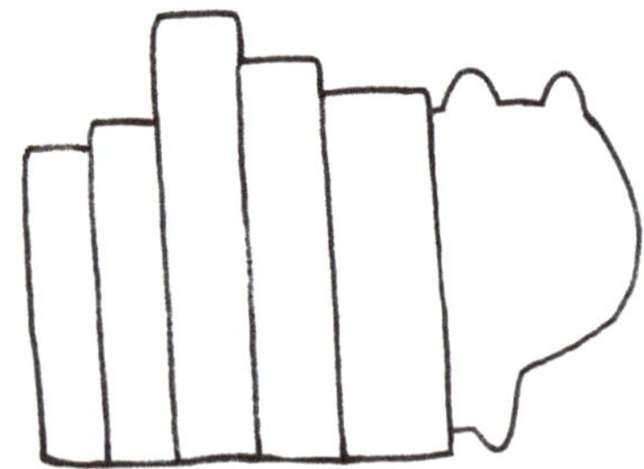

3
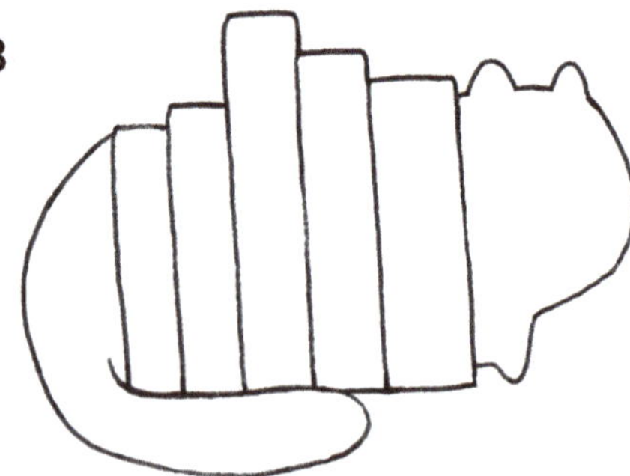

4
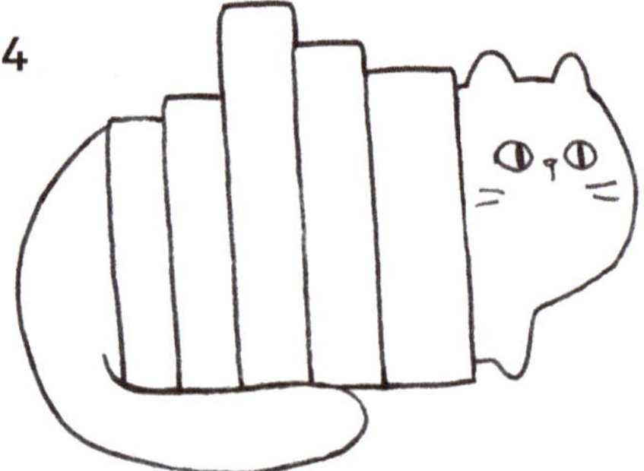

5
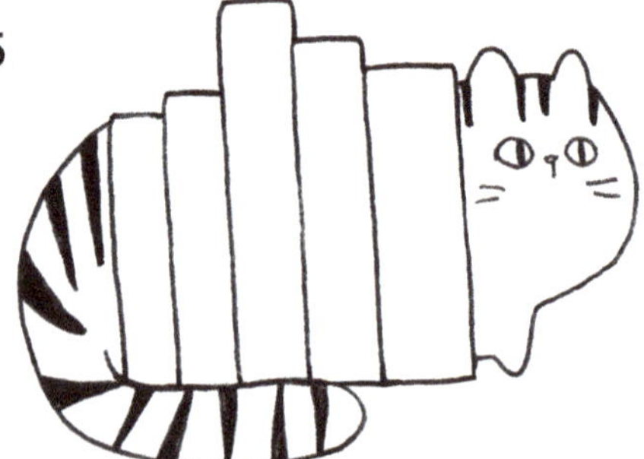

6
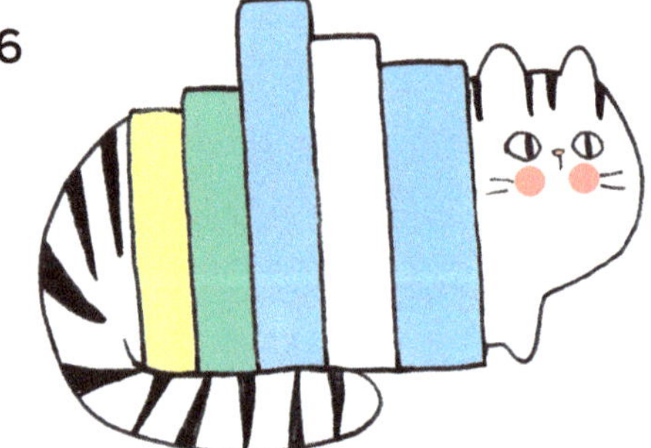

DESK LAMP

1
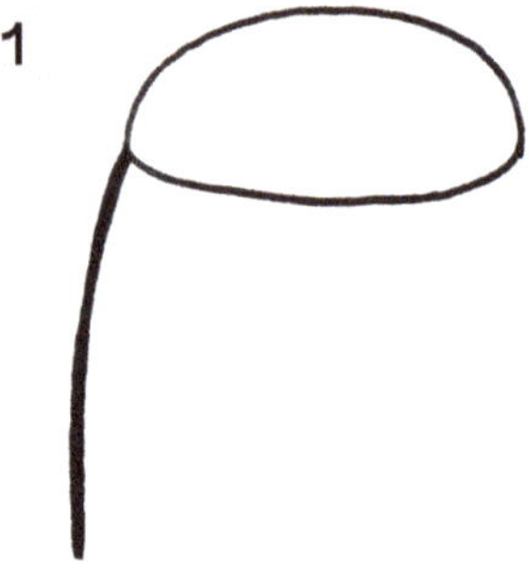

2
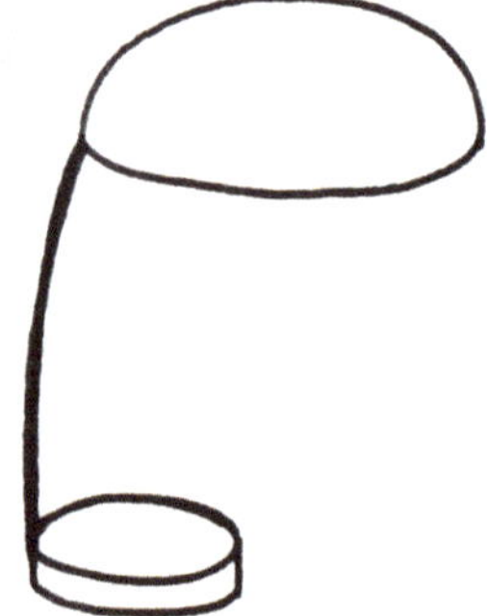

3
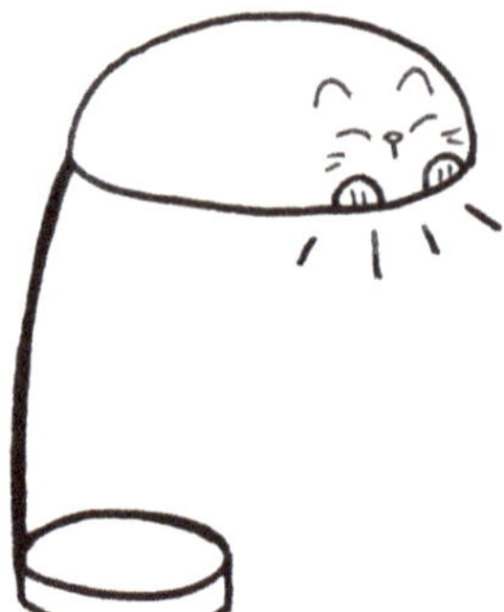

4
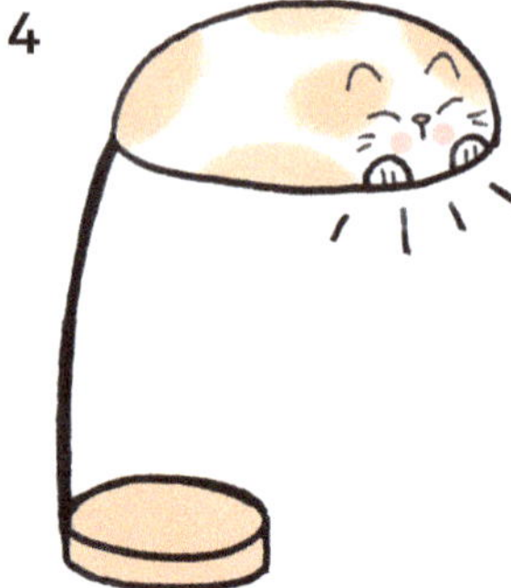

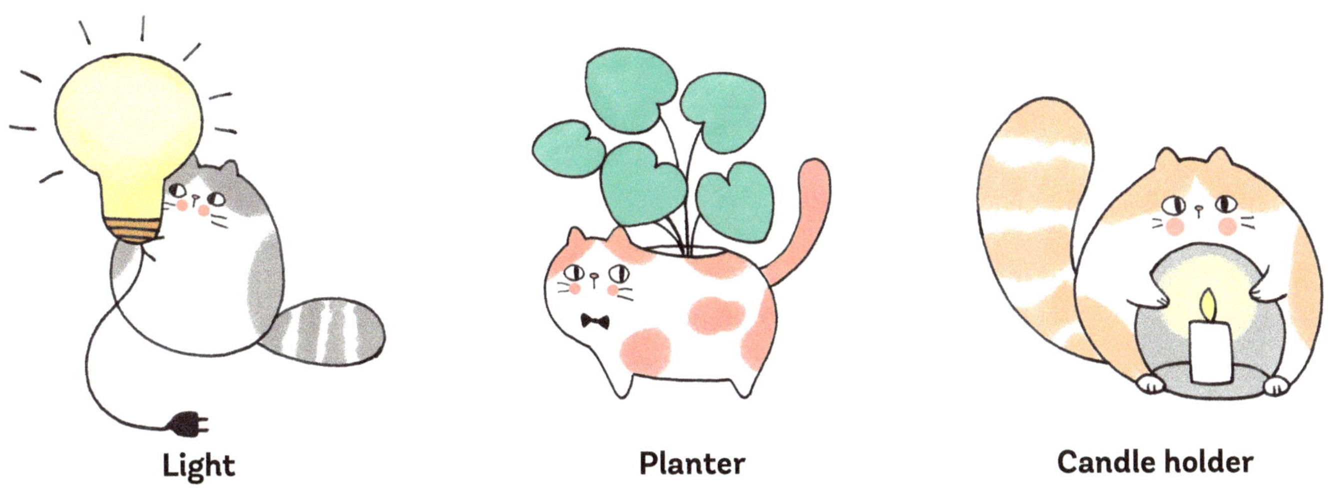

Light   **Planter**   **Candle holder**

Create and complete your own home accessories here.

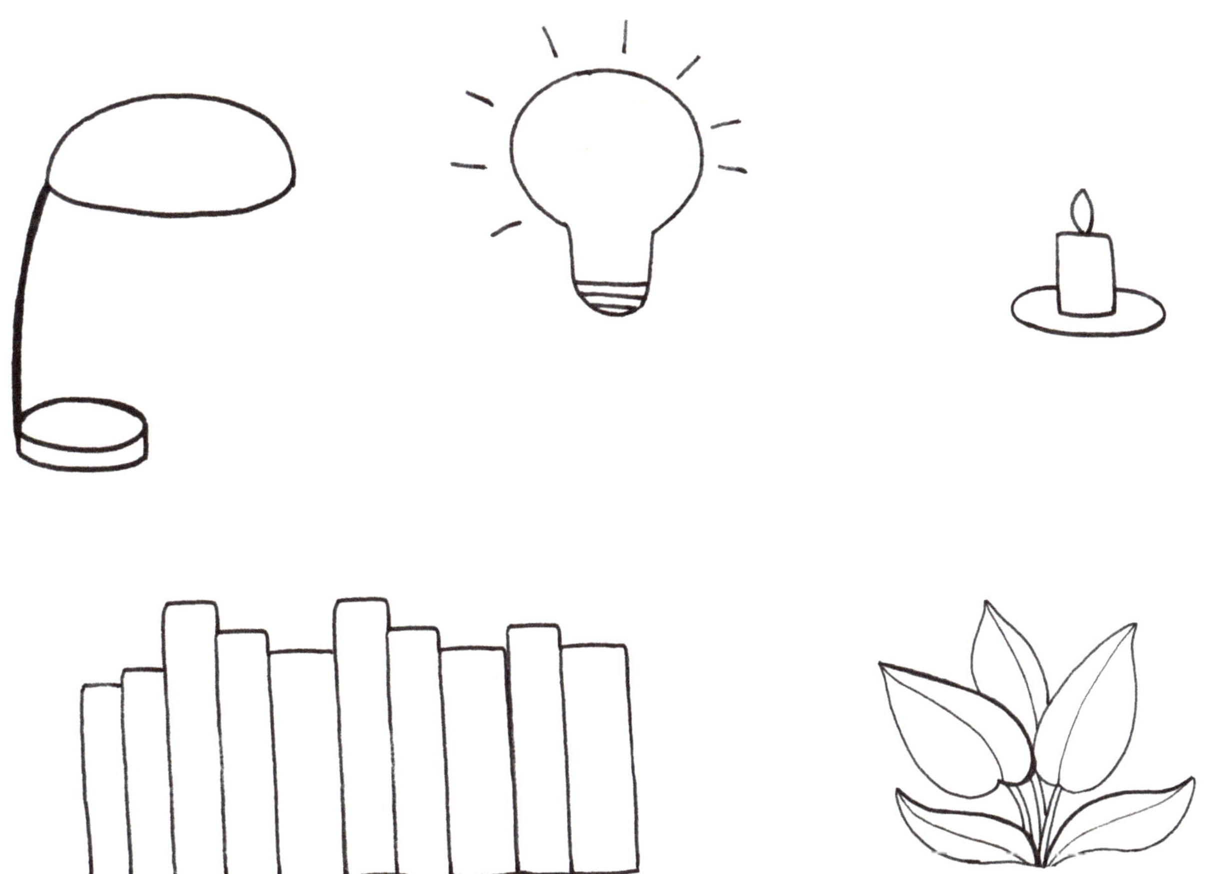

CHAISE LOUNGE

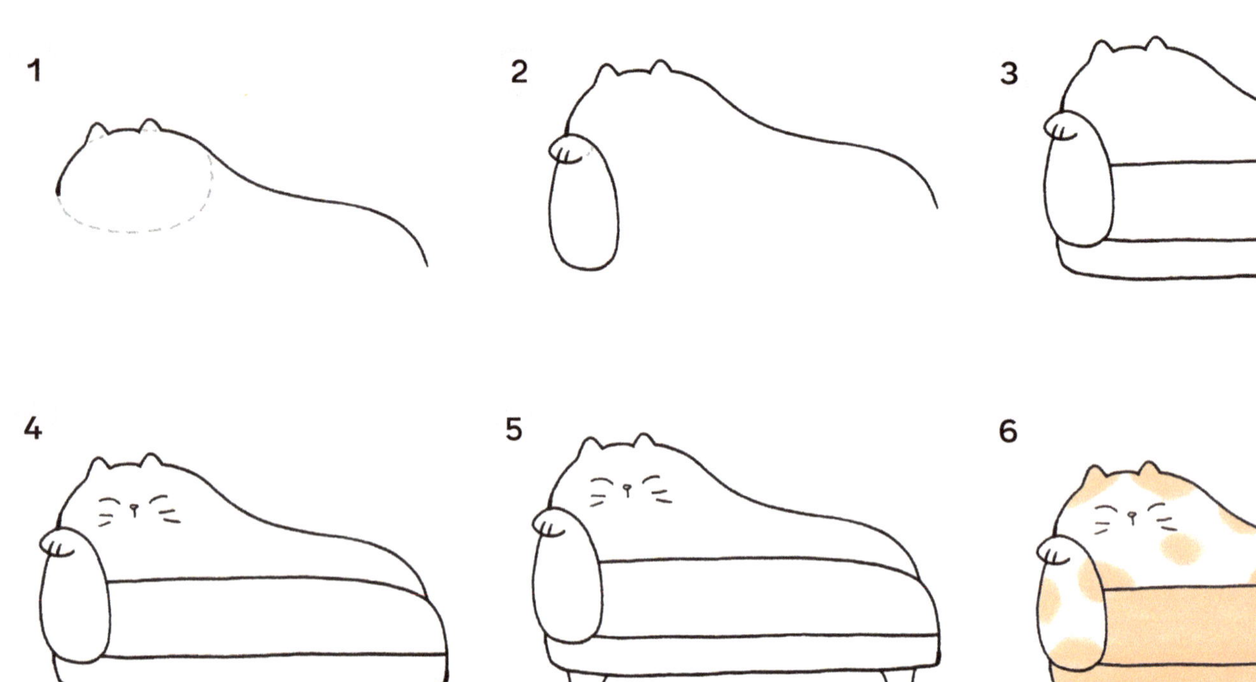

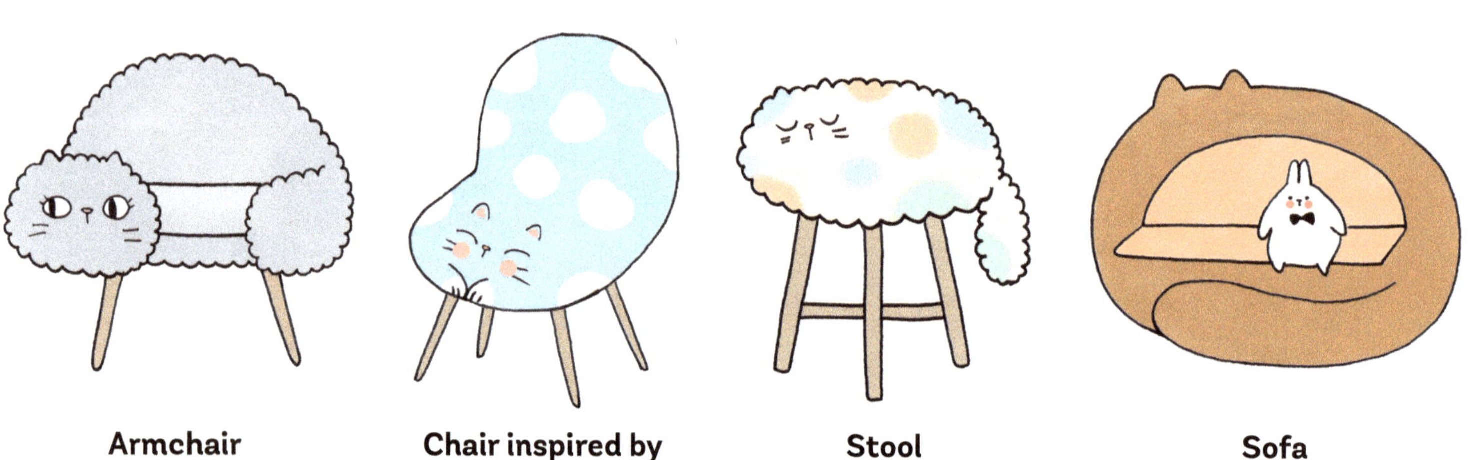

Armchair

Chair inspired by Arne Jacobsen

Stool

Sofa

Create and complete the cat chairs below. Why not add a little color and pattern too?

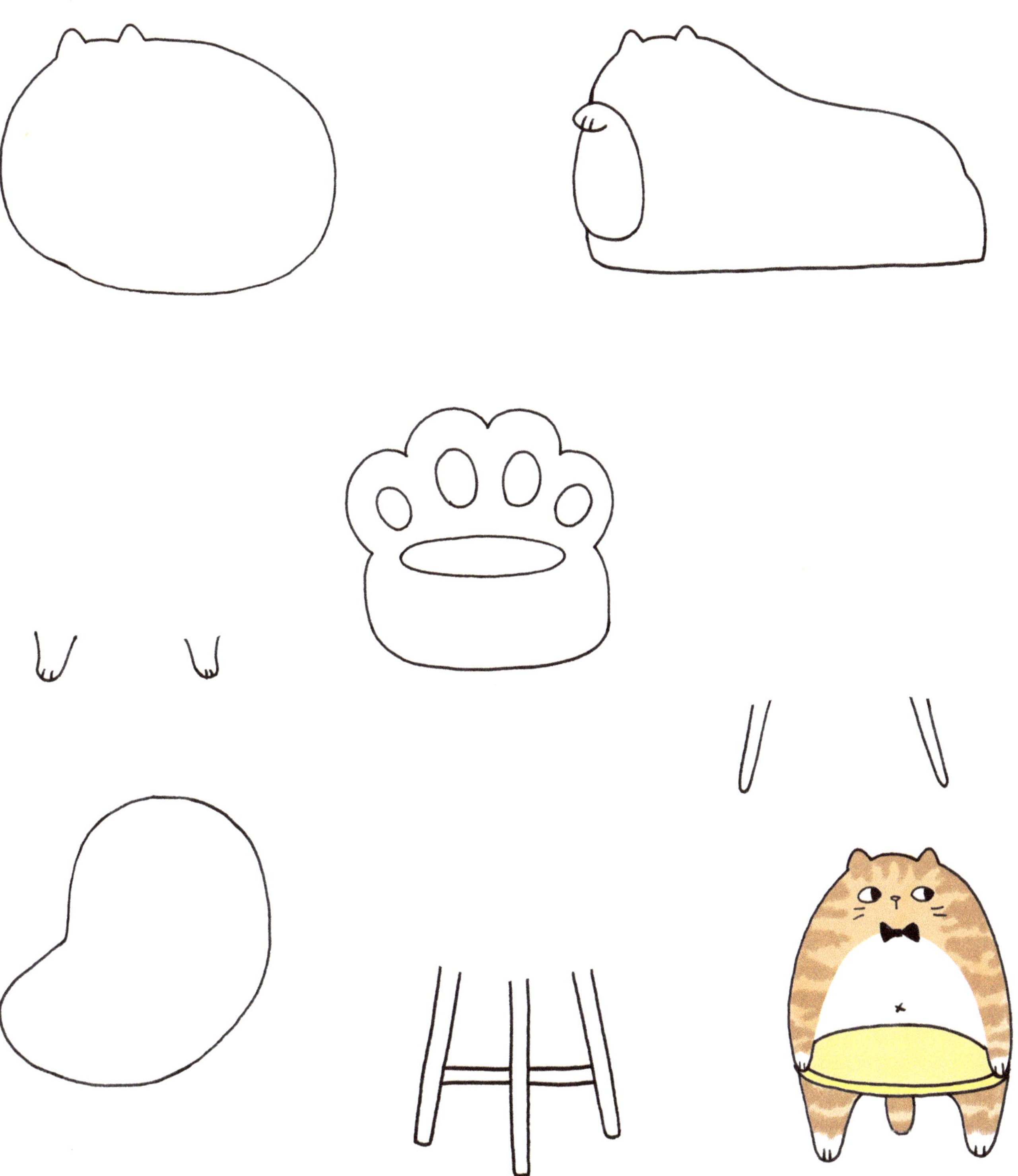

TOASTER

1 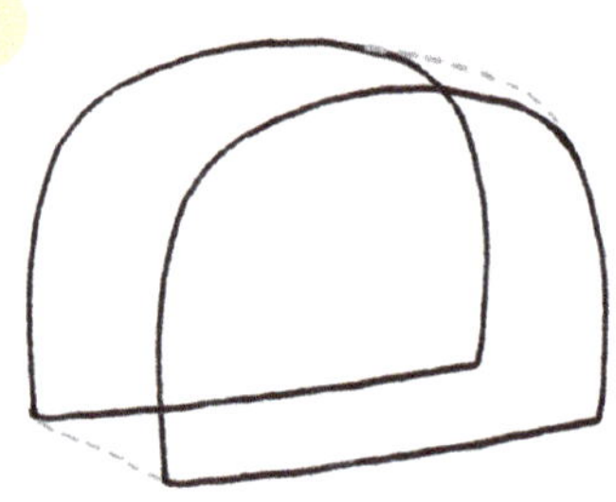
2 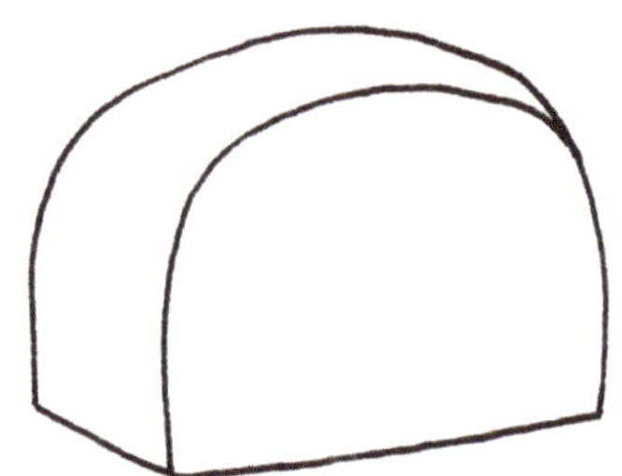
3 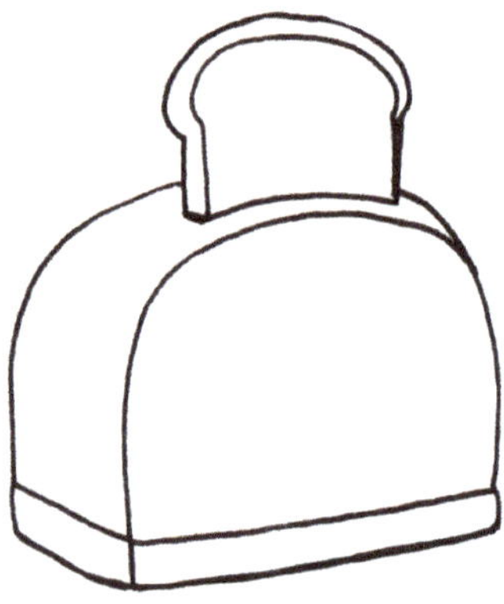

4 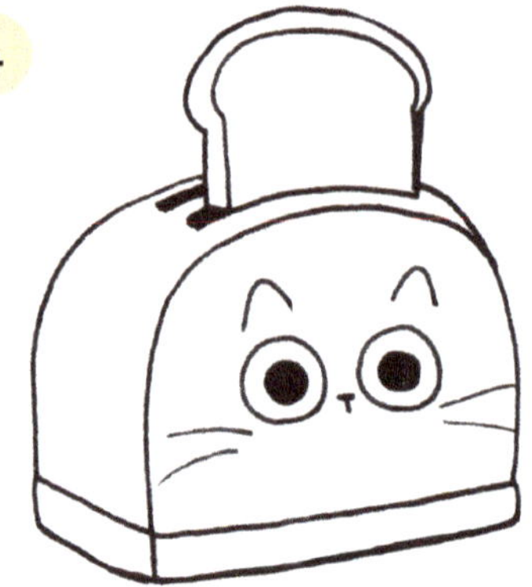
5 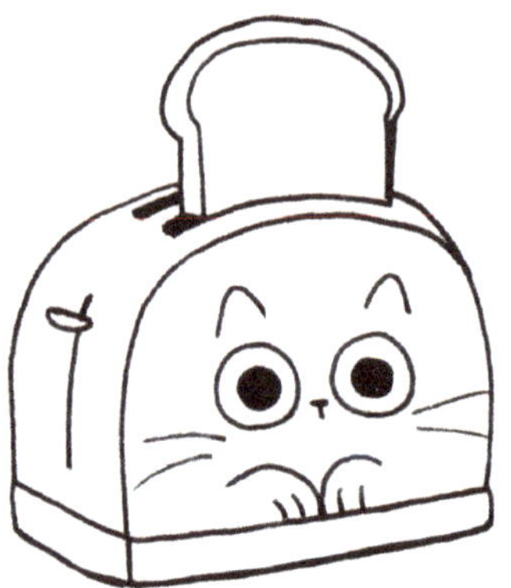
6 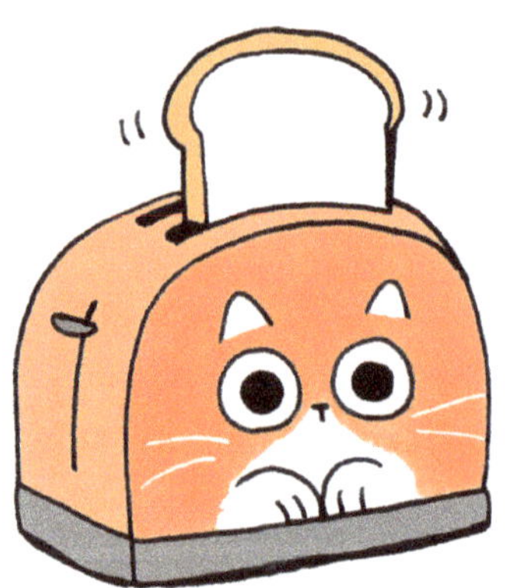

MIXER

1 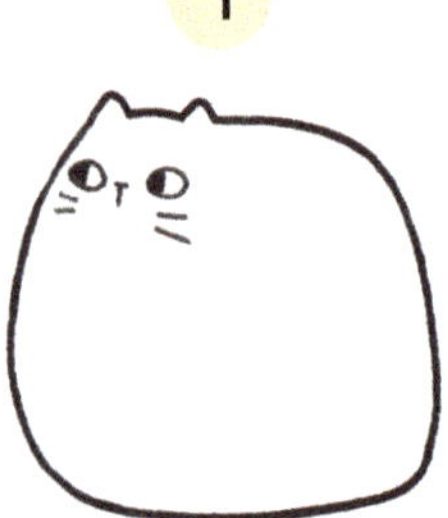
2 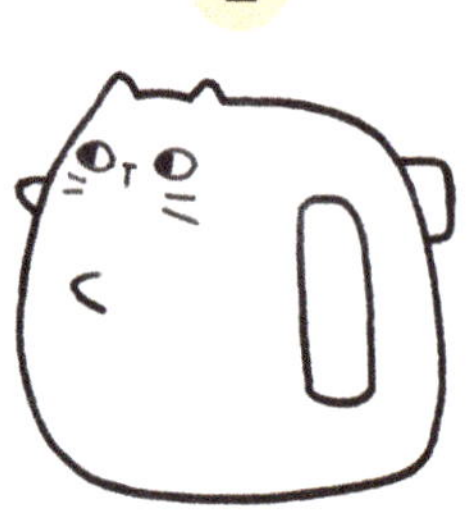
3 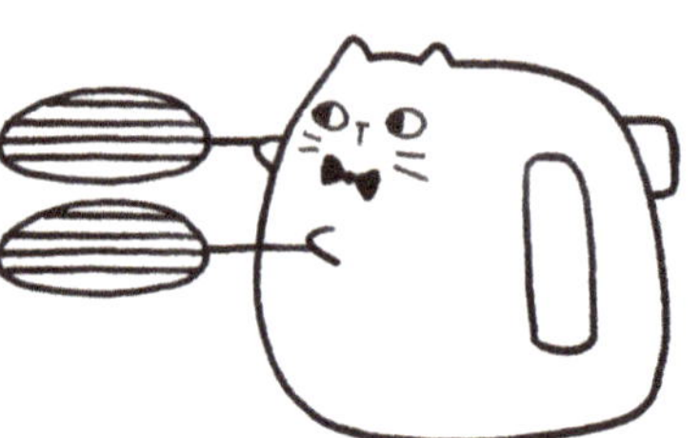
4 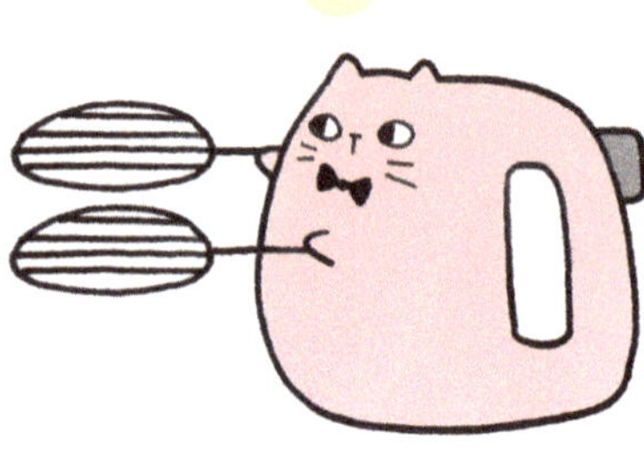

Let your imagination run wild and turn these shapes into cute appliances.

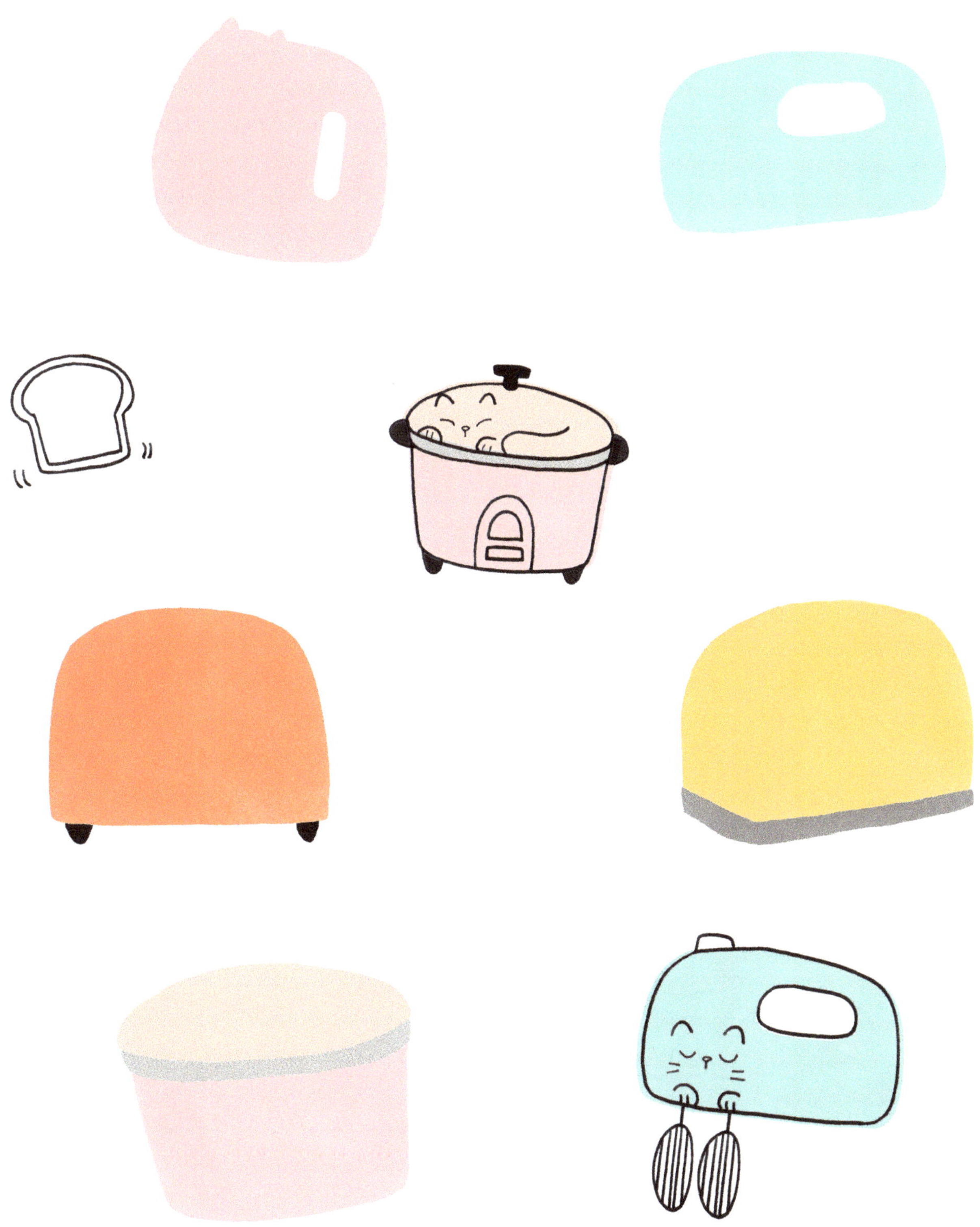

OLD-SCHOOL TELEPHONE

1
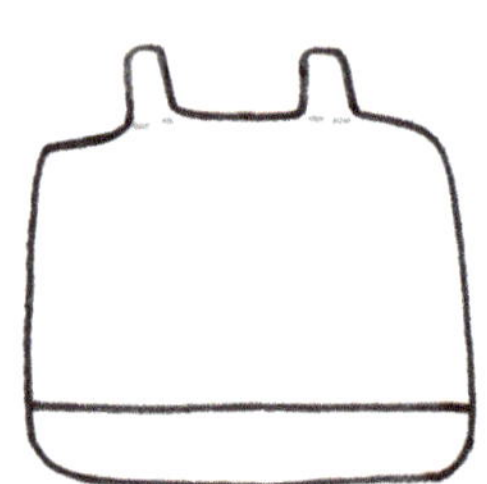

2
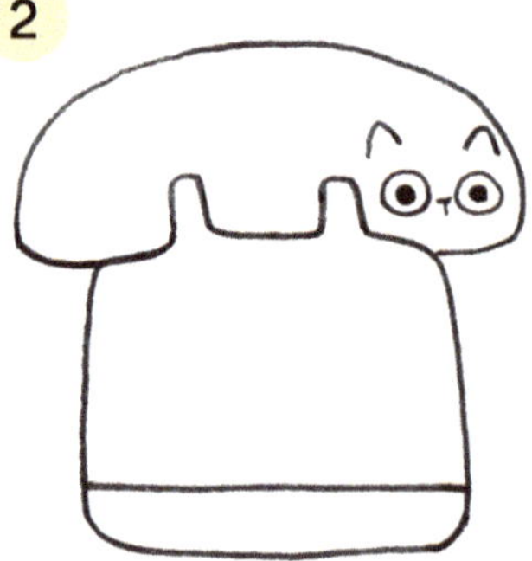

3
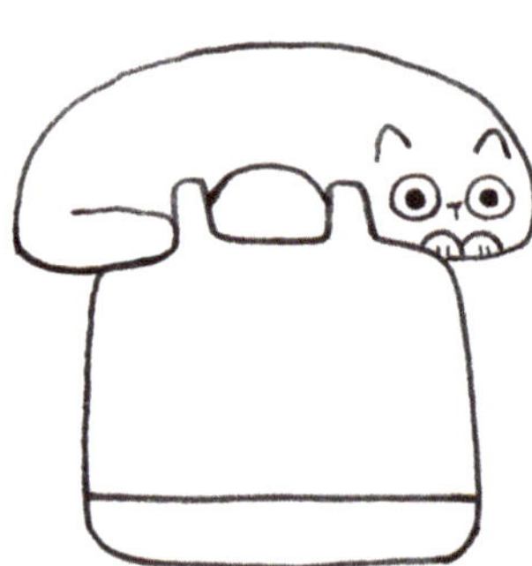

4
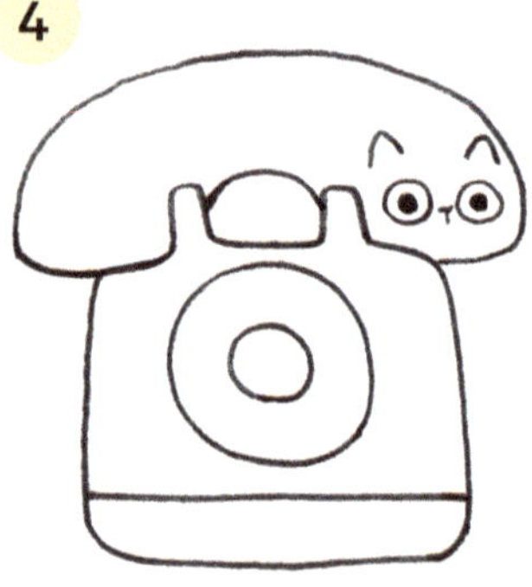

5
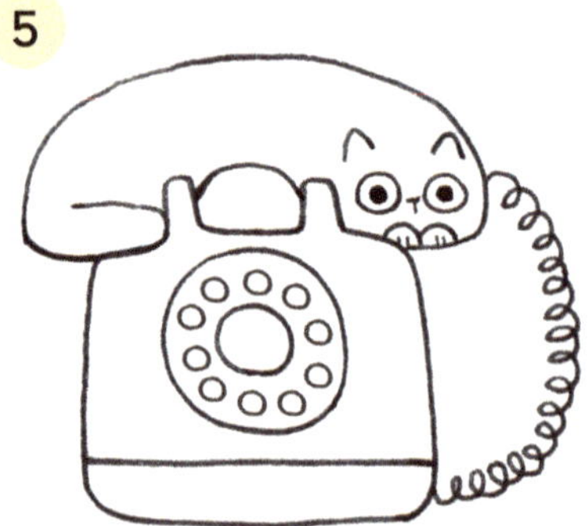

6
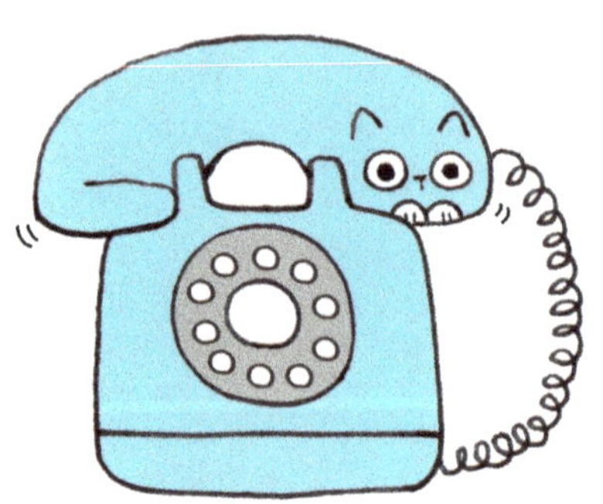

TEA KETTLE

1
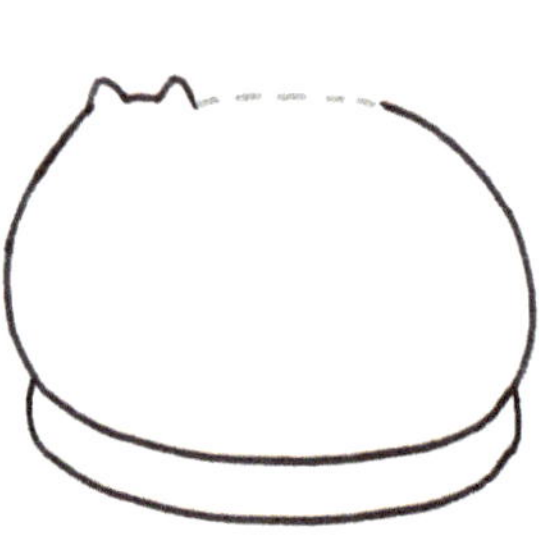

2
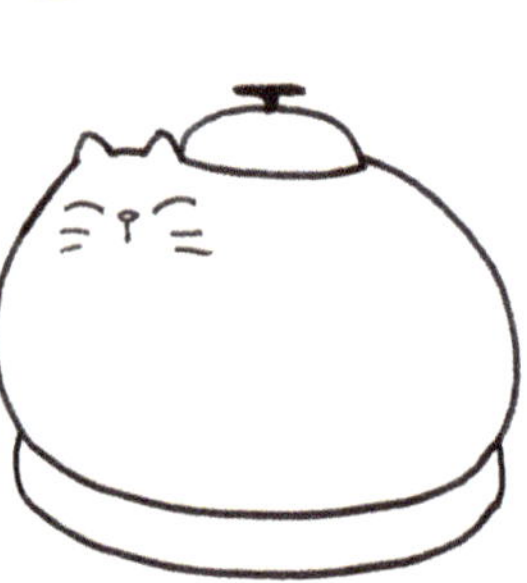

3
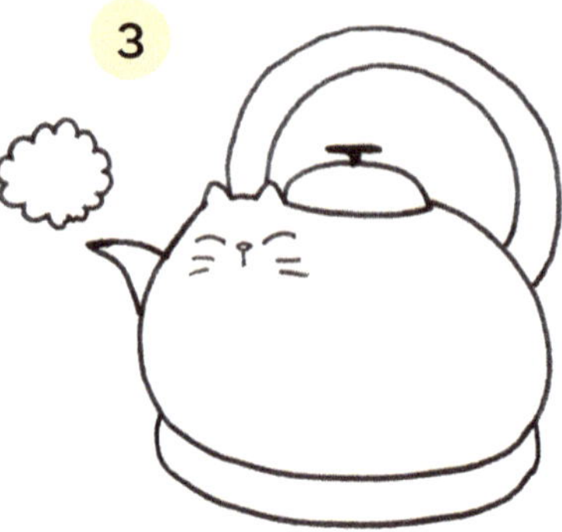

4
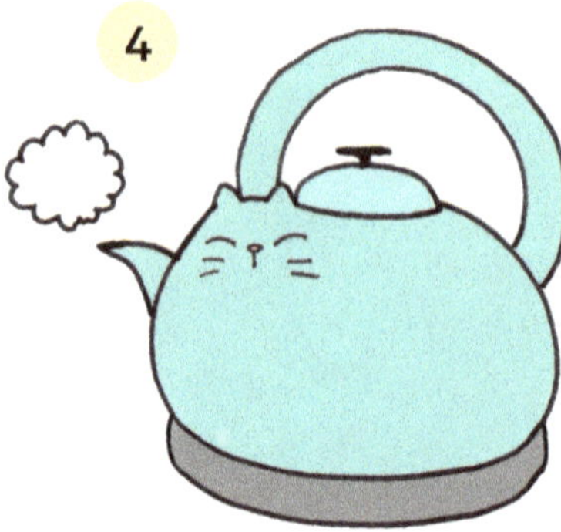

Design and complete your appliances here. Don't forget to add color!

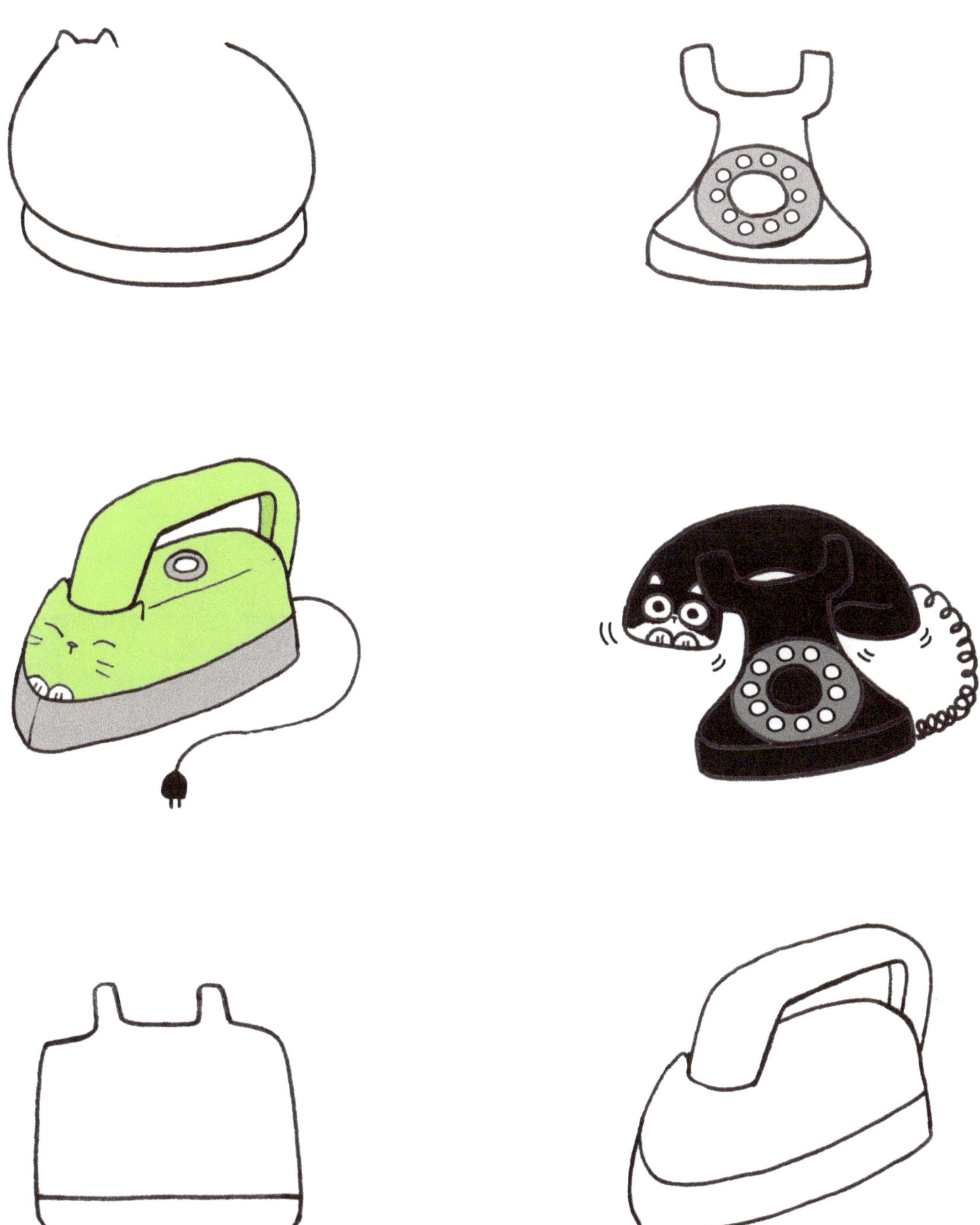

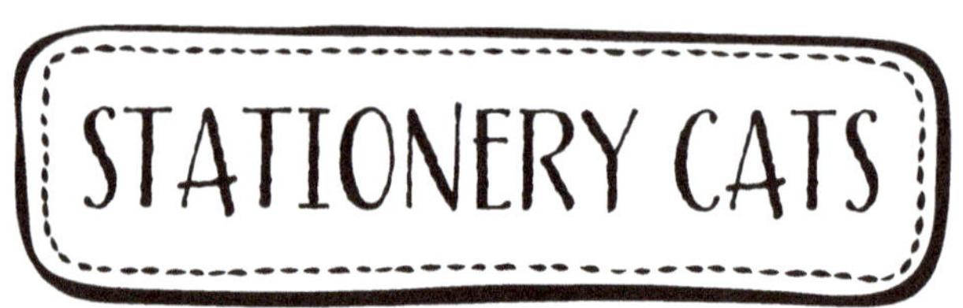

Follow the steps below to draw your own cat stationery.

PENCIL CASE

1 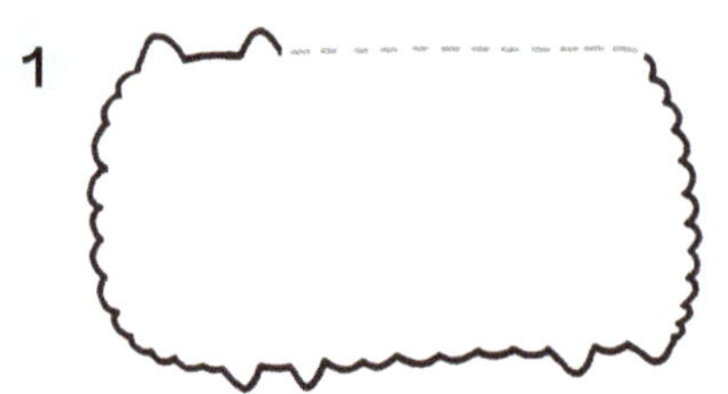 2 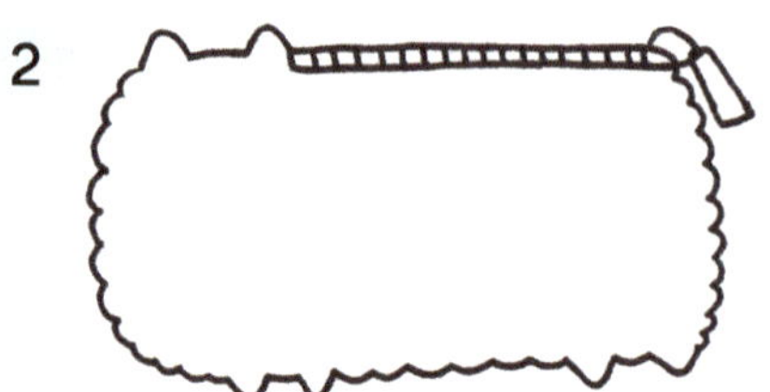 3 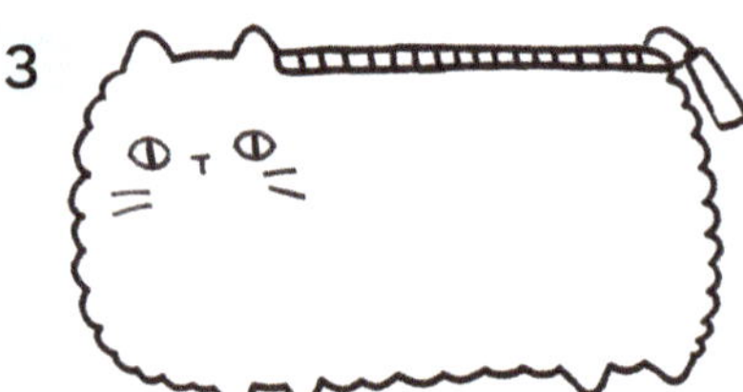

4 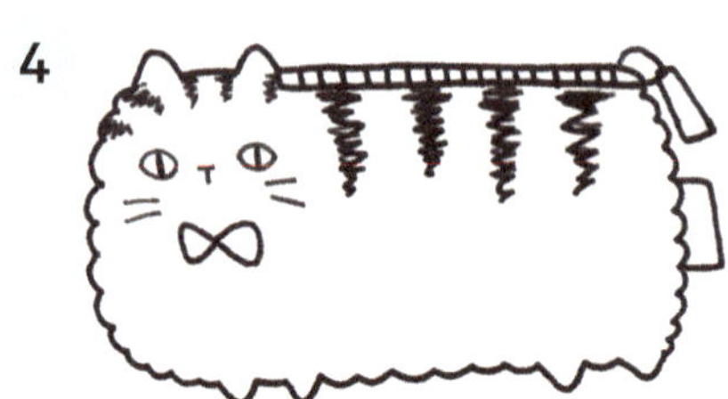 5 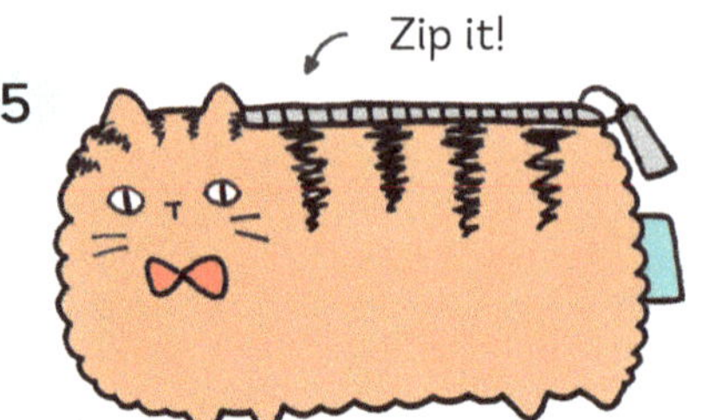

PENCIL SHARPENER

1 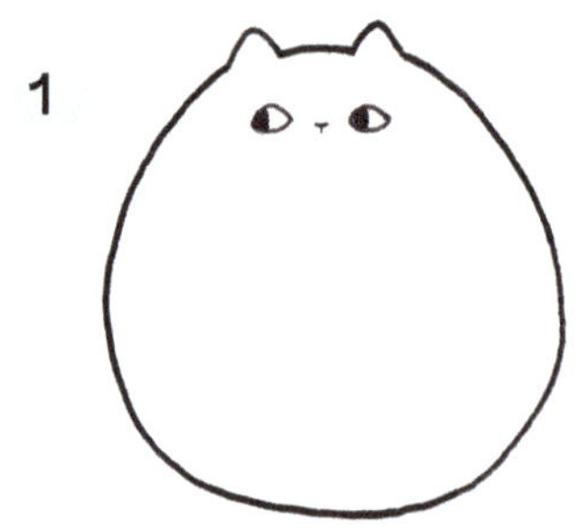 2 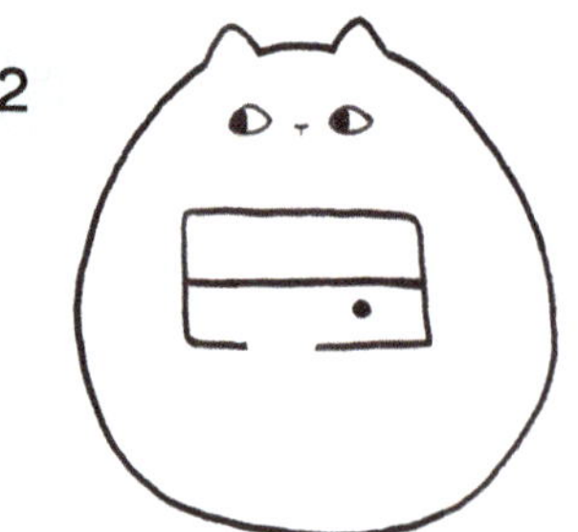 3 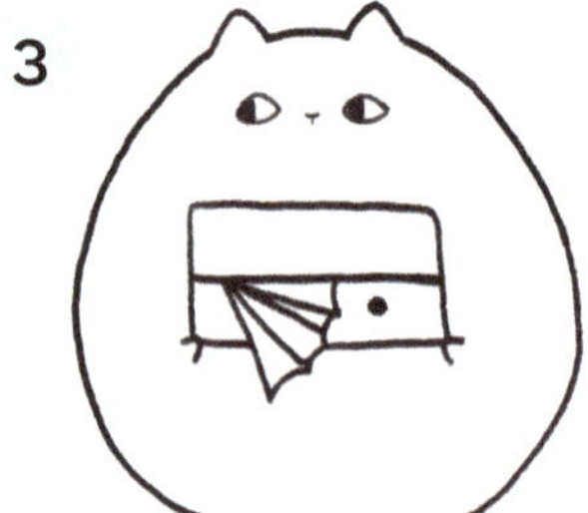

4 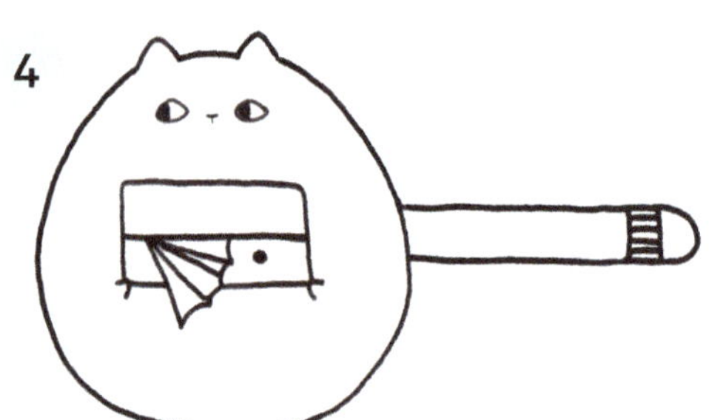 5 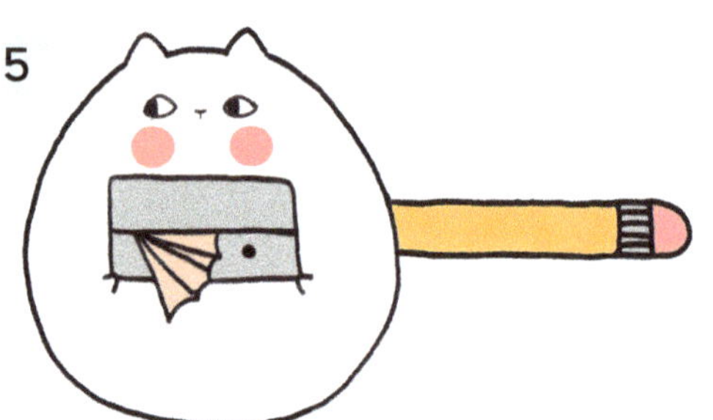

MECHANICAL PENCIL

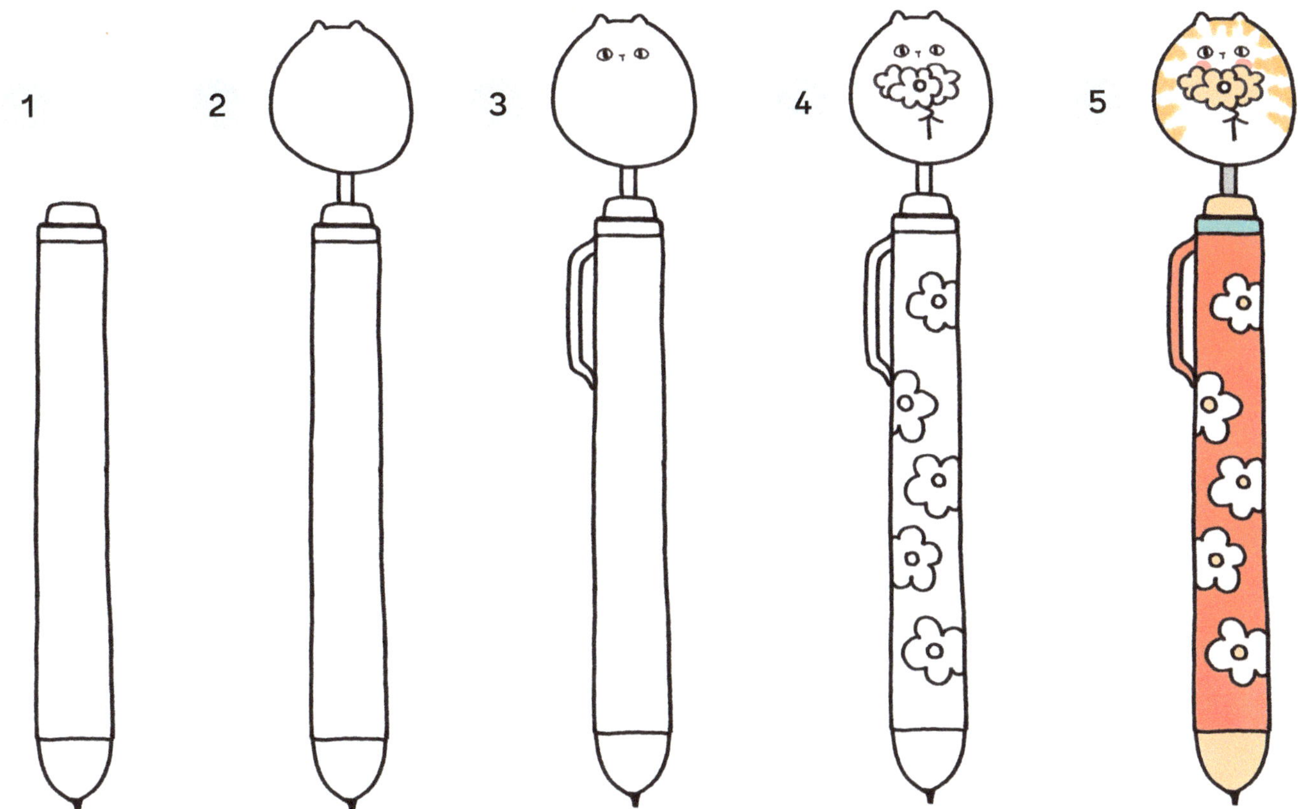

JOURNAL

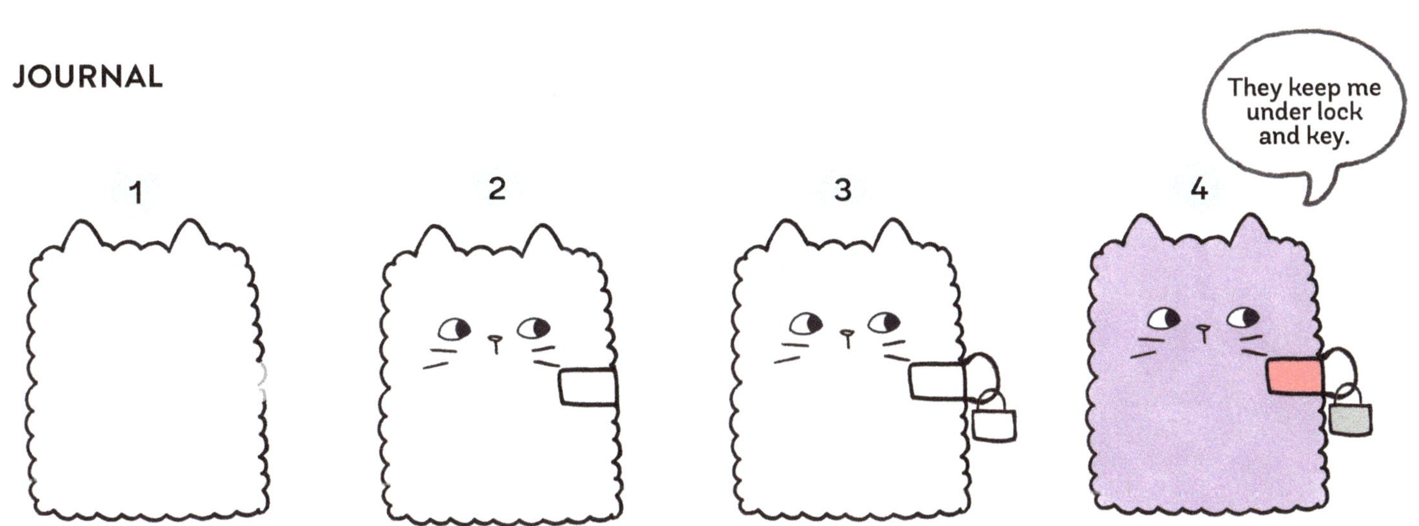

BINDER CLIP

1 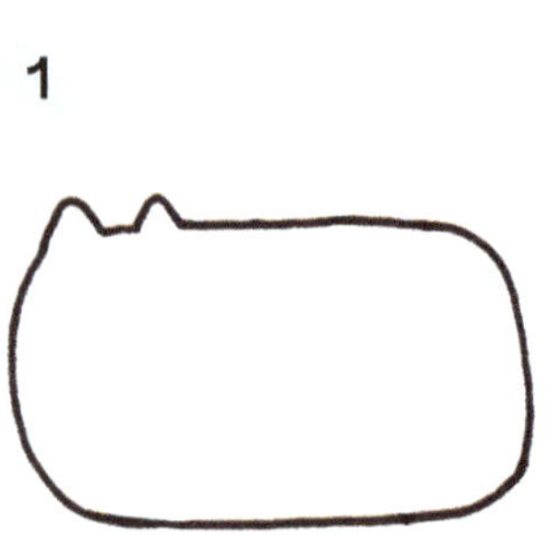

2 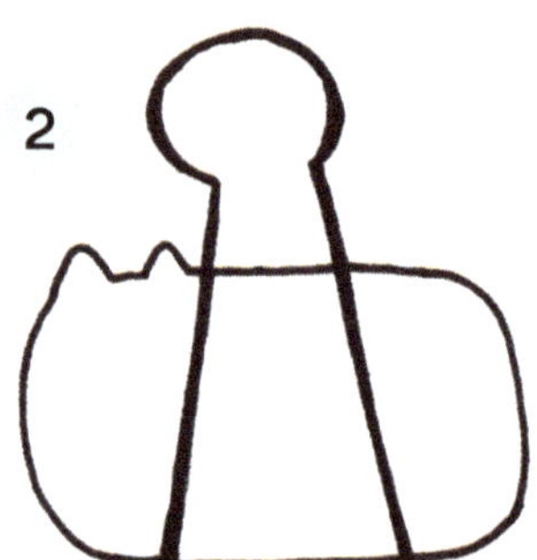

3 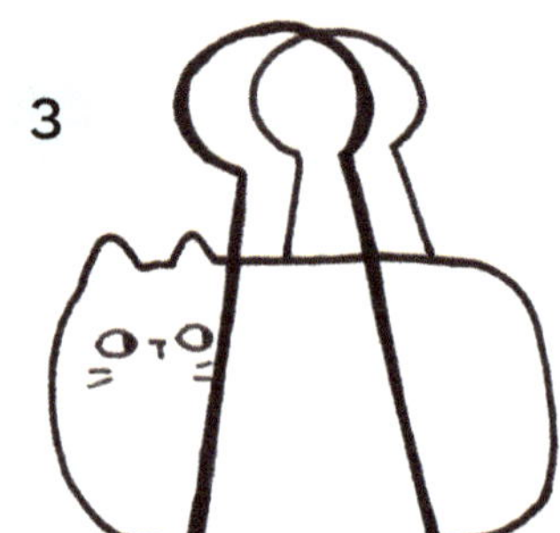

4 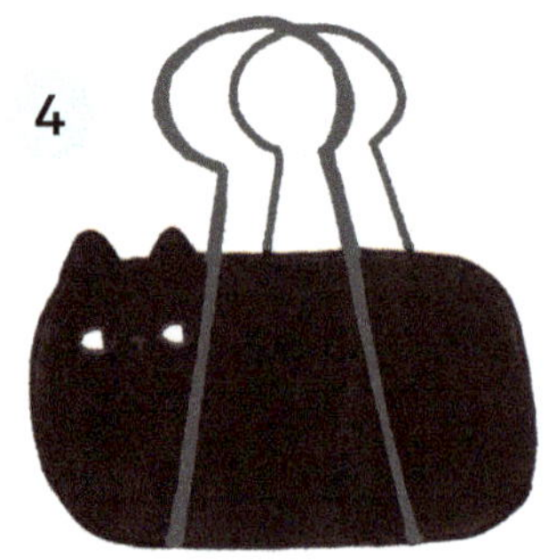

STAPLER

1 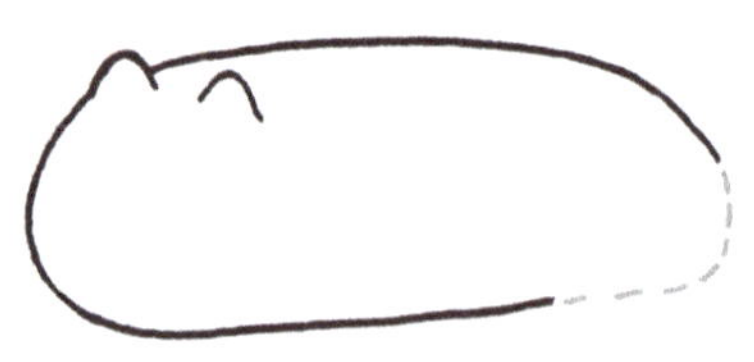

2 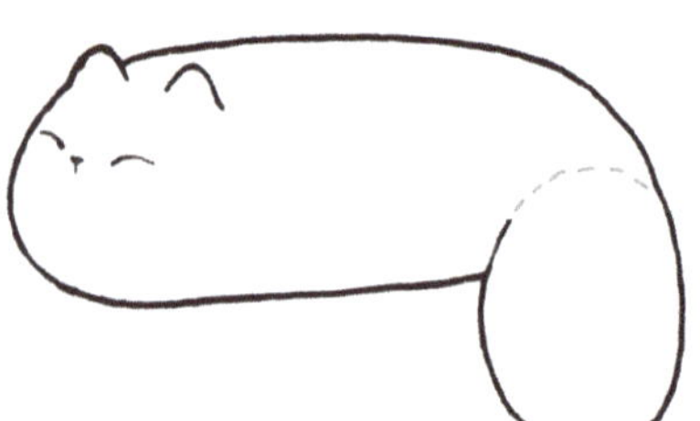

3 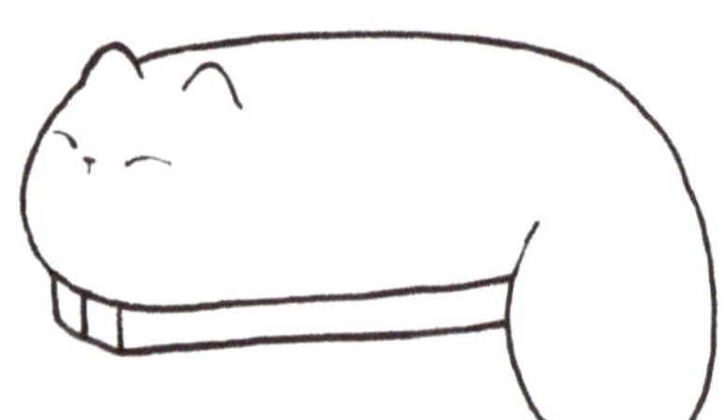

4 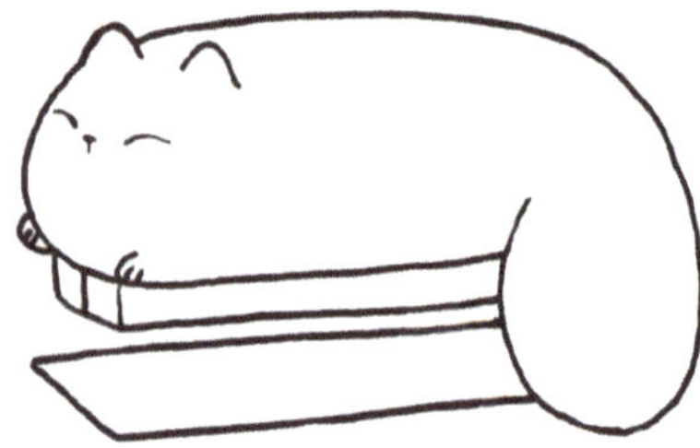

5 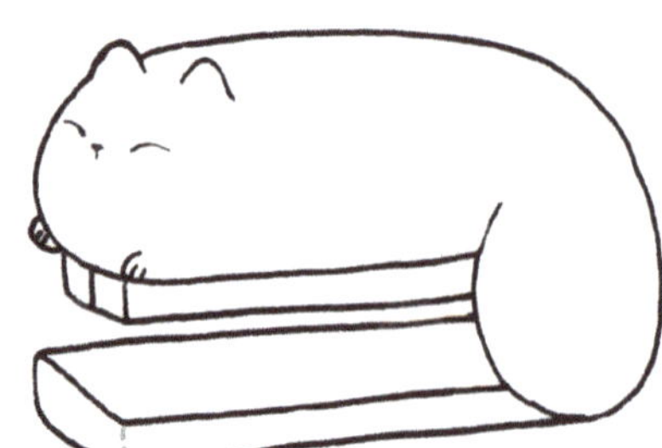

6 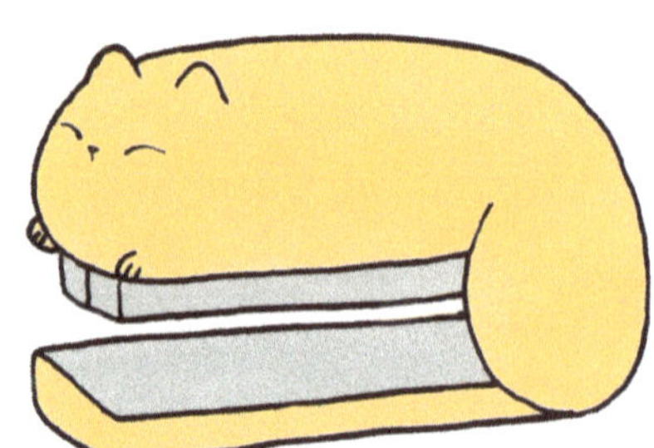

ERASER

1

2

3

4

PENCIL

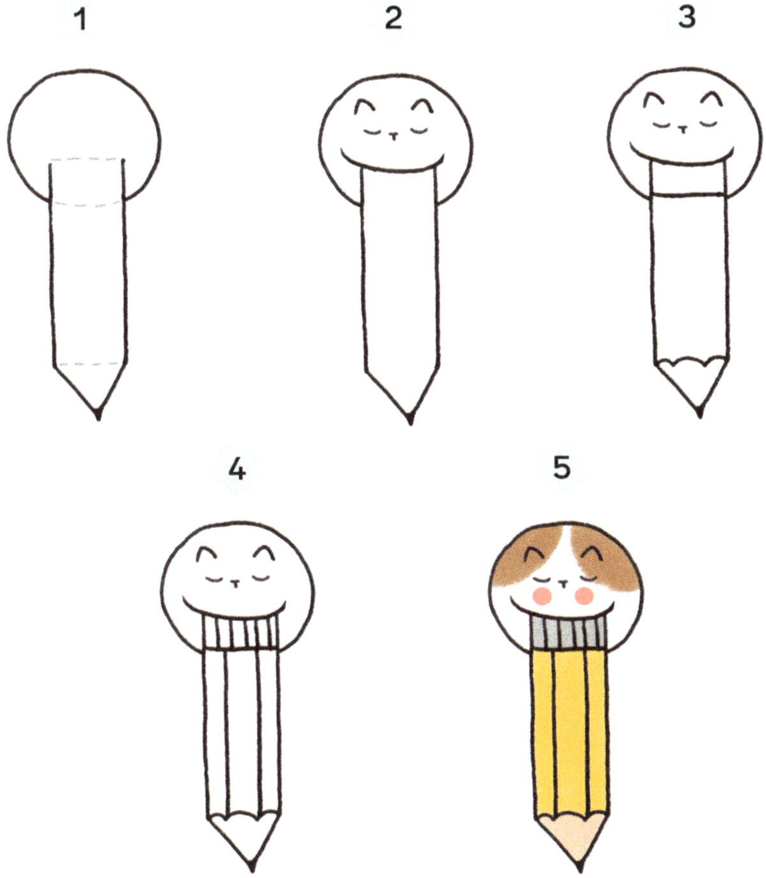

1

2

3

4

5

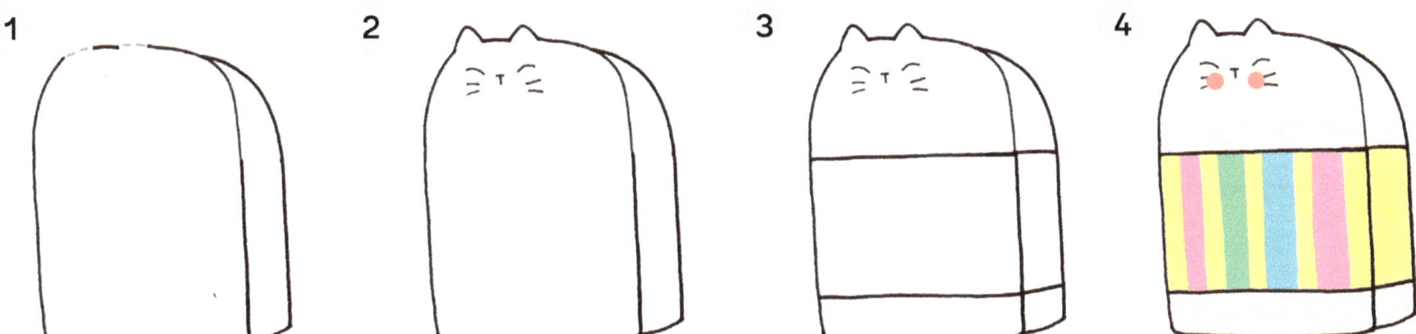

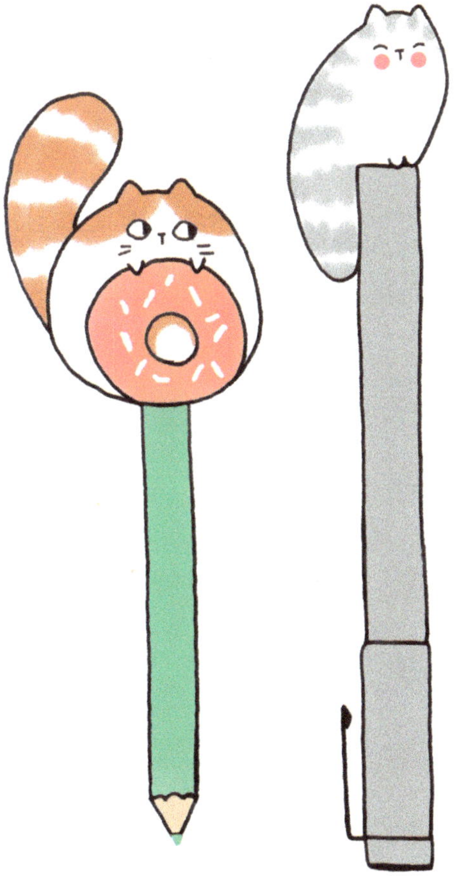

Colored pencil   **Liner pen**

Fill this spread with cat stationery doodles.

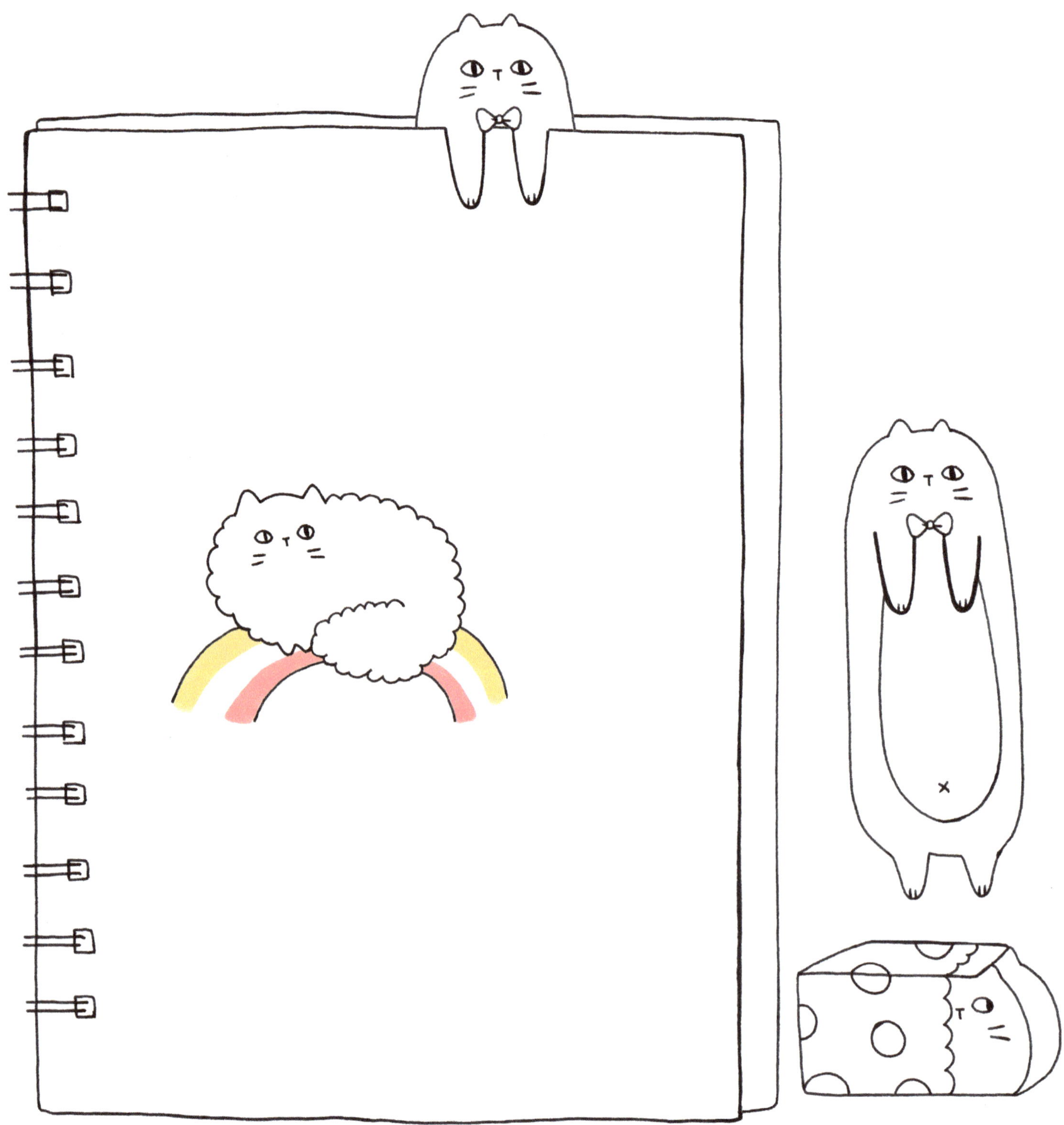

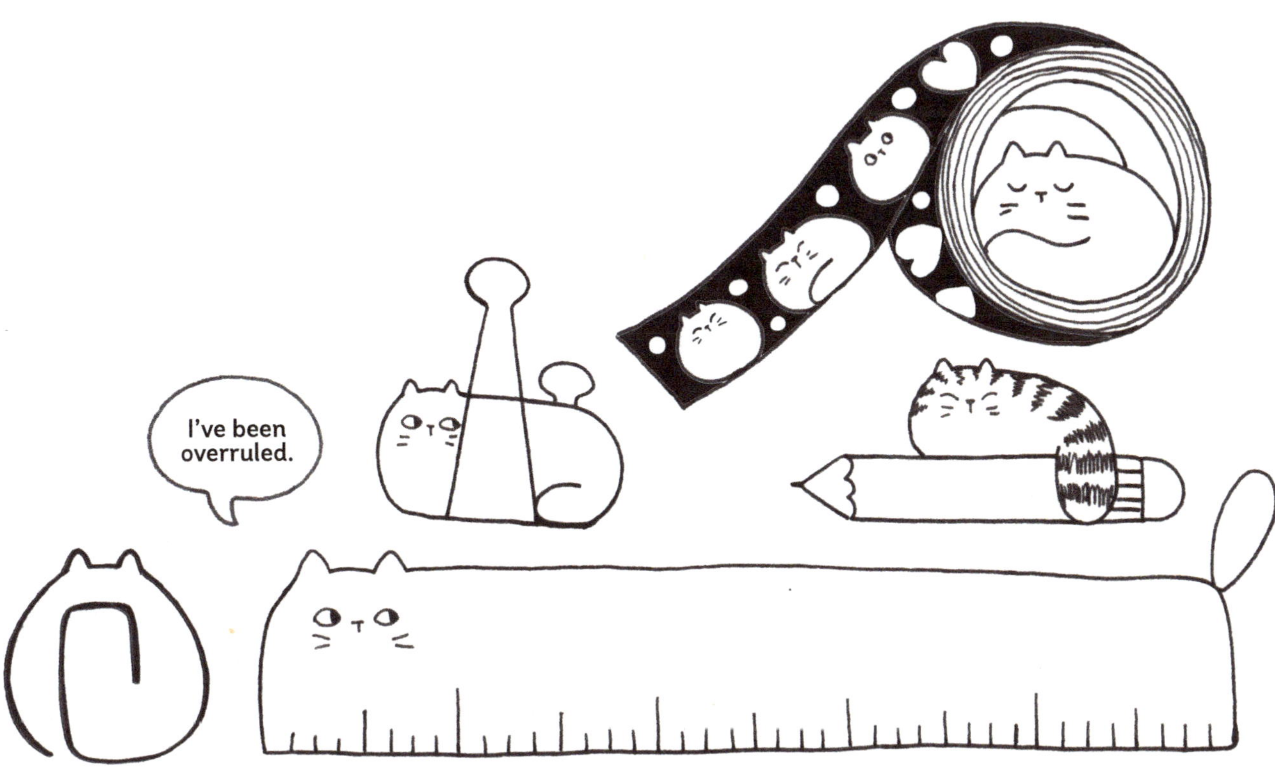

103

CHRISTMAS STOCKING

1 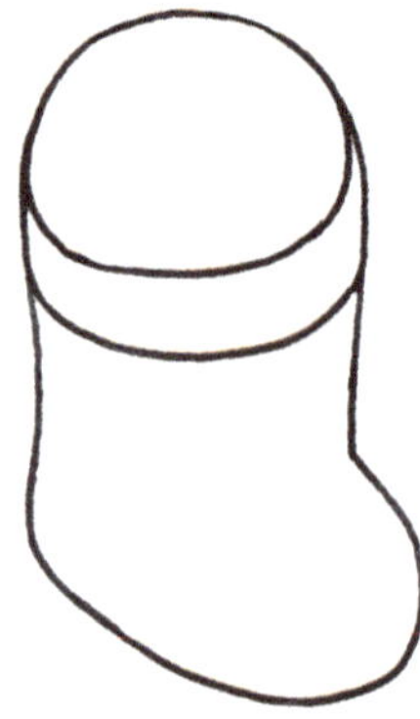
2 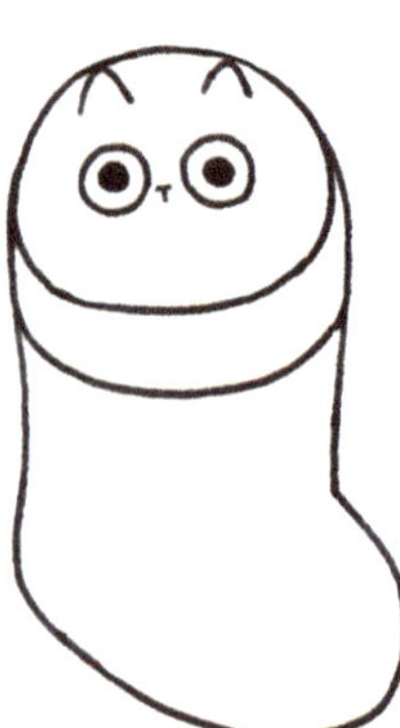
3 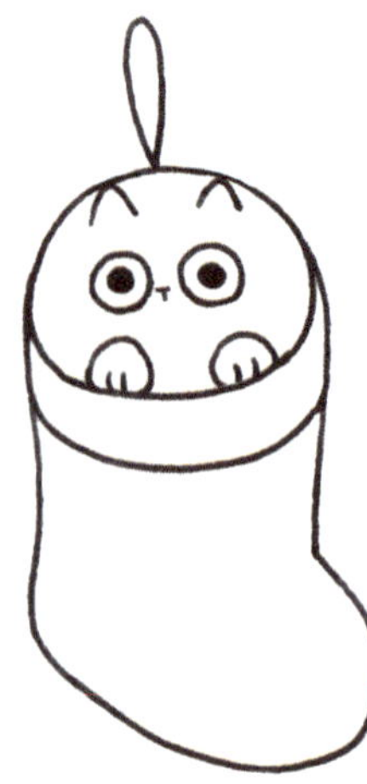
4 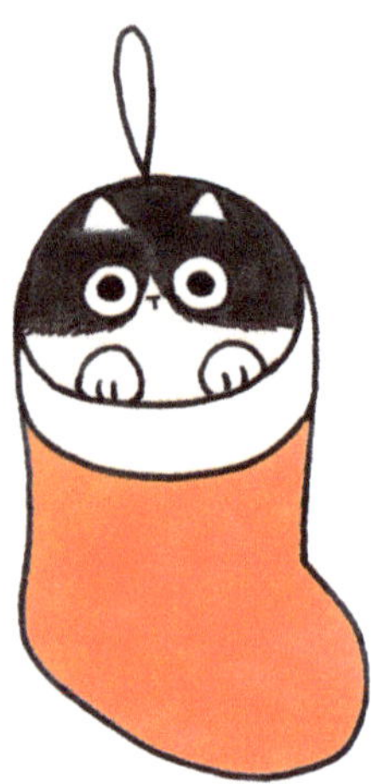

CHRISTMAS LIGHTS

1 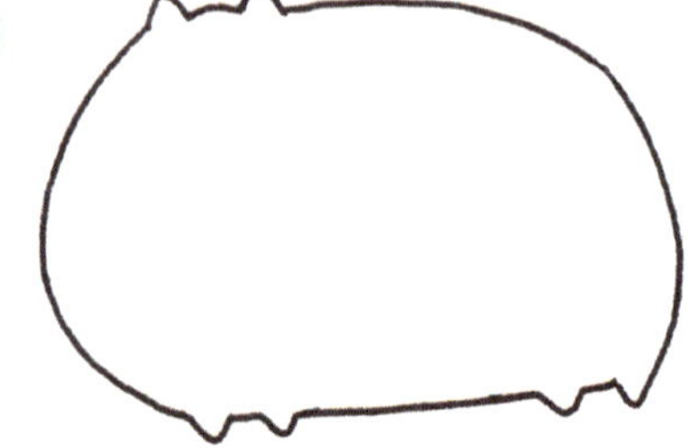
2 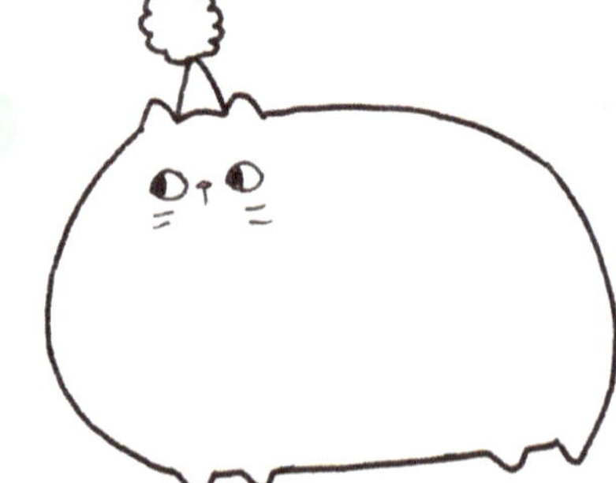
3 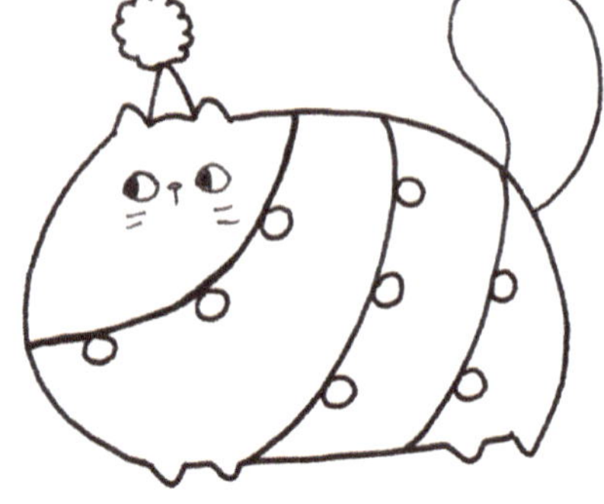
4 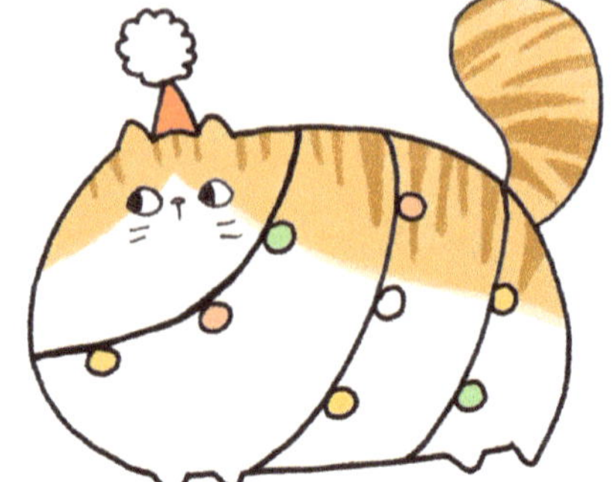

Merry Cat-mas!

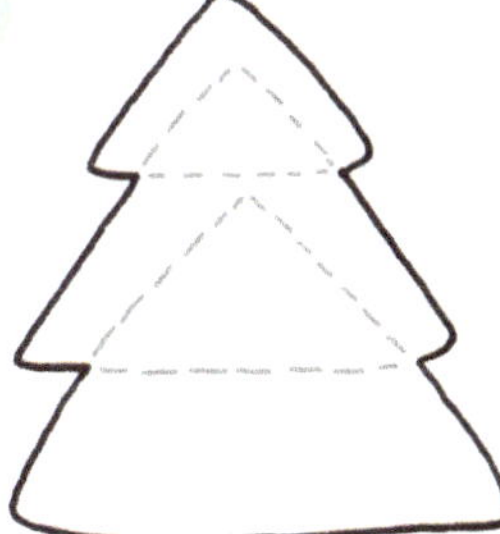
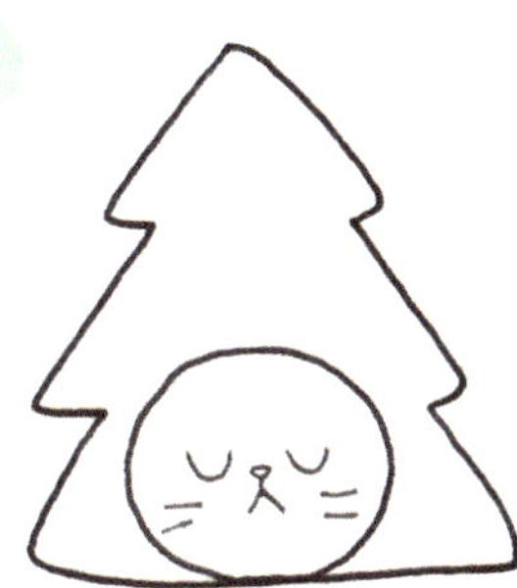
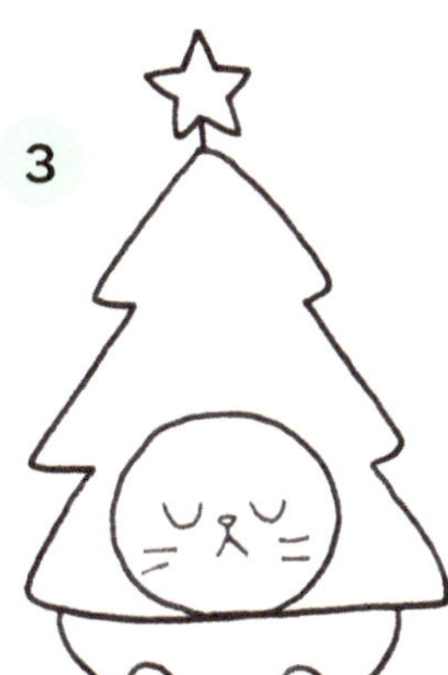
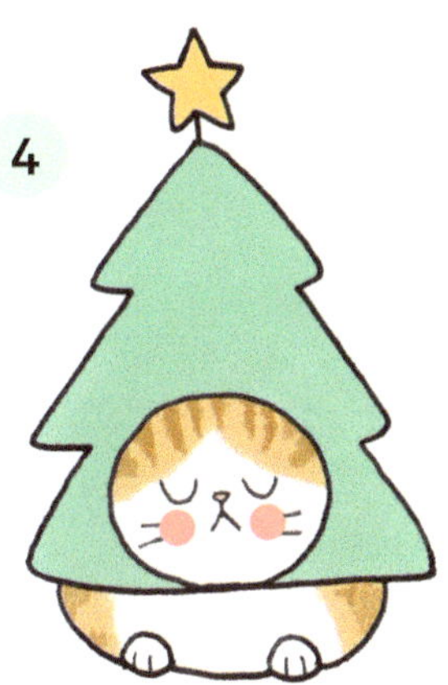

Turn these simple shapes into festive Christmas cats.

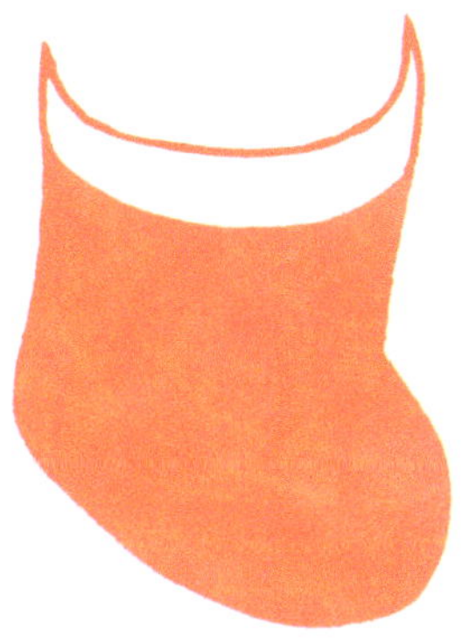

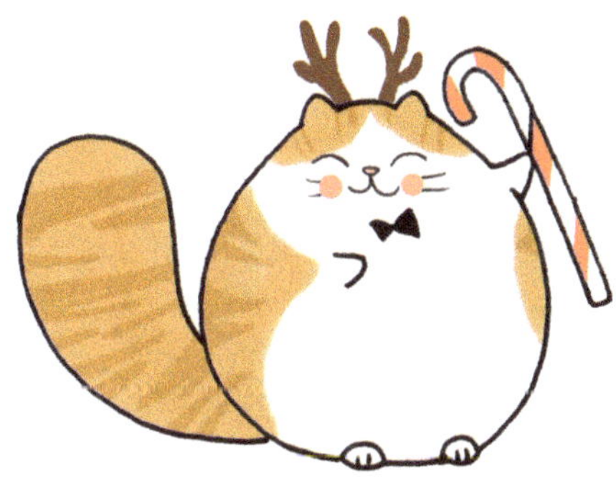

HALLOWEEN VAMPIRE BAT CAT

1
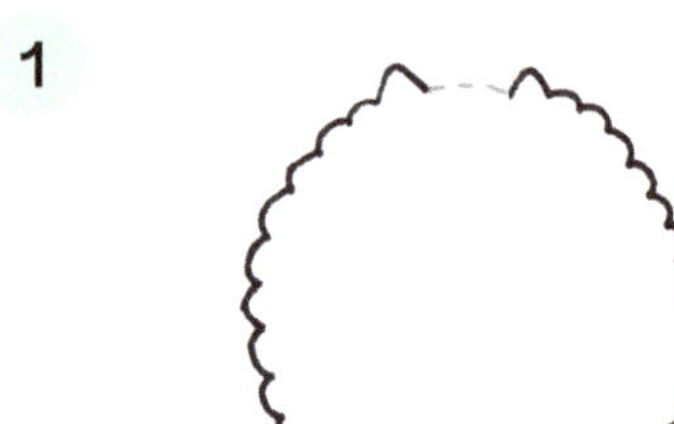

2
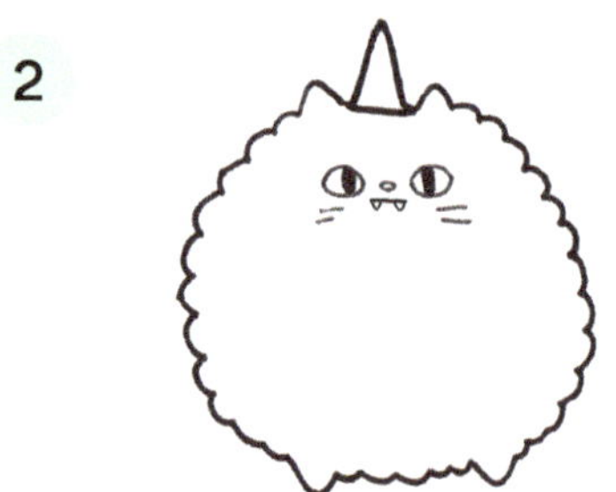

3
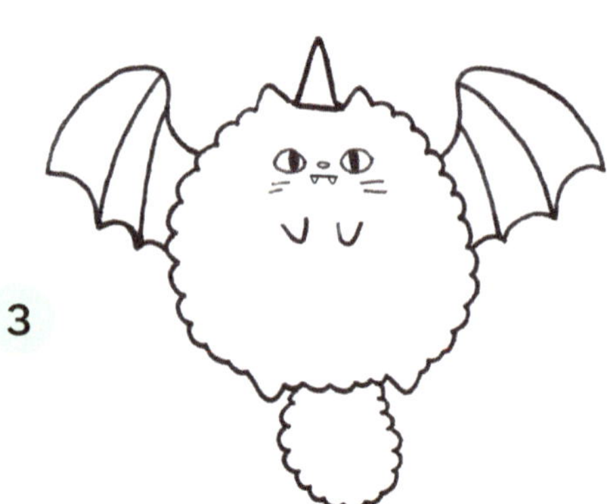

4
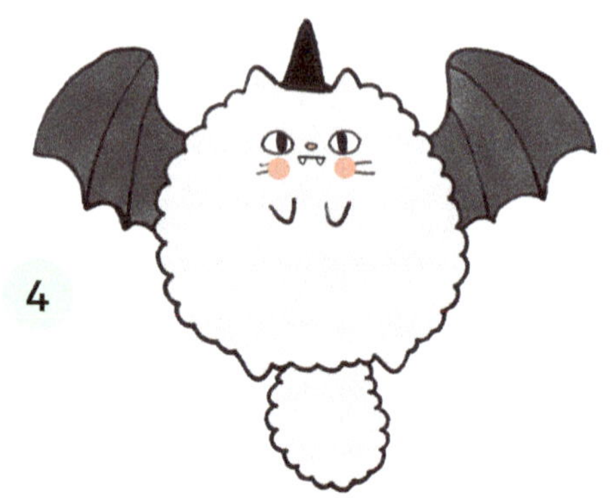

MUMMY CAT

1
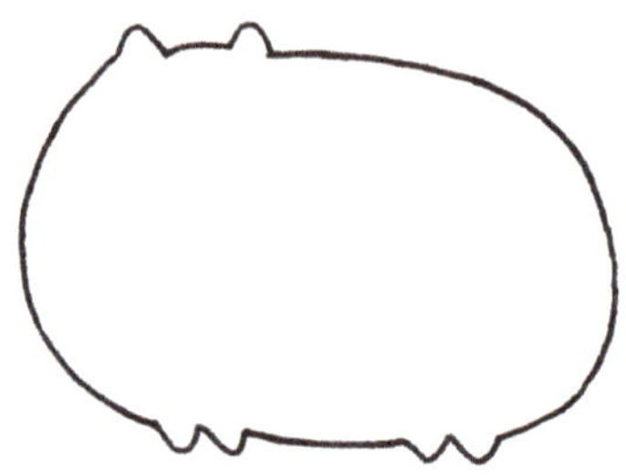

2
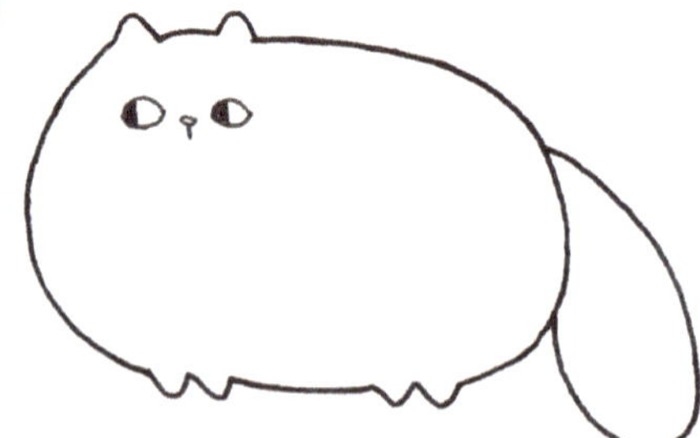

3
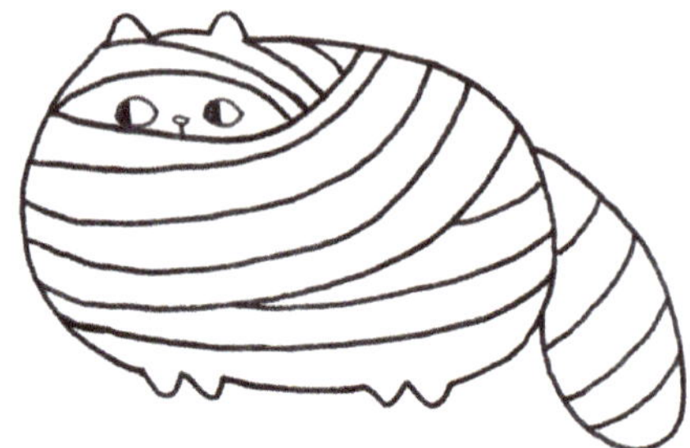

4
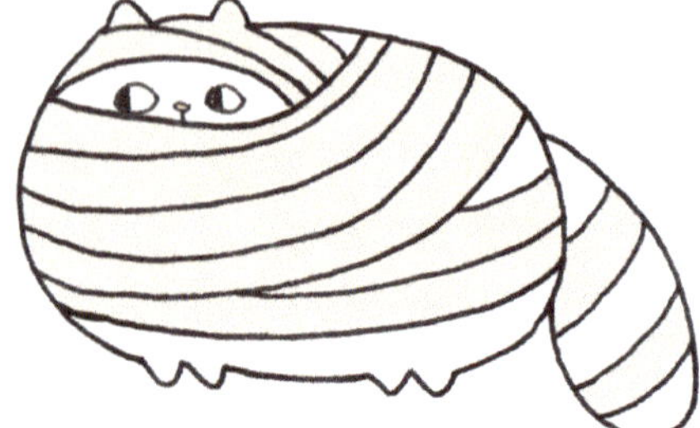

PUMPKIN CAT

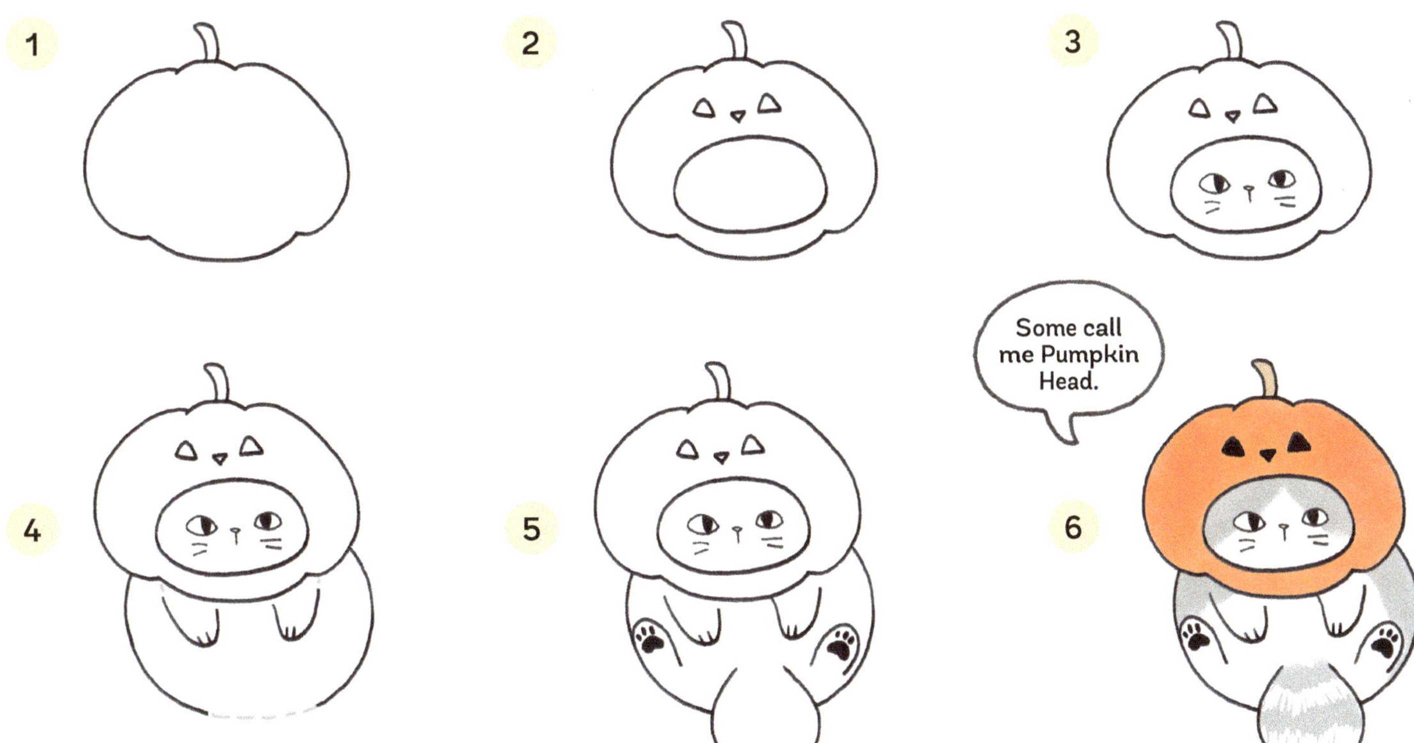

Complete your Halloween cats. Don't forget to color them in.

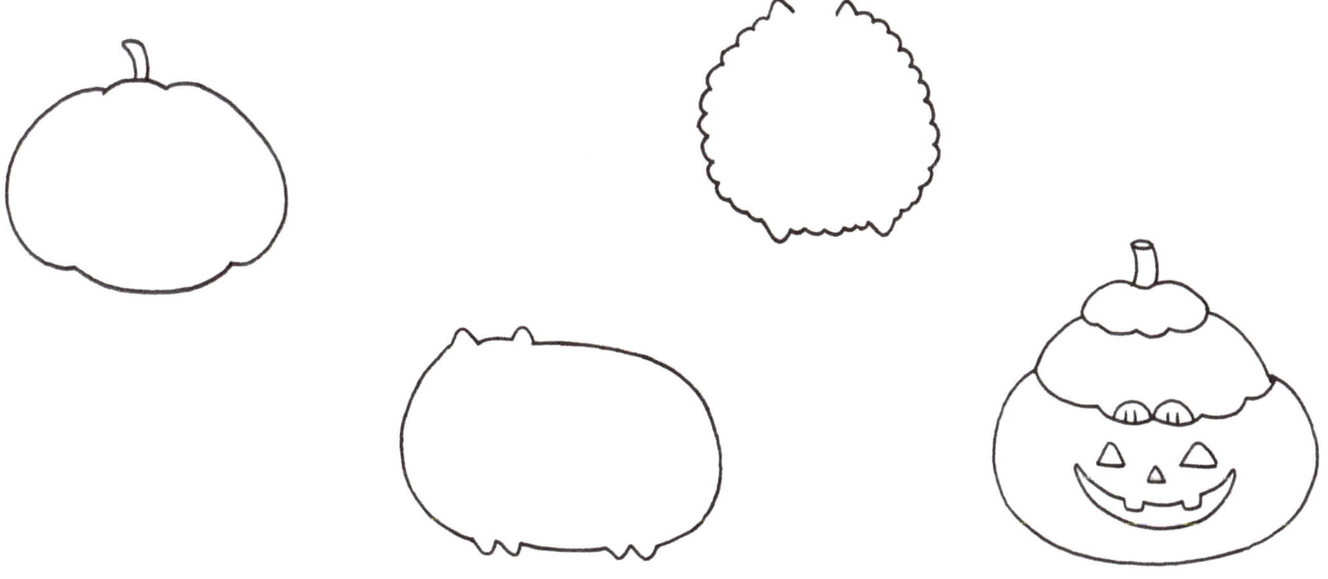

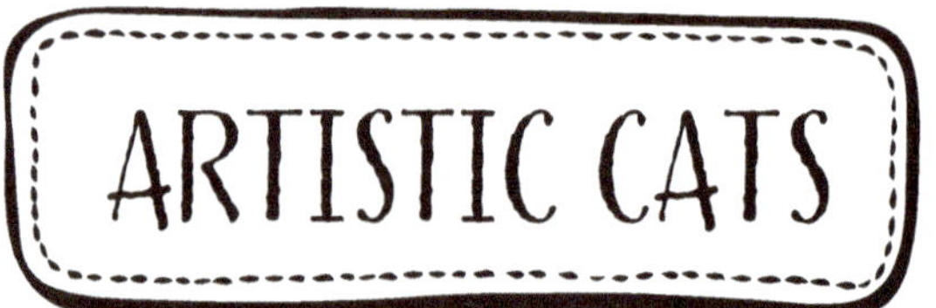

ARTISTIC CATS

Piet Mondrian is best known for his abstract geometric-inspired paintings. He developed a simplified style by restricting his palette to the three primary colors—blue, yellow, and red—on a grid of black vertical and horizontal lines on a white background. If he were to have drawn a cat, it probably would have looked something like this!

PIET MONDRIAN

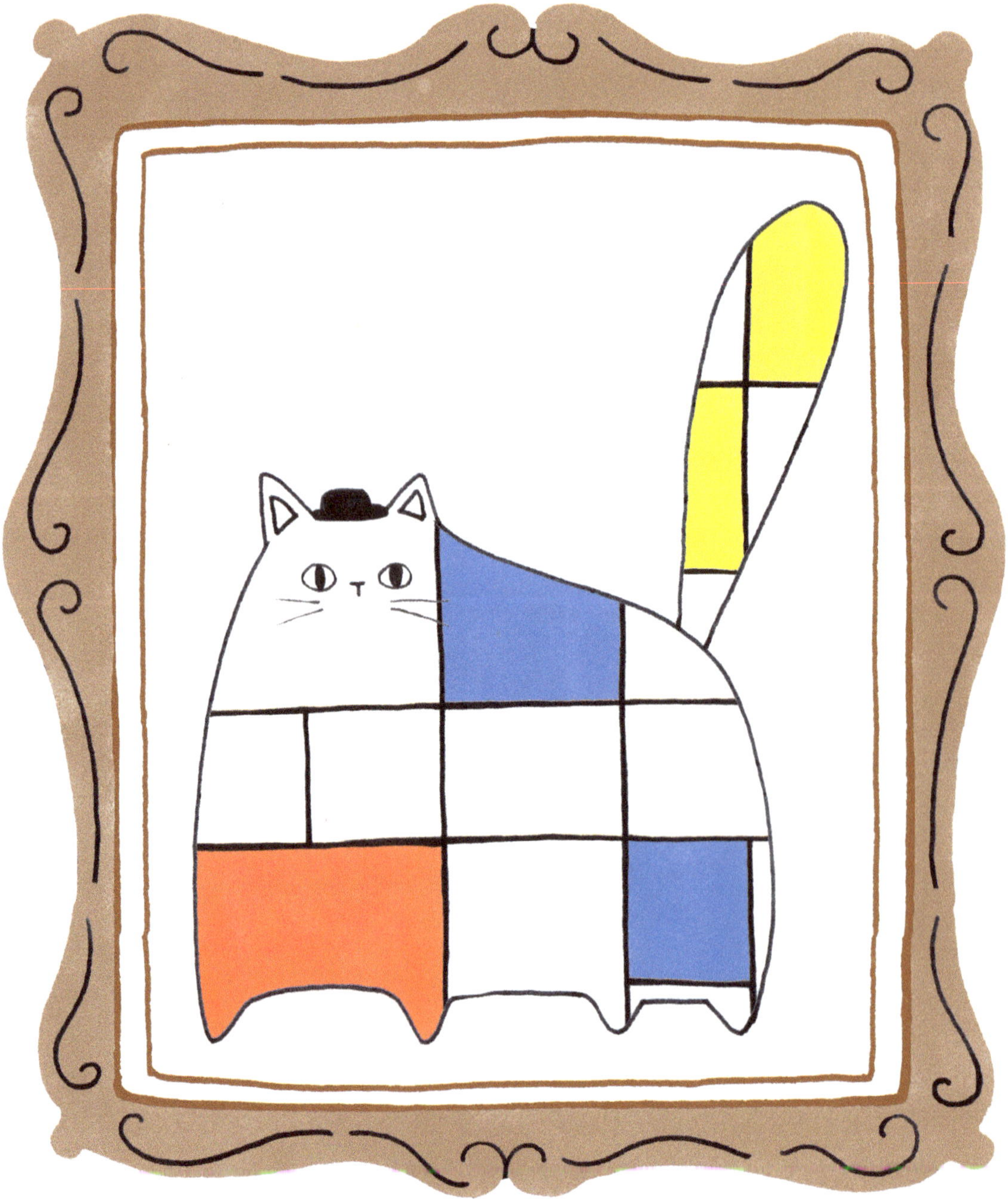

Doodle your Piet Mondrian cat here. Create a grid of black vertical and horizontal lines, and then color the blocks in red, yellow, and blue.

You can tell Yayoi Kusama's obsession with polka dots when you see her artworks. It's her most recognizable motif. Pumpkins are another trademark of her works; she started drawing them when she was a kid. This is my cat portrait inspired by Yayoi Kusama.

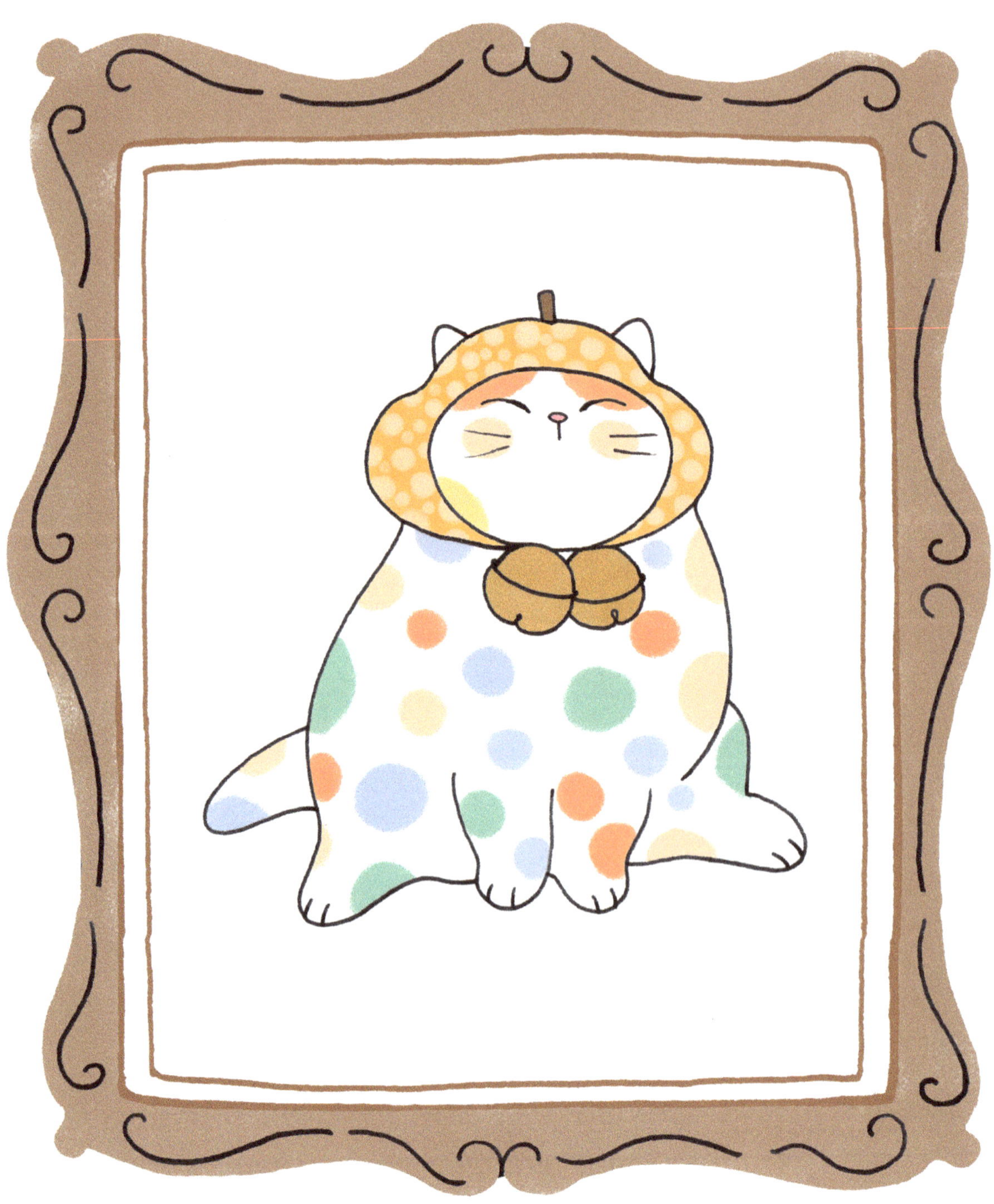

Fill the gallery with feline portraits inspired by the work of Yayoi Kusama or any of your favorite artists. Perhaps add polka dots of different sizes or pumpkins? Use all of your color tools, if you like!

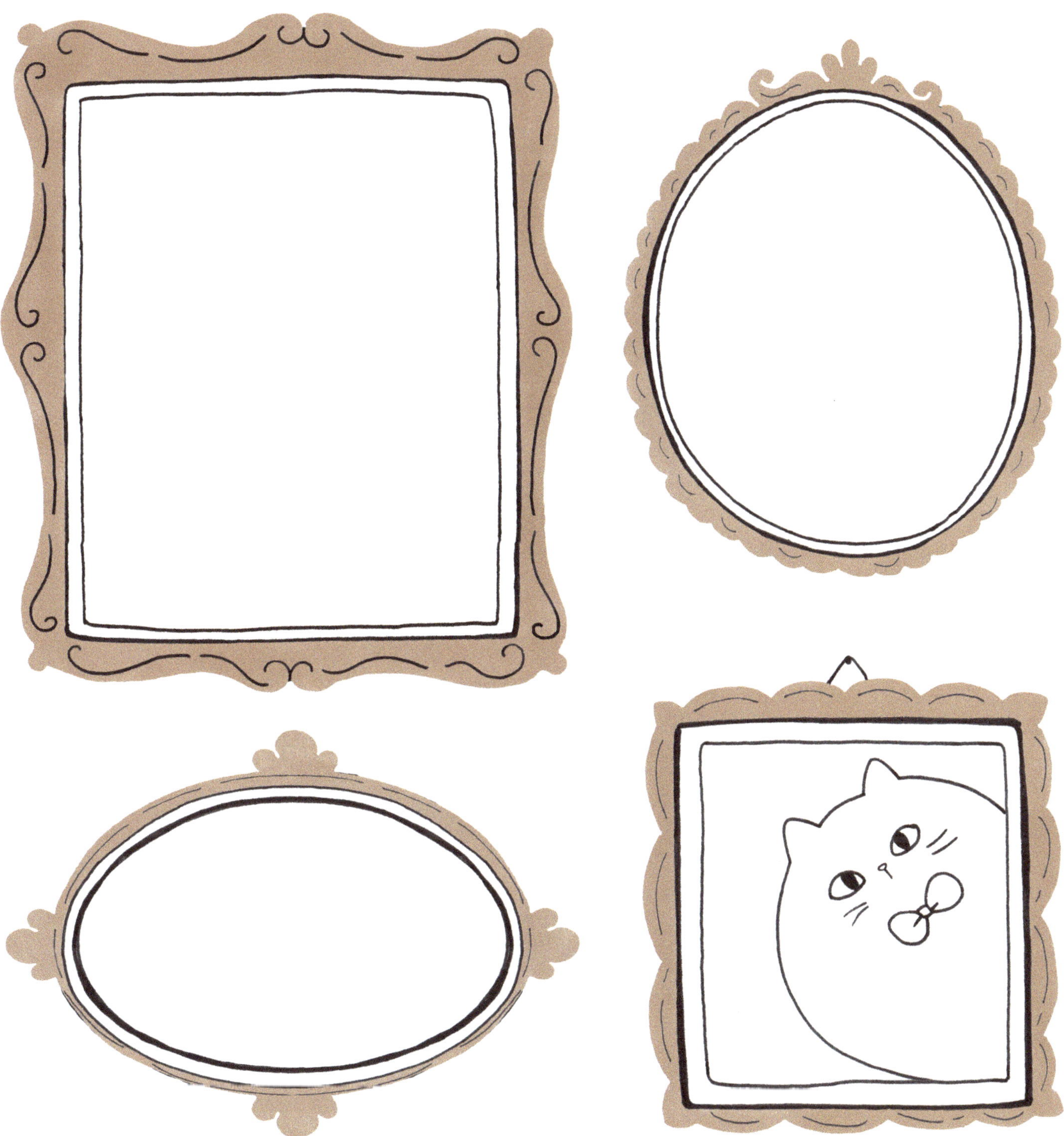

ABOUT THE ARTIST

Lulu Mayo is passionately committed to daydreaming in the fantasy art world where cats and mysterious creatures live. Cats have always been at the center of her works, and you will find them in each of the 20 books she has published worldwide, which have been translated and sold into more than 20 different territories. Follow Lulu on Instagram: @lulu_mayo_art or visit lulumayo.com.

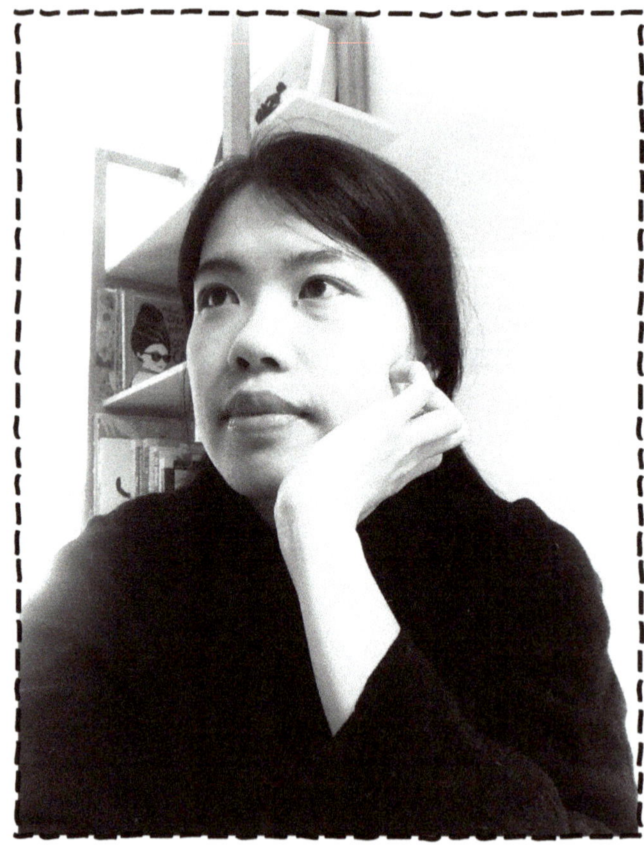